Good Cop, Bad Cop

David A. Schultz and Christina DeJong
General Editors

Vol. 10

PETER LANG
New York • Washington, D.C./Baltimore • Bern
Frankfurt am Main • Berlin • Brussels • Vienna • Oxford

Milton Heumann and Lance Cassak

Good Cop, Bad Cop

Racial Profiling and Competing Views of Justice

PETER LANG
New York • Washington, D.C./Baltimore • Bern
Frankfurt am Main • Berlin • Brussels • Vienna • Oxford

Library of Congress Cataloging-in-Publication Data

Cassak, Lance.
Good cop, bad cop: racial profiling and competing
views of justice / Lance Cassak, Milton Heumann.
p. cm. — (Studies in crime and punishment; vol. 10)
1. Racial profiling in law enforcement—United States.
2. Discrimination in criminal justice administration—United States.
3. Crime and race—United States. 4. War on Terrorism, 2001– I. Heumann,
Milton. II. Title. III. Studies in crime and punishment ; v. 10.
HV8141.C37   363.2'3'08900973—dc21   2003002788
ISBN 978-0-8204-5829-8
ISSN 1529-2444

Bibliographic information published by **Die Deutsche Bibliothek**.
Die Deutsche Bibliothek lists this publication in the "Deutsche
Nationalbibliografie"; detailed bibliographic data is available
on the Internet at http://dnb.ddb.de/.

Cover design by Dutton & Sherman Design

The paper in this book meets the guidelines for permanence and durability
of the Committee on Production Guidelines for Book Longevity
of the Council of Library Resources.

Printed in the United States of America

Contents

Acknowledgments

Writing this book was not easy. The issues are complicated, maybe intractable. Yet writing this book was also a joy. The complexity of the issues is the very thing that initially sparked our interest. We saw competing "goods" and we wondered what a closer look would reveal. Little did we know that the deeper we would dig, the more we found that there was to dig. Rarely in the past few years has a day or week passed without new information about racial profiling in the popular media, without some new spin or direction regarding the practice. And because we both are overwhelmed by so many other demands on our time, we came to appreciate even more, maybe treasure, the time we were able to spend on a project which increasingly puzzled us, troubled us, and fascinated us. The other reason that we came to love working on this project was the fact that we so loved our collaboration. It was—and is—a joy to jointly tackle the profiling issue as it is with the many other matters about which we talk, and occasionally, disagree. It may sound trite, but it is also true: we respect very much what each of us brings to the table and we are proud of the joint efforts that we can produce as a result. We have collaborated for over twenty years, and our joint work has never been anything but fun and (we hope) productive and valuable.

Because our work on racial profiling has spanned a number of years, there are many people to whom we are indebted. A number of friends listened to our thoughts and ruminations on this complex and always-expanding topic and shared their ideas on the swirl of issues surrounding profiling, some even voluntarily. At the risk of excluding some who deserve mention, we want to thank a number of people who were particularly generous with their time and attention: David Cassak, Jim Jacobs, Stephen Levin, Michael Paris, Eugene Schwartz and Tom Zimmerman. For her assistance with this research project in its several phases, we would like to thank Laura Bilotta. We would also like to thank Brian Pinaire, who read earlier drafts with great care and interest and who offered many helpful suggestions, and Zelia Giuliano, for her help in putting this book together. Portions of this book appeared in slightly different form in "Profiles In Injustice?—Police Discretion, Symbolic Assailants and Stereotyping," *Rutgers Law Review* 53 (Summer 2001) and "Afterword" *Rutgers Law Review* 54 (Fall 2001). We thank the editors of the Rutgers Law Review for permission to use that material in this book.

Finally we devote this book to the two people who have had to live with it, and us, for the past several years—of course, we mean our wives, Mary Brennan and Monica Friedman Heumann. Their endless patience for our endless ruminations, twists and turns, dead ends, and piles of new materials is remarkable and beyond praise. We promise to make order out of the roomfuls of "profiling stuff" which clutter our home offices, and we promise to never forget the unbelievable and invaluable support you gave us in this project. The book is dedicated to you.

Portions of the Preface and Chapters that follow are reprinted by permission of the Rutgers Law Review from "Profiles in Justice? Police Discretion, Symbolic Assailants and Stereotyping," Volume 53:4 of the *Rutgers Law Review,* and "Afterward: September 11th and Racial Profiling," Volume 54:1 of the *Rutgers Law Review.*

Introduction

Someone once said that history is mostly
guessing, the rest is prejudice. . . .
Ironically, many have said the same thing
about criminal profiling, and with good reason. [. . .][1]

As the twentieth century turns into the twenty-first, few topics of general public debate are more likely to stir emotions than racial profiling. "Racial profiling," wrote the author of a 1999 report for the New Jersey Chapter of the American Civil Liberties Union, "was born of slavery, raised by segregation, and has matured under pervasive, patently-false stereotypes of minorities, especially African-Americans and Latinos."[2] Not so, a former chief deputy sheriff would counter somewhat later, responding to a separate criticism of racial profiling, "Street police work is all about profiling . . . it has nothing to do with racial prejudice."[3] In recent years, racial profiling became perhaps the most hotly-debated issue in criminal law and justice, with the possible exception of the death penalty.

Such comments are not limited to those who toiled in the fields of law enforcement or assumed the mantle of guardian of our civil liberties but cut across broad swaths of the American public. By 1999, 2000 and 2001, articles in newspapers and magazines—not to mention coverage on television and radio—that discussed or debated "racial profiling" or incidents so labeled numbered more than a thousand each year. In early 2001, Jon Corzine, recently elected to the United States Senate from New Jersey, introduced the "End Racial Profiling Act" by saying that: "I rise on this historic day to speak about an issue that defines our health as a society—the issue of racial profiling." He went on to observe that "the practice of racial profiling is the antithesis of America's belief in fairness and equal protection under the law."[4] A few months later, the tragic events of September 11th significantly complicated and changed the debate over racial profiling.

As we shall see, the term "racial profiling" arose in the mid-1990s to describe specific types of police practices, although those practices actually began more than a decade before that. At first, the term was generally used as a shorthand label for the practice of law enforcement officers, who were searching for illegal drugs, of stopping minority motorists. That tactic of stopping motorists on the highway to search for drugs as initially conceived did, at least briefly, involve both a profile describing a number of the characteristics police thought marked those involved in illegal drugs, and race as a factor in the profile.

However, as the practice spread, whether the law officer's use of race in deciding whom to stop was *one* factor among many or the *sole* reason for the stop, became a key bone of contention. Anecdotal evidence, combined with statistical studies prepared for lawsuits challenging such highway stops in a few key states and other studies commissioned by state legislatures, appeared to show that although minorities constituted fewer than 20% of the drivers on the highways, they comprised three-quarters of the motorists stopped. Some of the incidents involved high-profile African American celebrities, including prominent athletes and movie stars.[5] Throughout the mid-1990s, stories of law enforcement targeting minority motorists increased, becoming so frequent and ubiquitous that the practice gave birth to its own contribution to the American lexicon, the purported offense of "Driving While Black."

In short order, however, as use of the term "racial profiling" became more frequent, the concept itself spread and became more diffuse and amorphous. Use of the term carried beyond traffic stops targeting minority drivers. By the end of the 1990s, "racial profiling" was used to describe just about any action by law enforcement that the speaker or writer believed involved the improper use or consideration of race. The shooting of four African American teenagers on the New Jersey Turnpike, police firing forty-one shots at an African immigrant in the vestibule of his apartment building after they mistook the man's wallet for a gun, the unsuccessful prosecution of an Asian American scientist on espionage charges, even the execution of an inmate on Texas' death row—all of these incidents, and many, many more, were denounced as "racial profiling."[6]

By 2000, racial profiling was an issue in the presidential election. In one of the debates during the Democratic primaries, former New Jersey Senator Bill Bradley scolded Vice-President Al Gore for not having walked down the hall to President Bill Clinton's office and demanded an executive order banning racial profiling. Gore responded in kind, warning Bradley that he was in no position to begin casting stones: "You know, racial profiling practically began in New Jersey." The issue carried over to the general election. In the second debate between the Democratic candidate Gore and Republican candidate George W. Bush, Gore responded affirmatively to the question of whether he would sign a federal law outlawing racial profiling; Bush went a step further, vowing "to do everything we can to end racial profiling." And in the debate between Vice-Presidential candidates Joseph Lieberman and Dick Cheney, both candidates strongly condemned racial profiling after the debate moderator invited the two men—both white, one nearly sixty years old and the other somewhat older, and both long ensconced as Senator and CEO of a billion-dollar oil company in upper-middle class America—"to imagine themselves black victims of racial profiling."[7]

Legislators at both the federal and state levels also took up the issue and passed many pieces of legislation to address the practice. The only branch of government that did not get caught up in the at-times cacophonous debate over racial profiling was the judiciary, especially the United States Supreme Court. While legislators, members of the executive branch and many in the general public saw racial profiling as a serious problem warranting some action— with or without careful consideration of the problem preceding that action—judges, more often than not and taking their lead from the Supreme Court, treated the problem as if it was nothing new and no big deal.

Finally, just as something of a consensus was emerging that racial profiling—even broadly and vaguely defined— should be done away with came the horrific events of September 11th. After nineteen Arab and Muslim men hijacked four commercial airliners and flew them into the World Trade Center in New York, the Pentagon and a field in Pennsylvania, the debate over racial profiling was reinvigorated and, for many, changed dramatically. As Americans struggled to determine whether the attacks of September 11th could have been prevented and, more importantly, how to stop future attacks, many who had previously condemned racial profiling now argued that race or ethnicity *might* be used legitimately in deciding whom to investigate. "Flying While Arab" threatened to replace "Driving While Black."

We began this volume with a simple though compelling observation: what experienced police officers—of all races—view as a necessary tool of law enforcement can be seen by critics as a pernicious singling out of persons based primarily on race and other physical characteristics. Studies have shown that, excluding those officers motivated by an explicitly racist interest, experienced police scrutinize potential wrongdoers and consider several attributes as they exercise their judgments. Race, the studies suggest, might be one of these attributes, and few scholars object to this sorting process. Yet, calls by politicians, pundits and many in the general public for banning all "profiling"—generally meaning *any* use of race by the police—have come in increasingly demanding tones.

This is the puzzle with which we began—the tension between what experienced police do and what some in the larger public debate say should never be done. As we continued to navigate the sea of profiling research, the waters became not clearer but more muddied. First, we learned that profiling was, and is, a laudable police practice, something quite different from the "profiling" of popular discourse. A "profiler" is, in fact, a skilled law enforcement officer trained in drawing inferences about wrongdoers in a patterned series of cases. This is a far cry from "profiling" on street patrol or on highways, though the term has been used in this context as well. Yet, we also found that "profiling" was increasingly becoming synonymous with racism. Any use of race in *any* way—whether in deciding who to stop or who might be a suspect, or in myriad other ways—was condemned as tantamount to discrimination. In short, the term itself, we found, could be anchored in praiseworthy police activities as well as in the rhetoric of racism.

Case law provided little help in sorting through the issues and arguments surrounding profiling. For the most part, courts either ducked the propriety of police use of profiles, or endorsed the inclusion of race as *one* of the factors, though not the only factor in a profile. Nor did an acceptable definition or illumination of the issues of profiling emerge from the more deliberative court opinions. Most often, consideration of the central issues was ducked; at best, when it did address profiling, the case law generally provided yet another "on the one hand, on the other hand" view of the propriety or acceptability of this police practice.

Finally, the events of September 11th further complicate the understanding of profiling. Before this horrendous day, matters were confused enough, but now police activities, the language of profiling, and popular reaction to the practices and the case law, all cast a new and different light on the acceptability of profiling, making it very difficult to balance the relevant cost and benefits. What was already difficult and complex before September 11th became exceedingly complicated after this watershed day in U.S. history. While there is certainly no reason to expect that one's views on profiling before the terrorist attacks would cohere with what one believed after September 11th· we have been intrigued by the disjuncture between beliefs in the abstract and expectations in more concrete situations—a phenomenon we see as a peculiar form of cognitive dissonance. Clearly, for many, the costs and benefits of using race (or ethnicity) in a profile have been altered, and this increased our fascination and bewilderment at the twists and turns taken during our profiling sojourn.

It is only appropriate in a book dealing with profiling generally, and racial profiling in particular, that we provide something of a road map for where we are headed. One of the aims of this book is to trace the development of profiling and a number of practices that eventually came to be called "racial profiling." Chapter 1 begins with a brief look at the development of criminal profiling, and then addresses a second line or type of profiling that began with the "skyjacker" profile in the late 1960s. We also look at standard police training and experience and how that influences the push to "profile." Chapter 2 looks at the next incarnation, the airport drug courier profile. Chapter 3 examines the adaptation of the airport drug courier profile to travel on the highways. Chapter 4 discusses the public debate over racial profiling and the evolution of the concept, which has come to describe, for many, any police or criminal justice practice that smacks of racial discrimination. Chapter 5 looks at how the legal system, particularly the United States Supreme Court, has dealt with the issue of race and how that has played into the larger public debate over racial profiling. Finally, in Chapter 6, we offer our own assessment of the costs and benefits of racial profiling, consider the effects of the horrible events of September 11th on the debate about racial profiling, and raise some final questions about what we have seen and where we are going.

CHAPTER 1

The Roots of Racial Profiling

If confronted directly, [profiling] is intractable—easy to forbid
in theory, impossible (and maybe inadvisable) to root
out in practice, for reasons that go to the heart of why
police officers do the things they do.[1]

Turning and turning in the widening gyre
The falcon cannot hear the falconer;
Things fall apart; the centre cannot hold;[2]

With everything that has been written in the past few years
about racial profiling—all of the questions raised, all of the accusations and allegations leveled—it is easy to forget that well
before anyone objected to the practice of "racial profiling,"
profiling *per se* was an accepted, if relatively little-debated,

tool in law enforcement that neither required nor even necessarily or usually involved consideration of a suspect's
race. Indeed, profiling is still practiced in far-off corners of
law enforcement investigative work that receive little publicity, even as racial profiling became a very highly visible
issue in law enforcement in the late 1990s and into the
twenty-first century.

One of the many questions that warrants attention in the
current debate over racial profiling is: How did profiling
change from a little-noticed practice of a relative few in law
enforcement into an allegedly widespread practice subject
to a scrutiny that has shaken the foundations of more than a
few state law enforcement agencies? The answer to that
particular question is useful in addressing the other questions that swirl around the current debate.

To a large extent the answer lies in a characteristic of the
legal landscape upon which racial profiling has played out, a
characteristic that is not unique to law but one that is important to it. Law's tendency to evolve or, in a more neutral
sense, expand, is a source of fascination for some and frus-
tration for others. Basic concepts and principles move beyond the situation that spawned them and are constantly
tested and re-tested as new players in new factual settings
with different agendas and interests enter the fray.[3]

The same process of evolution can be seen with regard to
profiling, generally, and racial profiling, specifically. Profiling began as a supplement to traditional law enforcement
investigation techniques. In its original incarnation, in the
second half of the twentieth century, it operated essentially
in a reactive fashion in a limited number and type of cases
and was the province of a small group of criminologists and
psychologists, sometimes self-identified as "elite" units. But
by the 1990s, profiling, both among law enforcement professionals and, more importantly, the public at large, came
to be used in a much broader range of cases and as a proactive device, not simply to solve a known crime but to find
crimes that had not yet been detected or to stop crimes that
had not yet been committed. Moreover, profiling was no

longer the responsibility of an "elite" unit, but of all, or at least most, law enforcement agents. In addition, the focus of profilers moved from internal psychological characteristics to external characteristics, events, or circumstances that were both observable by laypersons and, to a great extent, in themselves perfectly innocent. And, perhaps most important, race was introduced into the equation.

As the term and practice has spread, profiling, like Yeats' falcon, has moved ever further away from its original moorings. The term "racial profiling" has come to be applied to a range of police behavior bearing no, or only the slightest, resemblance to profiling as initially conceived and understood. What was once a unique and little-known investigative technique has become the most-talked about and debated public policy issue in law enforcement short of the death penalty.

In the Beginning

Before there was racial profiling, there was criminal profiling, or just plain profiling. Criminal profiling has been described as the "process of inferring distinctive personality characteristics of individuals responsible for committing criminal acts."[4] In order to legitimate the practice, therefore, supporters of criminal profiling like to invoke the names of some of the most famous practitioners in nineteenth-century detective fiction, such as C. August Dupin from Edgar Allan Poe's classic "The Murders in the Rue Morgue," and Sir Arthur Conan Doyle's Sherlock Holmes.[5] As a more practical, if less literary, matter, the roots of profiling are more accurately traced to the mid-twentieth century.

In the 1940s and 1950s, "The Mad Bomber," believed to be responsible for more than thirty bombings over a fifteen-year period, bedeviled New York City. Frustrated by their failure to identify, much less capture, the bomber, police turned to Dr. James A. Brussel, a psychiatrist in Greenwich Village, to assist them in their search for the Mad Bomber. Law enforcement asked Brussel to look at photographs of the crime scenes and letters the Bomber had sent to news-papers regarding his deeds.

From his study of the photographs and of the letters, Brussel concluded that the Bomber was a paranoid who hated his father but obsessively loved his mother. He also opined that the Bomber was a heavy-set, single, middle-aged Roman Catholic of foreign birth who lived in Connecti-cut with a brother or sister. Brussel even predicted that when the police found him, "chances are he'll be wearing a double-breasted suit. Buttoned." Armed with that analysis, and starting from the assumption that the Bomber was a disgruntled former employee of Consolidated Edison, the police used the conclusions drawn by Brussel, and iden-tified and arrested the Mad Bomber. Brussel had been cor-rect about all of his conclusions, except one (he lived with two maiden sisters, not one), down to the double-breasted suit, buttoned, that The Mad Bomber wore as the police es-corted him from his home.[6]

Dr. Brussel is frequently credited with being a trailblazer in the use of behavioral science in criminal investigations, and his work in the Mad Bomber case has been cited as the first effort to solve a criminal case by criminal profiling. More important, his success in the Mad Bomber case jump-started the new investigative approach. It led, for instance, to his working on other cases, including the efforts to find the Boston Strangler in the 1960s. Also during this period, other pioneers in the field also became actively involved in the efforts to develop investigative techniques that em-ployed behavioral sciences, including psychiatry, in criminal investigations.[7]

One of them was Howard Teten, who studied with Brus-sel, and began using a multi-disciplinary approach to foren-sic science and knowledge of psychiatry in the investigation of crimes in the San Leandro, California Police Department. In 1962, Teten moved to the Federal Bureau of Investigation and began developing techniques of what is now viewed as criminal profiling, first in New York and later at the FBI Na-tional Academy in Quantico, Virginia. By the early 1970s he was training other FBI agents in criminal profiling techniques as aids to criminal investigations, primarily through a course called Applied Criminal Psychology. Teten worked with other colleagues at the FBI, such as Pat Mullaney, Robert Ressler and John Douglas, in a special unit, the Behavioral Sciences Unit, devoted to exploring the use of behavioral sciences in the investigation of crimes.

Douglas became head of the BSU in 1977, eventually changing the name of the unit to the Investigative Support Unit, and advanced criminal profiling a step further by taking it out of the classroom and applying it in the real world. When the BSU first started, its instructors were almost exclusively that—instructors—as had been the case since Teten first came to the FBI's National Academy. Although they consulted on actual cases occasionally, they worked on real crimes very sporadically at first. Under Douglas, the BSU became involved more and more in actual investigations as well as teaching responsibilities. By the end of the 1970s, the BSU was getting more and more requests for help in developing profiles of suspects in individual cases. In 1979, the BSU received fifty requests for assistance in actual cases, which instructors tried to fulfill while continuing their teaching. The number of requests doubled the next year and again the year after, and by the early 1980s Douglas had given up his teaching responsibilities and was working solely on investigations. At that point, the FBI hierarchy was still somewhat skeptical of the practice, concerned that its effectiveness was hard to assess and that it might be the "fuzzy math" of criminal investigation. But strong praise from law enforcement officers in the field who received the help of the BSU personnel persuaded the FBI that the program was worth continuing.[8]

As it developed in the 1960s, 1970s, and 1980s from these beginnings, criminal profiling took shape as a scientific approach to crime solving and criminal investigations, involving experts trained in and drawn from a number of fields, most prominently criminologists, psychologists and psychiatrists and those trained in the forensic sciences.[9]

The purpose of profiling is not specifically to identify the person or persons who may have committed a particular crime but "rather, describe the type of person most likely to have committed the offense."[10] As summarized by one student, a defender of criminal profiling, the creation of a profile by the FBI is comprised of "five overlapping stages," which, like any good scientific model, involve the accumulation and assessment of data, the formulation of a hypothesis, and the testing of that hypothesis:

> A profile begins with the "Profiling Inputs Stage." This step involves the accumulation of crime scene evidence, victimology, forensic information, preliminary police reports, and photographs. Once all of the information is collected, the profiler begins the "Decision Process Model Stage." In this stage, the profiler organizes and arranges the information into a meaningful pattern. This process includes determining the type of crime committed, the primary intent of the offender, the risk of the victim, the willingness of the offender to take a risk, and the time and location factors involved in the offense. Based on this information, the profiler classifies the crime in the "Crime Assessment Stage." This includes a reconstruction of how the crime took place, the type of crime, the level of organization at the crime scene relative to the victim's risk level, the control of the victim and sequence of events, the staging and the motivation for committing the crime, and the dynamics of the crime scene. Upon completion of the classification of the crime, the profiling process continues with the "profile stage." This stage generates the actual profile, which includes information such as demographics, educational level and intellectual functioning, criminal history, military history, family history, habits and social interests, residence in relation to the crime scene, type of vehicle owned, personality characteristics, and suggested interview techniques. [. . .]
>
> Once a profile is created it is sent to the investigating officers for their investigative use. In addition, the profiler rechecks all of the profile information so that there are no inconsistencies.[11]

It should be noted that criminal profiling has its critics as well as its supporters. Some object that it is more art than science and adds little to the concrete information already in the possession of the police from which profilers work. Former New York City Police Commissioner Patrick V. Murphy

has offered the following assessment of psychological profiling: "I suppose it's useful in a very, very limited sense. You
might develop a few leads." Even some profilers claim only
that profiling is little more than making educated guesses.
And, notwithstanding the stunning accuracy of Dr. Brussel
in the Mad Bomber case, many profiles turn out to be incorrect, with, critics contend, the potential to lead police in the
wrong direction.[12]

In sum, criminal profiling, as it was originally conceived,
had a number of important features. First, profiling was limited to specific types of crimes—primarily murder, arson,
and rape, particularly when committed by a serial offender.
Second, it was largely reactive. That is, criminal profilers
were brought into a case in response to a known crime (or
crimes) that they attempted to solve and used what was
known to that point as the backdrop from which to work.
Indeed, individual characteristics of the specific crime already committed were, as we have seen, critical to the work
of the profiler. Third, criminal profiling was essentially a scientific exercise, largely the province of special "elite" units,
composed mostly of experts or law enforcement personnel
trained in one or more of the behavioral sciences.

The Next Steps: *Terry v. Ohio*, the War on Drugs, and Airline Hijackers

The road from profiling to racial profiling did not follow a
straight path. While Teten and his colleagues at the FBI
were honing their skills in psychological profiling during the
1970s, developments in the practice of creating profiles
traveled simultaneously down another path. Profiling became an increasingly popular tool for law enforcement. Profiles were developed for a wide variety of crimes beyond the
serial murderers, rapists, and arsonists with whom the practice was originally concerned and conceived. Among the
other types of profiles created were those for persons who
smuggle illegal aliens into the country, operators of drug
smuggling vessels, battering parents, car thieves, poachers

and child molesters. The most prominent and, for understanding racial profiling, the most important profile, however, is the one developed to catch those involved in trafficking in illegal drugs, most commonly referred to as "the drug
courier profile."[13]

As we will discuss shortly, the development of the drug
courier profile as part of the effort to stop the trade in illegal
narcotics, represents something of a midway point for what
has come to be called "racial profiling." Three key events,
seemingly unrelated, occurred in the late 1960s and early
1970s that led profiling as a practice away from the type
conceived of at the FBI's BSU to a separate strain embodied
in the drug courier profile. Those three events were the decision of the United States Supreme Court in *Terry v. Ohio,* the
commencement of the War on Drugs, and the development
of a profile to stop airplane hijackers. The Court's decision
in *Terry,* provided (perhaps unintentionally) the legal basis
or justification for law enforcement stops using profiles by
giving constitutional validity to a type of police encounter—
the investigative stop—that did not quite amount to a full-
blown arrest. The War on Drugs, on the other hand, provided the impetus for the rise of the new kind of profiling by
giving it a stage—aggressive efforts at drug interdiction—on
which to play out and also creating the Drug Enforcement
Agency, which would assume a critical role in the development of these types of profiles. Finally, the airport hijacker
profile provided a model for an effective profile that, many
believed, could be adapted to the War on Drugs.

Terry v. Ohio

The Supreme Court's decision in *Terry v. Ohio*[14] stands as
something of a second-tier landmark decision of the Court
under Chief Justice Earl Warren. In its sixteen-year history,
the Warren Court revolutionized a number of areas of law,
not the least of which was criminal justice and, specifically,
the law regarding police tactics.[15] The Court's decision in
Terry came in 1968, essentially at the end of the Warren

Court's tenure (although he stayed one more term, Chief Justice Warren announced his intention to retire three weeks after the decision he authored in *Terry* was handed down[16]), and, while it has not generated quite the same degree of attention, debate, and passion as some other Warren Court decisions, the decision is justly recognized as one of the most important decisions of the Court, one that continues to influence greatly the law of police tactics to this day.

Some Fourth Amendment General Principles

To understand and appreciate what *Terry* wrought, we need to recall where the law of search and seizure stood before the decision. The Fourth Amendment to the United States Constitution provides that,

> The right of the people to be secure in their persons, houses, papers and effects, against unreasonable searches and seizures, shall not be violated, and no Warrants shall issue but upon probable cause, supported by Oath or affirmation, and particularly describing the place to be searched, and the persons or things to be seized.[17]

Justice Robert Jackson succinctly described the importance of the protections afforded by the Fourth Amendment to our basic liberties:

> [They] belong in the catalog of indispensable freedoms. Among deprivations of rights, none is so effective in cowing a population, crushing the spirit of the individual and putting terror in every heart. Uncontrolled search and seizure is one of the first and most effective weapons in the arsenal of every arbitrary government. And one need only briefly to have dwelt and worked among a people possessed of many admirable qualities but deprived of these rights to know that the human personality deteriorates and dignity and self-reliance disappear where homes, persons and possessions are subject at any hour to unheralded search and seizure by the police.[18]

Nonetheless, despite the importance of these rights, for much of the nation's history, the Fourth Amendment, along with guarantees of the other rights secured by the Bill of Rights, applied only to actions of the federal government, not the states.[19] But in a series of cases in the twentieth century, the Supreme Court came to hold various amendments in the original Bill of Rights applicable to the states through the Fourteenth Amendment to the Constitution, among them, the Fourth Amendment, in one of the Warren Court's first significant decisions in the area of criminal justice.[20]

Unfortunately, efforts by the Supreme Court and lower courts to interpret the language of the Fourth Amendment have produced something less, indeed considerably less, than a clear set of rules as to what the amendment allows and prohibits, so that any effort to summarize the state of the law is necessarily qualified with numerous exceptions, caveats and disclaimers.[21] Still, as the Court approached the issues posed in *Terry,* there were essentially two types of constitutionally permissible police-citizen encounters. One allowed for purely consensual encounters: police may always to approach a person and ask that person questions, and, without more, the person has the right to answer or refuse to answer as he or she sees fit. However, police were allowed to subject a person to an involuntary stop only if the arrest was "reasonable," and there was probable cause for it; there was also a strong preference that the police have a warrant authorizing the arrest.

The rules were similar for searches: generally speaking, searches either had to be performed with the consent of the person being searched (or the owner of the thing to be searched) or had to be reasonable, and supported by a validly issued warrant. Of course, the general principles on their own terms raised an endless numbers of issues—such as what type of restraint constitutes an "arrest," what constitutes "probable cause," and how to judge whether a warrant has been validly issued and executed—and came with numerous exceptions, particularly for searches and seizures conducted under "exigent circumstances,"[22] which threaten to swallow the rule. But, generally speaking, that was the relevant legal landscape the Court confronted as it decided *Terry v. Ohio.*

The Decision in *Terry*

Terry involved a challenge to the actions of a Cleveland, Ohio, police detective, Martin McFadden, and a street-level encounter with two men, John Terry and Richard Chilton.[23] The facts are worth considering in some detail in light of *Terry*'s subsequent relation to the law enforcement practices that have garnered the label "profiling."

McFadden was a veteran plainclothes detective, patrolling an area of downtown Cleveland with which he was very familiar. McFadden spotted two men (Terry and Chilton) whom he did not recognize and who seemed to be acting suspiciously near some retail establishments. As the Court's opinion quotes McFadden: "they didn't look right to me at the time." At first McFadden did nothing more than continue to observe the two men, whom he watched walk back and forth, more than a dozen times, between the street corner and the window of a local store, sometimes stopping to talk to a third man named Katz. McFadden had not yet seen the men commit a specific crime but was concerned that they were "casing" the store, preparing for a robbery. At that point, according to the Court, McFadden "considered it his duty as a police officer to investigate further." He approached the men, stopped them, and asked their names, to which the men mumbled a response. Following that brief exchange, McFadden moved quickly and patted the men down, finding guns on Terry and his companion, Chilton, resulting in charges against them for carrying concealed weapons.[24]

Because McFadden did not have probable cause for the initial stop and pat down, Terry and Chilton, in the ensuing criminal prosecution, brought a motion to suppress the guns McFadden found on them, challenging the initial "stop and frisk" as an unreasonable search and seizure that violated their Fourth Amendment rights. (It was generally agreed that once McFadden found the guns, he had probable cause to arrest the men and lawfully subject them to a full search incident to an arrest.) The state trial court and a lower appellate court upheld the initial stop and search, essentially because such practices had been recognized at common law and in statutes in a number of states. The Supreme Court of Ohio dismissed the appeal because it found that the case raised "no 'substantial constitutional question.'"[25]

The United States Supreme Court took the constitutional issues much more seriously. Chief Justice Earl Warren wrote the majority opinion in the 8–1 decision that upheld the stop and frisk despite the lack of probable cause for either the search or the seizure. Warren framed the issue for decision as the "narrow question posed by the facts before us: whether it is always unreasonable for a policeman to seize a person and subject him to a limited search for weapons unless there is probable cause for an arrest."[26] Warren first dismissed the argument put forward by the prosecution that the "stop" part of a "stop and frisk" is not a seizure for purposes of the Fourth Amendment. Noting that an arrest could occur in ways other than as traditionally understood as a trip to the stationhouse, Warren stated "It must be recognized that whenever a police officer accosts an individual and restrains his freedom to walk away, he has 'seized' that person."[27] Then, operating from the premise that the ultimate inquiry was the reasonableness of McFadden's actions, Warren described the balancing test that inquiry required,

> In order to assess the reasonableness of Officer McFadden's conduct as a general proposition, it is necessary "first to focus upon the governmental interest which allegedly justifies official intrusion upon the constitutionally protected interests of the private citizen," for there is "no ready test for determining reasonableness other than by balancing the need to search [or seize] against the invasion which the search [or seizure] entails."[. . .] And in justifying the particular intrusion the police officer must be able to point to specific and articulable facts which, taken together with rational inferences from those facts, reasonably warrant that intrusion.[28]

Warren went on to identify the governmental interest at stake, in terms that foreshadowed (certainly inadvertently) many of the arguments later made in favor of profiling, as follows:

> One general interest is of course that of effective crime preven-
> tion and detection; it is this interest which underlies the recog-
> nition that a police officer may in appropriate circumstances
> and in an appropriate manner approach a person for purposes
> of investigating possibly criminal behavior even though there is
> no probable cause to make an arrest. It was this legitimate in-
> vestigative function Officer McFadden was discharging when
> he decided to approach petitioner and his companions. He had
> observed Terry, Chilton, and Katz go through a series of acts,
> each of them perhaps innocent in itself, but which taken to-
> gether warranted further investigation.[29]

And, after describing what it was that McFadden saw that would reasonably lead him to suspect something suspicious was afoot, Warren concluded, "It would have been poor po-lice work indeed for an officer of 30 years' experience in the detection of thievery from stores in this same neighborhood to have failed to investigate this behavior further."[30]

In the end, the practical effect of the Court's ruling in *Terry*, and what gives the decision its lasting importance, was to create a new category of constitutionally permissible seizures, a midway point between purely consensual police-citizen encounters and full arrests based on probable cause. Since *Terry*, limited investigative stops by law enforcement, short of arrests, have been held not to run afoul of the Fourth Amendment as long as the law enforcement officer is able to articulate facts sufficient to demonstrate a "rea-sonable suspicion" that criminal activity has occurred or is about to occur. The basis for the stop must be more than "an inchoate or unparticularized suspicion or 'hunch.'"[31] There is some irony in this. For one thing, Warren never em-ployed the words "reasonable suspicion" in the *Terry* deci-sion; for another, the actual holding of Warren's opinion is arguably narrower than that, focusing largely on the justifi-ability of the frisk, rather than the stop.[32] Indeed, there is some evidence that Warren initially envisioned a more am-bitious decision, hoping to do for the practice of "stop and frisk" what the Court had done for police interrogations in

Miranda v. Arizona.[33] However, there was such deep division among the Justices about the permissible scope of the investigative stops that Warren ultimately tried to avoid the issue of whether the initial stop and questioning of Terry and Chilton was constitutional.[34]

Terry is a very rich opinion, one well worth the continued study and scrutiny it has received. It reflects, overall, a very pragmatic approach to the many issues raised by this type of police practice. Thus, the Court devoted significant attention to why some of the staples of Fourth Amendment jurisprudence—such as the exclusionary rule[35] and the warrant requirement—were not practical or effective in the type of street encounter involved in the case. And, although subsequent cases have extended the permissible scope of a frisk, the Court's original reason for allowing frisks was concern for the safety of the police officers involved. Although some have viewed *Terry* as consistent with the rest of the Warren Court's work in criminal justice, more frequently the decision is described as one of the few pro-law enforcement decisions handed down by the Warren Court, having been decided against a backdrop of rising crime rates, social unrest, and, especially, the very pointed criticisms leveled against some of the Court's earlier criminal justice decision, especially *Miranda.*[36] Subsequent cases in the decades that followed the decision have extended the reach of *Terry* to cases involving less serious crimes, including drug-related offenses. For our purposes, however, *Terry* is most important for creating a new category of investigative stops that are permissible on less than probable cause. In so doing, the decision established the legal basis for profiles such as the drug courier profile that followed.[37]

Richard Nixon's War on Drugs

If *Terry v. Ohio* created the legal basis for the drug courier profile, Richard Nixon's decision to make law and order, and particularly illegal drug use, a part of the agenda for his first administration was the catalyst for the creation of the profile.

Early Law Enforcement Efforts

Until the twentieth century, the use of what we now consider illegal drugs was largely legal. Substances such as cocaine, opium, morphine, and even heroin were found in a number of items for regular consumption, such as physician-prescribed medicines, patent medicines, and even consumer products such as hay fever remedies and Coca-Cola (until 1903). Before the Industrial Revolution, social and cultural norms were the most important tools in regulating drug use. Before the 1890s, state and local laws regulated the use of such substances but generally did not prohibit their use. In the final decade of the nineteenth century, some states passed laws to outlaw the use of certain narcotics as concerns about drug abuse grew, but even then many Americans associated abuse of drugs with "outsiders," such as foreigners and African Americans.[38]

The federal government became more heavily involved with the passage of statutes early in the twentieth century, such as the Opium Exclusion Act in 1909 and the Harrison Narcotic Drug Act in 1914, and with the creation of the Federal Bureau of Narcotics in 1930. But the early drug laws were largely tax laws and contained many compromises and exceptions—such as those in the Harrison Act that exempted patent medicines sold over the counter and by mail order and allowed physicians to sell narcotics by way of prescriptions—that took away much of their force. Passage of the Harrison Act—the first major federal effort to prevent the use of illegal drugs—generated considerable debate among certain constituencies such as reformers, physicians, and trade groups, and in the international community, but was not a matter of wide public interest in the United States. At the time of the passage of the Harrison Act, use of drugs elicited much less concern than consumption of alcohol, and many viewed the passage of the act as "a routine slap at a moral evil, something like the Mann Act or the Anti-Lottery Acts."[39]

Moreover, authority to enforce the narcotics laws was

placed not in the Justice Department but in the Treasury Department, along with the primary responsibility for laws governing Prohibition. Leaving enforcement of the drug laws to the Treasury Department—whose efforts in enforcing the liquor laws were initially resisted by the then-Secretary of the Treasury Carter Glass, received inadequate funding from Congress and were notoriously ineffective—suggests that prevention of illegal drug use was not a very high priority for the federal government. Even when crime control became a significant issue in the 1960s during the administration of Lyndon B. Johnson and enforcement of the drug laws moved to the Justice Department, the 1967 report of Johnson's crime commission devoted relatively little attention to the problem of drugs.[40] Johnson took some steps to increase federal efforts to stop drugs—such as creation of the Bureau of Narcotics and Dangerous Drugs (BNDD) in the Justice Department—but it was slow going, as evidenced by the refusal of J. Edgar Hoover to get the FBI heavily involved in drug enforcement, despite Johnson's efforts to persuade him to help with the problem. By the end of the 1960s, as one prominent student of criminal justice notes, "drug cases were still a small part of most criminal dockets," comprising fewer than 5% of the criminal charges brought by state prosecutors as late as 1971.[41]

The War on Drugs

This foot-dragging at the federal level would soon change, however, for not only did the Supreme Court decide *Terry v. Ohio* in 1968, but it was also an election year. America's participation in the Vietnam War figured to be the big issue in the campaign of Richard Nixon, the nominee of the Republican Party, but mishaps in the progress of the war (such as the Tet Offensive early in the year) and the resultant growing dissatisfaction with the war and President Johnson's decision not to seek re-election, made it a difficult issue for Nixon to articulate an attractive position, effectively eliminating that as the central issue in his campaign. Nixon found the perfect substitute in calling attention to everything he claimed was going wrong in America, including the declining effectiveness of law and order. And a critical component of his campaign for law and order was the illegal use of drugs.[42]

Late in the summer, shortly before Election Day, Nixon delivered a speech at Disneyland in Southern California. "As I look over the problems in this country," Nixon announced to a group of Republican supporters, "I see one that stands out particularly. The problem of narcotics." He continued, describing the illegal use of drugs as "among the modern curse of the youth, just like the plagues and epidemics of former years," concluding that "they are decimating a generation of Americans." He also blamed drug addicts for half the crime in New York City and vowed to fight drug use aggressively in his new administration.[43]

There was, perhaps not surprisingly, little if any support for Nixon's claims about the harmful effect of drugs at the time he made them. As far as decimating the youth of America, as one student of the drug wars has noted, "drugs were so tiny a public health problem that they were statistically insignificant: far more Americans choked to death on food or died falling down stairs as died from illegal drugs."[44]

The same could be said of Nixon's efforts to tie drugs to the commission of other crimes such as theft or violent crime. A generation later, the causal connection between the use of drugs and other types of crime appears fairly certain,[45] though at the time of Nixon's speech social scientists had not yet demonstrated this connection. The argument may have had some intuitive appeal, but, in the late 1960s and early 1970s, there was little hard evidence to support Nixon's proposed nexus. Some studies provided evidence that drug addicts were also likely to commit other crimes, but such studies failed to ask critical questions, such as whether the use of drugs by addicts actually *caused* other types of crime.[46] Thinkers as ideologically different as Ramsey Clark and James Q. Wilson, did not mention or cast doubt upon drug use as a cause of other crimes. Indeed, a study on the relation of drug use to other types of crime, in a 1967 symposium on "Combating Crime" in the *Annals of the American Academy of Political and Social Science,* concluded that "[n]o known drug, by itself, can be shown to 'cause' crime [. . .]" Studies were more likely to tie causation to economic conditions than to drug use and to discuss drug use as a separate offense unrelated to the commission of other crimes.[47] Even a 1972 report by the White House's own National Commission on Marijuana and Drug Abuse concluded that use of drugs did not lead to other crimes and that marijuana use, if anything, inhibited criminal behavior; Nixon found the report unpersuasive.[48]

Whether or not drugs caused public health problems or crime as Nixon claimed, he had found an issue that touched a nerve. The use of illegal drugs, particularly marijuana and LSD but also speed and heroin, was seen as both a contributor to and a symbol for much of the social unrest and cultural turmoil of the 1960s. For that reason alone, use of illegal drugs was a subject of concern in the mid- to late 1960s, and in particular, a source of tension between the young and old. "The popularity of drugs among the young induced panic in the old," historian William O'Neill has written, "[t]he generation gap widened." With its triumvirate partners, sex and rock and roll, drug use was a cornerstone of the counterculture that arose in the middle of the decade.[49] As such, problems associated with drug use—on its own or tied to other phenomena—received significant attention in the press and resonated with broad segments of the public.

Upon taking office, Nixon kept his promise to combat drugs, staffing the effort with enthusiastic young men devoted to the task.[50] Three developments in Nixon's War on Drugs would come to play a critical role in the evolution of profiling.

First, and most important, was the creation of the Drug Enforcement Agency (DEA). Like that of his predecessors, the Nixon administration's initial efforts to fight the use of illegal drugs were spread among a number of agencies, in-

cluding the BNDD and the Office of Drug Abuse Law Enforcement (ODALE). In 1973, the War on Drugs became the
responsibility of the DEA, an agency that was an amalga-
mation of the BNDD, ODALE and the responsibilities of the
Customs Service devoted to enforcement of the laws
against illegal drugs.[51]

The DEA was created after agents for ODALE, in the
spring of 1973, staged raids in the middle of the night on
two residences in Collinsville, Illinois, a suburb of St. Louis,
certain that they had located major drug dealers. The
ODALE agents—with long hair and dressed in shabby street
clothes in an effort to blend into the milieu of the people
they were after—stormed into the homes heavily armed
and dragged the occupants out of bed, shouting at them
and verbally abusing them in the process. The sight of five
long-haired men, dressed as they were and brandishing
weapons, initially led one of the homeowners to believe
that hippies were attacking him and his wife. Unfortunately,
the ODALE agents had the wrong houses and succeeded
only in terrorizing the residents. This created a furor in
Washington, particularly after it was learned that this was
not the first time ODALE agents had raided the wrong residences. Later that year, Congress created the DEA and
placed restrictions on its operations, ironically, in part out of
a desire to better safeguard civil liberties in the effort to
track down major players in the drug trade.[52]

Two other aspects of Nixon's War on Drugs would also
influence the development of profiling. From the beginning, the Nixon administration sought to work with state
and local law enforcement agents in the battle against
drugs, expanding similar initiatives begun under the Johnson administration. Indeed, this tack had been one of the
cornerstones of ODALE's efforts to stop drug dealers. In
fact, it ironically led ODALE to borrow from local law enforcement offices and press into service precisely the type
of poorly trained and poorly disciplined officers who were
the key participants in the Collinsville raids that led to
ODALE's demise.[53]

Finally, the eager young operatives formulating policy and strategy for the War on Drugs in the Nixon White House saw the opportunity to "field test new tactics and weapons."[54] Using a proposed crime bill for the District of Columbia as something of a testing ground, the White House pushed for, and got, a number of aggressive law enforcement techniques that had heretofore been rejected by Congress. Those new law enforcement techniques included preventive detention for suspects of crime and "no knock" raids by law enforcement. White House officials also considered such things as "loose search warrants" that allowed police to search for things not specifically mentioned in the warrant and expanded wiretaps for conversations generally thought of as privileged, such as those involving a suspect's doctor, lawyer or clergy.[55] One of the new law enforcement techniques eventually adopted for use in the War on Drugs, a creation of the DEA, was the drug courier profile.

TABLE 1 Key Developments in President Nixon's "War on Drugs"

Development 1

Establishment of the Drug Enforcement Agency (DEA)—1973
> An amalgamation of the Bureau of Narcotics and Dangerous Drugs (BNDD) and the Office of Drug Abuse Law Enforcement (ODALE), the DEA was created by Congress in order to fight the war on drugs.

Development 2

Cooperation at the Federal, State and Local Levels
> Like its predecessor, ODALE, the DEA forged relationships with state and local law enforcement officers. The DEA, however, had been created, in part, to avoid the abuses and embarrassments that resulted from earlier cooperative endeavors, and thus agents had to be careful to maintain federal oversight.

Development 3

New Tactics and Weapons
> Charged with winning the War on Drugs, the DEA used a variety of tools and strategies. Techniques such as preventive detention and "no-knock" raids were approved by Congress, and with its expanded authority, the DEA eventually created the drug courier profile.

The Airplane Hijacker Profile

If *Terry v. Ohio* provided the legal basis for the drug courier profile, and Nixon's War on Drugs the impetus for it, development of a profile to detect airplane hijackers (also sometimes called "skyjackers") provided the model. The late 1960s, it is important to recall, witnessed not only the decision in *Terry* and the start of the War on Drugs but a dramatic increase in the number of commercial airline flights that were hijacked, that is, in which one or more passengers used violence or threats of violence to force an airborne flight from its original destination to a different one chosen by the hijacker. In the late 1960s crime generally appeared to be flourishing. Still, even in that atmosphere, skyjacking drew special attention; at a time when other types of crime, such as theft and forcible rape, increased by about 15% to 20%, the number of airplane hijackings rose exponentially. "Between 1950 and 1967," William Manchester noted, "the airlines reported an average of 2.3 attempted skyjacks a year. In 1969 there were 71, of which 58 went to Cuba—three times as many as the year before."[56]

Creation of the Skyjacker Profile

In October 1968, the federal government created a Task Force to study the problem and devise a way to stop the increasing number of skyjackings. The Task Force was comprised of representatives from a number of different agencies, including the Department of Justice, the Federal Aeronautics Administration, and the Department of Commerce, and included people trained in a variety of disciplines, including psychology, law and engineering. The Task Force came up with a multi-step procedure to identify skyjackers before they boarded the plane. A profile of potential skyjackers became a critical element of those procedures.[57]

Under the procedures established by the Task Force for "discouraging and apprehending potential hijackers," all passengers about to board a plane had to pass through a magnetometer (commonly referred to as a metal detector) and were observed to see whether they matched the characteristics set out in the hijacker profile. If a passenger met the profile characteristics *and* triggered the metal detector, the passenger was "interviewed" by airline personnel. If airline personnel were then satisfied that the person was no threat to hijack the airplane, he or she was allowed to board the plane. However, if airline personnel still had concerns, the person was not allowed to board and the United States Marshal's Service was called. One or more officers with the United States Marshal's Service then made a further attempt to determine the identification of the passenger and would ask the person to proceed again through the metal detector. If the person refused or, upon complying, still set off the machine, the officer frisked the person. If no weapon was found, the person was allowed to board the plane. However, if a weapon or other item that might be used in a hijacking was found, the person was detained.[58]

The characteristics of the hijacker profile were carefully drawn from a study of previous skyjackings. The Task Force used statistical, sociological, and psychological data to come up with twenty-five to thirty characteristics by which skyjackers appeared to differ from ordinary air travelers. From those twenty-five to thirty characteristics, the Task Force came up with a shorter list to create the profile used by airline personnel. The initial profile was, in turn, tested against a sample of the historical cases involving hijackers to determine its reliability, and it was found that over 90% of the sample group met the profile. The profile was also subsequently reevaluated in light of new hijackings and changes in the trends of hijackings.

The Task Force was very sensitive to the large number of travelers who posed no risk to others and was intent on minimizing the burden to them.[59] Hence, the procedures, including the profile, were also tested to make certain they were as unobtrusive as possible:

One sample consisting of 500,000 screened passengers showed that only 1,406 satisfied the profile—.28%. Approximately one half of those were nevertheless permitted to board immediately after failing to activate the magnetometer, leaving 712, or .14%, to be interviewed. Of those interviewed, 283, approximately one-third, were actually searched. Therefore, only .05% of the sample was ultimately subjected to a preventive weapons frisk. Twenty persons were denied boarding—approximately 1/15 of those searched, and of those, 16 were arrested. In sum, almost everyone (99.86%) of the one-half million persons passed swiftly through the boarding process without even being asked a question and 99.95% boarded without being searched.[60]

Moreover, the procedures appeared to be effective. In *United States v. Lopez,* an early legal challenge to the procedures, the Honorable Jack B. Weinstein, a highly-respected judge in the federal district court with jurisdiction over, *inter alia,* LaGuardia and Kennedy International Airports in New York, noted that "[n]o flight fully protected by the program has been hijacked" and that in 1970 hijackings overall appeared to decline by 50% over the past year.[61]

An Initial Challenge; Some Early Warning Signs

The legal challenge to the FAA's procedures, including the skyjacker profile, over which Judge Weinstein presided in *Lopez,* involved the temporary detention and search of a passenger at Kennedy International Airport who, based on the profile, was suspected of being a potential hijacker. He was not a hijacker, but he *was* carrying a package of heroin concealed beneath his clothing. The defendant was prosecuted for carrying heroin and he moved to suppress the evidence found as a result of the search undertaken because he met the characteristics of the skyjacker profile, challenging the FAA procedures as violation of his Fourth Amendment rights to be free of unreasonable search and seizure.

Judge Weinstein rejected Lopez's general challenge to the FAA's skyjacker profile, deciding that the profile and the procedures established by the FAA constituted a reasonable attempt to combat skyjacking. The court also found that the

preventive detention features and search for weapons con-
templated by the procedures were consistent with the "stop
and frisk" principles set forth in *Terry v. Ohio,* going so far as
to rule that it made no difference that the search for weapons in the course of the FAA's procedures was for a purpose
(to prevent skyjacking) other than to protect law enforcement personnel, which had been the justification for the
frisk given by the Supreme Court in *Terry.*[62]

Still, Judge Weinstein expressed some qualms about the
path upon which law enforcement was embarking:

> We reach this conclusion recognizing that the system used is
> disquieting. Employing a combination of psychological, soci-
> ological, and physical sciences to screen, inspect and categorize
> unsuspecting citizens raises visions of abuse in our increasingly
> technological society. Proposals based upon statistical research
> designed to predict who might commit crimes and giving them
> the special attention of law enforcement agencies is particularly
> disturbing.[63]

And, while approving generally of the procedures established by the Task Force, including the creation and use of a
hijacking profile, Judge Weinstein actually ruled for the defendant in *Lopez* for reasons that bode ill for the path profiling generally was to take. The court held that, in implementing the procedures, airline personnel violated the
defendant's right to be free of unreasonable search and seizure by unilaterally adding two elements to the profile established by the FAA: an unspecified "ethnic element for
which there is no experimental basis" and a second element that required the airline personnel to exercise some
discretion in making the decision to detain the defendant.
This, Judge Weinstein stated, crossed the line: "The approved system survives constitutional scrutiny only by its
careful adherence to absolute objectivity and neutrality.
When elements of discretion and prejudice are interjected,
it becomes constitutionally impermissible."[64]

It warrants mention that not every court expressed similar concerns about the use of the hijacker profile. For exam-

ple, a panel of the Court of Appeals for the Fifth Circuit described the profile as "a valuable and useful tool in the hands of the airport security officers."[65] And another appellate court opined that the "potential for great and immediate harm" presented by skyjacking, along with the "unusual detection problems" and the escalating frequency of the practice had created a "crisis" in law enforcement sufficient to justify the profile.[66]

The hijacker profile is an important early step in the evolution of profiling, with much to teach, at least in hindsight, about what eventually was to become, first, drug courier profiling and, later, racial profiling. In some regards the hijacker profile draws upon the type of criminal profiling being done by Teten, Douglas, and the others in the FBI's BSU. A team of experts drawing upon historical data and experience and methodologies in the social sciences, including psychology, carefully conceived the profile. Moreover, it was carefully tested to determine its validity, shown to be reliable, and attempted to be as precise and accurate as possible.[67]

In other important ways, however, the hijacker profile moved away from those criminal-profiling moorings. For one thing, the profile was essentially proactive, rather than reactive; that is, it was used to detect and prevent a future crime rather than to determine who had committed a known crime. Moreover, the elements of the profile were things readily observable to lay persons, rather than the type of observations only a carefully trained law enforcement official would pick up on. Rather than profiling being the tool of a highly trained "elite" team of experts, the hijacker profile was to be used by laypersons. In other words, profiling was increasingly less the reactive application of information and methodologies by specialists, drawing from the behavioral sciences in the course of a crime investigation, and more the proactive approach by law enforcement personnel generally (and those working with them) to uncover planned or potential criminal activities.

The Lessons from Police Behavior and Training

The development of the skyjacker profile was a dramatic departure from the original conception of profiling, but one quite consistent with what research on police teaches about "street level" practices. The police behavior literature describes how police invariably use their experience to identify potential criminals.

Indeed, our interest in profiling began with a puzzling contrast. On one hand, the standard criminal justice studies on police behavior detailed how experienced cops constructed "pictures" of "typical offenders" and how these pictures shaped police behavior. Nowhere in this classic literature[68] was to be found a condemnation of the reliance on these stereotypes; in fact, learning to form such stereotypes was considered essential to good policing and these shorthand evaluations were part and parcel of the judgments of an experienced police officer. In recent years, though, with the surfacing of racial profiling as a concept, the product of years of police work has come to be condemned as a form of outright racism. On one hand then, the practice of profiling seemed to be a predictable, perhaps laudable part of what police do; on the other, it has increasingly been construed as racially discriminatory behavior. To understand further the roots of racial profiling we turn now to a review of the classic literature on appropriate police practices.

Racism, Pigeon-Holing, and Police Experience

It would be easy and tempting to say that the problems identified with racial profiling is simply the work of a few bad cops. Many of the harshest critics of racial profiling see it as nothing more than unbridled racism, while many who defend the police argue that a small number of cops involved in some unfortunate and highly publicized events have unjustifiably tarred an entire profession. However, one cannot simply dismiss racial profiling as the product of a few rogue cops. As we shall see in this section, before the debate over racial profiling began traditional police practices encouraged law enforcement officers to use experience and training to interpret available information in such a way as to identify "symbolic assailants." Whether what has come to be called "racial profiling" is totally different from traditional police practices and training, whether it is a corruption of those practices and training, or whether it is a legitimate part of a more systematic approach to policing are important issues that have received much less attention than they deserve.

Arguments and explanations abound as to the use of race by police. If we view police behavior as operating along an imaginary continuum, the most crass and least defensible use of race would involve racist officers who relied on race *exclusively*.[69] Some police are said to stop individuals simply because of their race, because the cops are themselves racist. They prefer to pick on minorities, primarily because of the attitudes they bring to the job, essentially because of a person's race as opposed to any particular insights about crime or wrongful behavior.

Then there are those police officers who operate on "hunches," and for whom race looms large in the hunch. The officer has some kind of intuitive belief about an individual's culpability, and his intuition, on average, is also linked to race. The hunch differs a little from simple racist behavior in that it is not necessarily driven by an antipathy toward a minority group, but by a belief that a member of a minority is likely to be guilty.

Finally, race plays a major role in many police decisions because police are taught, usually by their on-the-job experience, that race, along with some other variables, is related to the probability of guilt. This is very important for it is, we believe, at the heart of what makes profiling so complex, so intriguing, and so debatable an issue. It is easy to condemn it and conclude that racist behavior is unacceptable. Similarly, though we might occasionally be attracted to the notion of "hunch" decision making,[70] due process almost always requires something more than a mere hunch before a police officer can act on his suspicions.

But profiling on the basis of police experience is a different matter. Though race could also be used alone, for the most part (and for the purposes of this discussion) we assume that race is used along with a number of other variables in helping police identify suspects. The police officer—either formally through police department directives and training, or through what he learns from experience on the street—comes to identify certain packages of defendant variables as being associated with a higher probability of defendant culpability.[71] Jerome Skolnick coined the term for this kind of stereotyping in his classic book, *Justice Without Trial*. The police officer sees the defendant as a "symbolic assailant," a suspect more likely to be culpable than an individual without the attributes his experience associates with this criminal behavior. In Skolnick's words,

> The policeman, because his work requires him to be occupied continually with potential violence, develops perceptual shorthand to identify certain kinds of people as symbolic assailants, that is, as persons who use gesture, language, and attire that the policeman has come to recognize as a prelude to violence. [. . .] The disposition to stereotype is an integral part of the policeman's world. [. . .] Ethnic stereotypes become part of the armory of investigation.[72]

Thus, Skolnick makes the case for the alert and seasoned police officer who is able to register new situations through the lens of past experiences. Other scholars echo these words but add some additional nuance to the explanation. Roy Roberg and Jack Kuykendall, building on Skolnick, note:

> Who is a dangerous person [to the police officer]? Those "types" of people with whom the officer has the most dangerous or troublesome experiences become in effect, that officer's symbolic assailants. It may be a certain type of person other officers have identified as dangerous. It may be a person the officer stereotyped as dangerous prior to police employment.

Factors that become important in determining danger are a
person's actual behavior, language, dress, area, and in some
situations, age, sex, and ethnicity.[73]

Reflecting on the ways that officers come to identify certain
"types" and situations, William Muir, Jr. writes of the
pigeon-holes police develop over time. Based on his extensive interviews with policemen, Muir concludes:

> To anticipate what was going to happen, policemen developed
> a sense for the patterns in human affairs. They formed con-
> cepts, or classifications, which helped them assimilate and dis-
> tinguish discrete persons and events . . . the methods by which
> policemen developed their judgments were intricate, and their
> procedures and categories changed over the long period of
> their careers. As they matured in their jobs, however, their con-
> cepts became habits and got locked more and more securely
> into place. . . . [Policemen] form concepts: inventing a series of
> pigeonholes into which they slotted similar persons and events.
> Then, they apply the concepts: that is, they consign a particular
> person or event to a particular pigeonhole.[74]

In two other classic studies of police behavior, James Q.
Wilson and Jonathan Rubinstein explicitly confront the way
race may enter into police stereotyping. Wilson observes
that

> The line between prejudging them [people] purely on the
> basis of police experience and prejudging them on the basis of
> personal opinion (showing prejudice) is often very thin. [. . .] [If
> a police officer] believes with considerable justification that
> teenagers, Negroes and lower-income persons commit a dis-
> proportionate share of all reported crimes [. . .] then being in
> those population categories at all makes one, statistically, more
> suspect than other persons.[75]

And Rubinstein writes of police stops in neighborhoods
when they see something out of the ordinary (e.g. seeing a
white person in a black neighborhood—the police assume
he is there to buy drugs or sex). The police officer

> knows that many people would think him prejudiced or cynical
> for harboring such thoughts, but he also knows that these peo-
> ple have not seen what he has seen. [. . .] For the policeman

these judgments are rooted in the reality of city life. He is not
making a moral judgment (regardless of what his private opinions are) but is responding to what he sees daily on the street.[76]

We think these excerpts capture the predominant
themes about police categorizing in the major empirical
studies of police behavior. Much of this groundbreaking research was conducted several decades ago, but we do not
think (based on our observations and interviews with police
within the past few years) that much has changed.[77] Experienced police still sort cases along many variables, and ethnicity and race may be among these. What is striking is that
as we look back at the literature neither endorsements of
nor attacks on these sorting processes are to be found. Consistent with the spirit of the tenets of a neutral social science, what the police did was presented and explained.
Systematic normative assessments of this behavior were
few and far between. Experienced cops not driven by racism sorted along lines that may include race. Experience
was the teacher; making judgments the lesson. Studies almost never said whether this behavior was objectionable or
o.k., whether reliance on variables that might include race
was not just explainable, but was, in fact, an acceptable police practice.

Judicial Attitudes Toward Police Experience

Appellate courts have adopted a similar posture toward the
general lessons of police experience, and have gone beyond
the social science literature by often endorsing the worthi-
ness of what experience has taught police. The Supreme
Court, for example, has frequently noted that trained law
enforcement officers may be "able to perceive and articulate meaning in given conduct which would be wholly innocent to the untrained observer."[78] Other examples from the
Supreme Court and the lower courts express similar sentiments as well:

Whether certain facts viewed as a whole establish reasonable
suspicion must be determined by viewing them in light of a law

enforcement officer's experience and familiarity with the practice of narcotics couriers.[79]

In evaluating the facts giving rise to the officer's suspicion of criminal activity, courts are to give weight to "the officer's knowledge and experience" as well as "rational inferences that could be drawn from the facts objectively and reasonably viewed in light of the officer's expertise."[80]

In reviewing the propriety of an officer's conduct, courts do not have available empirical studies dealing with inferences drawn from suspicious behavior, and we cannot demand scientific certainty from judges or law enforcement officers where none exists. Thus the determination of reasonable suspicion must be based on commonsense judgments and inferences about human behavior.[81]

Police, then, are applauded for the subtlety of judgments they learn to make based on their training and this street experience. Appellate courts and the police hierarchy acknowledge the value of this experience and endorse its centrality to valid police decision-making. Finally, academics, who have time and again "discovered" the way police "sort" defendants, have rarely found fault with this practice. In short, police construction of "symbolic assailants" seems to receive unqualified acceptance in police practices, in judicial decisions, and in the research products of social scientists.

CHAPTER 2

The Airport Drug Courier Profile

As we described last chapter, in the 1970s one strand of profiling began to veer away from the more scientific model developed at the FBI's BSU. Down that separate path law enforcement created the practices that would become what we today call racial profiling.

Creation of the Drug Courier Profile

By 1974, the War on Drugs was bogging down, and the DEA was looking for something to increase its effectiveness. With the skyjacker profile as a model, the DEA developed a "drug courier profile": that is, a set of characteristics that would enable agents to distinguish between regular airline passengers and drug couriers—persons involved in the purchase or sale of illegal drugs—who were traveling to and from cities in which illegal drug use was thought to be rampant. DEA Special Agent Paul Markonni is generally credited with coming up with the drug courier profile when he was working out of the airport in Detroit. After devising the profile, Markonni trained other DEA agents in its use so that, by the end of the decade, the drug courier profile was being used in more than twenty airports nationwide.[1]

In a certain respect, it was a logical step from the sky-jacker profile to the drug courier profile, for, as in the *Lopez* case, many of the passengers stopped because they met the skyjacker profile did not intend to hijack the airplane but *were* carrying drugs. Indeed, the skyjacker profile caught many more people carrying drugs than attempting a sky-jacking: in late 1972, a study of 6,000 arrests resulting from the use of the skyjacker profile showed that more than a third of the people were arrested for carrying drugs, while fewer than a fifth were arrested on charges related to airline safety.[2]

In coming up with the profile, Markonni consulted with fellow DEA agents, informants, defendants in prior drug cases and airline personnel to determine what to look for in passengers attempting to board to tell if any of them were carrying drugs or were on their way to purchase drugs. The procedures used by the DEA agents in connection with the drug courier profile were similar to those used with the sky-jacker profile, except for the use of a metal detector. DEA agents staked out locations in airports and watched travel-ers as they attempted to board and exit planes. Much of the initial effort to gather information involved no confronta-tion, but an effort to learn, simply by observation, relevant facts about the person and the trip he or she was taking. If a person met the profile, agents approached, identified themselves, and attempted to elicit more information to see what, if anything, that person was up to. If additional questioning did not allay the agents' suspicions, they asked the person for permission to search him or her and any carry-on bag or luggage. If he or she refused to consent, the person was frequently told to remain while the agents sought a search warrant; occasionally, the person was told he was free to leave, but his luggage was not.[3]

Rounding Up the Usual Suspects; The Characteristics of the Drug Courier Profile

What were the characteristics of the drug courier profile as developed by Markonni and used by the DEA? Answers to that critical question vary. In the first reported challenge to the drug courier profile, the court, based on testimony by DEA agents, identified four main components of the profile. By the end of the decade, court testimony put the number of characteristics at more than double that original assessment.[4]

One frequently cited opinion from the United States Court of Appeals for the Fifth Circuit, *United States v. Elmore,* also drawing upon testimony from DEA agents including Markonni, identified seven "primary" characteristics and four "secondary" characteristics of the DEA drug courier profile. The "primary" characteristics were (1) arriving from or departing for an identified source city; (2) carrying little or no luggage or large quantities of empty suitcases; (3) traveling by an unusual itinerary such as rapid turnaround time for a very lengthy airplane trip; (4) use of an alias; (5) carrying unusually large amounts of currency worth many thousands of dollars, usually on the suspect's person, in briefcases or bags; (6) purchasing airline tickets with a large amount of small denomination currency; and (7) showing nervousness beyond that ordinarily exhibited by passengers. The "secondary" characteristics were (1) the almost exclusive use of public transportation, particularly taxicabs, in departing from the airport; (2) immediately making a telephone call after deplaning; (3) leaving a false or fictitious telephone number with the airline; and (4) excessively frequent travel to source or distribution cities. A number of studies have pointed to the list of characteristics set out in the *Elmore* opinion as an essentially reliable summary of the contents of the DEA profile developed by Markonni. This is not to say that all of those characteristics were employed in every case; indeed, one in-depth study found that only two of the characteristics—travel involving a "source" city and unusual nervousness—appeared in more than half of the cases.[5]

TABLE 2 "Primary" and "Secondary" Characteristics of the DEA's Drug Courier Profile

Primary Characteristics

1. Arrival from or departure to an identified "source city"
2. Little or no luggage; large numbers of empty suitcases
3. Unusual itinerary, such as rapid turnaround time for lengthy flights
4. Use of an alias
5. Carrying unusually large amounts of currency, generally on the person, or in a briefcase or bag
6. Purchasing a ticket with a large amount of small denomination currency
7. An unusual degree of nervousness or anxiety

Secondary Characteristics

1. Almost exclusive use of public transportation, particularly taxicabs, when departing from the airport
2. Immediate telephone call upon deplaning
3. Leaving a false or fictitious number with the airline
4. Excessively frequent travel to source or distribution cities

Not everyone agreed that the characteristics of the DEA drug courier profile could be reduced to a definite and specific set of characteristics. Instead, some courts described profiles as "rather loosely formulated" and "an informal, apparently unwritten, checklist."[6] Courts and commentators alike noted that components in profiles could change depending on a number of variables, including the region of the country involved, the airport involved, and the method of transportation (planes vs. automobiles), as well as from judicial district to judicial district, the agent, and the law enforcement agency (federal, state or local) involved. An individual agent might even have multiple profiles that he or she used in different cases.[7] And it has been suggested that some of the characteristics of the drug courier profile are confidential and were not even mentioned in the reported cases.[8] In fact, in the petition for certiorari prepared by the government in *United States v. Mendenhall,* the first Supreme Court case involving a challenge to the drug courier profile (a case we discuss in detail below), the Solicitor General's office stated that "there is no national profile; each airport unit has developed its own set of drug courier characteristics on the basis of that unit's experience. [. . .] Furthermore, the profile is not rigid, but is constantly modified in light of experience."[9] As one court concluded,

> It is important to remember that a profile is, in essence, a fact and not a legal principle. As a fact, it is as susceptible to change as the seasons. Telltale characteristics in one region or milieu may be very different from those in others. As counter-measures are constantly devised to meet the tactics of the opposition, the telltale characteristics of last year may not be the telltale characteristics of next year. Because of this inherent fluidity, it is particularly unfit for being frozen into a legal principle.[10]

The large and often varying number of characteristics frequently identified as components of the airport drug courier profile was not always viewed as a positive development. In fact, the highly malleable nature of profiles, along with the "corresponding exponential propagation of characteristics,"[11] provoked sharp criticism in some quarters. One particularly strong rebuke came from Judge George Pratt of the United States Court of Appeals for the Second Circuit, dissenting from a decision by the court to uphold as constitutionally valid a stop and search made by police based on the use of a drug courier profile. In his dissenting opinion, Judge Pratt forcefully stated the problem he (and many others) saw with the drug courier profile:

> To justify their seizure of Hooper's bag the agents testified he had come from a "source city" and fit the DEA's "drug courier profile." Yet the government conceded at oral argument that a "source city" for drug traffic was virtually any city with a major airport, a concession that met with deserved laughter in the

courtroom. The "drug courier profile" is similarly laughable; because it is so fluid that it can be used to justify designating anyone a potential drug courier if the DEA agents so choose. "The
[DEA] has not committed the profile to writing" and "the combination of factors looked for varies among agents." . . . Moreover, a canvass of numerous cases reveals the drug courier profile's "chameleon-like way of adapting to any particular set of
observations."

Then, drawing upon a survey he made of cases involving
airport drug courier profiles, Judge Pratt proceeded to list all
of the contradictory factors in the different profiles:

> arrived late at night . . . arrived early in the morning; one of
> then first to deplane . . . one of the last to deplane . . . deplaned
> in the middle; used a one-way ticket . . . used a round-trip
> ticket; carried brand-new luggage— carried a small gym bag;
> traveled alone . . . traveled with a companion; acted too ner-
> vous . . . acted too calm; wore expensive clothing and gold jew-
> elry . . . dressed in black corduroys, white pullover shirt, loafers
> without socks . . . dressed in dark slacks, work shirt and hat . . .
> dressed in brown leather aviator jacket, gold chain, hair down
> to shoulders . . . dressed in loose fitting sweatshirt and denim
> jacket; walked rapidly through airport . . . walked aimlessly
> through airport; flew to Washington National Airport on the La-
> Guardia shuttle; had a white handkerchief in his hand.[12]

Others have made the same point. Reviewing the cases,
one commentator discovered even more examples of the
factors irksome to Judge Pratt, thus creating an even-larger
list of contradictory features found in various profiles.[13] Testimony by DEA agents could sometimes add to the skepticism of critics that the DEA's drug courier profile was actually comprised of definite characteristics. Thus, one agent
testified that, as summarized by the court, "the profile in a
particular case consists of anything that arouses his suspicion," and in other cases agents showed a marked confusion about or ignorance of what characteristics were to be
found in the profile. Indeed, another agent, after testifying
that the defendant was stopped for meeting the characteristics of a profile, later admitted on cross-examination that
there was no profile.[14]

The composition of the drug courier profile drew other crit-icisms. For one thing, the profiles failed to make clear how many of the various characteristics one had to meet to trigger suspicion or how the various components were to be weighed.[15] "[W]e know little or nothing about the characteris-tics that make up the profile," complained one judge. "Nor do we know about the standards or criteria that guide an agent's application of it to particular individuals. We have only broad, self-serving police assurances that reliance on the profile and the agent's judgment is well founded."[16] Moreover, testimony by DEA agents themselves frequently undermined the reli-ability of the profile characteristics allegedly used. Thus, as a commentator summarizes, in one case, a DEA agent

> admitted that by necessity someone is always first off the plane and someone is always last; that people often walk briskly at airports; and that it is not unusual for someone disembarking from an airplane to look around the terminal. Similarly, a drug agent admitted that jogging to the airport restroom to use the urinal is as "consistent with the actions of a man in a hurry to use the bathroom . . . as it is with an intent to dispose of illegal narcotics by flushing them down the drain."[17]

Other courts also noted that the characteristics relied upon in the profile were as consistent with innocent behavior as criminal conduct.[18] Nonetheless, and despite the flaws, the airport drug courier profile was a frequently used law en-forcement tool in the War on Drugs.

Criminal Profiling vs. the Drug Courier Profile

The airport drug courier profile, like its ancestor the sky-jacker profile, represented a further departure from the type of criminal profiling conducted by law enforcement agents such as the FBI's BSU. Like the skyjacker profile, the drug courier profile was proactive rather than reactive; that is, agents employed the profile without any initial inkling that the person under observation had committed or was about to commit a crime. And, also like the skyjacker profile, the components of the profile were comprised of conduct and characteristics readily observable by ordinary persons as opposed to those evident only to elite units of experts specially trained in the behavioral sciences.

But the drug courier profile is distinguished in more important ways from earlier criminal profiling efforts. For one thing, behavioral science specialists were not involved in the crafting or implementation of the courier profile. Moreover, the profile was never carefully tested to determine its validity, nor was clear evidence gathered that demonstrated that the drug courier profile was reliable. Further, the DEA did not keep statistical data on the success rate of the drug courier profile. What testimony there is points in different directions. Thus, in the first challenge to the profile in *United States v. Van Lewis,* the court produced some reasonably impressive statistics in its defense of the effectiveness of the drug courier profile. The court asserted that "[s]ince the initiation of the DEA airport detail, agents have searched 141 persons in 96 airport encounters prompted by the use of the courier profile and independent police work." The 96 encounters further resulted in 77 searches in which drugs were found. In another case, a DEA agent testified that he found drugs in 60% to 70% of the people he stopped. But another case produced evidence that 30% of the stops and searches produced drugs, 30% of the stops and searches produced no drugs, 30% of the stops did not lead to a subsequent search, and in the remaining 10% of the cases, the person approached refused to stop for the officers.[19]

Finally in this regard, the arguably highly amorphous nature of the drug courier profile, with its endlessly proliferating set of characteristics, departed from the attempt of the skyjacker profile to be as precise as possible. In that regard, the drug courier profile introduced and, indeed, exacerbated that element of discretion in deciding whom to stop and search that Judge Weinstein had found troubling in his opinion in the *Lopez* case.

Race and the Drug Courier Profile

What about the other element to which Judge Weinstein had objected in his *Lopez* decision: the "ethnic" element as part of the profile used in that case? Did DEA agents, in using the drug courier profile to decide whom to stop and question at the nation's airports, use race or ethnicity as a characteristic? Although the formal list of primary and secondary characteristics set out in the *Elmore* case does not include a racial or ethnic component, there is significant evidence that race or ethnicity *was* a part of the drug courier profile, at least a consideration, if not formally one of the initial characteristics.

That evidence comes in part from the testimony of DEA agents, including Paul Markonni. In at least two cases, Markonni presented testimony suggesting that race had been a factor. In one case, Markonni testified that blacks preferred heroin to cocaine, and thus, "a black arriving from a major heroin distribution point arouses greater suspicion, *ceteris paribus* [all things being equal] than one arriving from a major cocaine distribution point." In another case, Markonni testified that most drug couriers were African American females. A racial element was apparent in other ways as well: for example, a police officer offered testimony that 75% of the persons stopped at the Memphis airport were African American, and a survey of cases in the early 1990s in which the drug courier profile was used showed that sixty out of sixty-three stops, more than 95% of the stops, involved minorities.[20]

Testimony and other evidence simply describing the recurring pattern of racial characteristics of those stopped may, strictly speaking, stop short of identifying race as a formal component of the drug courier profile. Still, it is significant proof that the race of those under observation played some role in the decision to stop. Indeed, given the observation and consideration of a host of small details inherent in implementing the drug courier profile—from how the person paid for his ticket to how he was dressed to whether he stopped to use the phone—it would be remarkable if law enforcement failed to notice or ignored the race of those they were watching. The conclusion by one scholar expressed almost a decade after the drug courier profile was first created and used—that the use of race as part of the profile had become "common or routine"[21]—may not be far off the mark. (Indeed, it has long been the fact that a number of profiles used by law enforcement, less prominent than the drug courier profile, have racial components, which have attracted little or no attention or criticism. For example, it is part of the standard profile of serial killers that the typical offender is white.[22]) What is remarkable, however—if the use of race was a common component of the drug courier profile—is that it received little if any mention by either the popular media or the courts for much of the 1970s and 1980s.

The Drug Courier Profile and the Courts

The courts are generally viewed as playing critical roles not simply in resolving legal disputes, but in articulating general legal principles and educating the public about those principles. This is especially true of the Supreme Court, described in a famous formulation as a "republican schoolmaster" and in another as conducting a "vital national seminar." This is particularly true when the Court is called on to handle issues involving rights secured by the United States Constitution. In those disputes involving the Constitution, the Court is afforded the opportunity to educate the public about the fundamental principles that guide us as a nation. Unfortunately, the Court does not always take up that opportunity. As one scholar has noted, "the Court has not always realized this noble intention. On occasion what it has taught the citizenry has served more to jeopardize than to sustain republican principles."[23]

The Supreme Court first confronted the practice of profiling in two cases in the spring of 1980, *United States v. Mendenhall* and *Reid v. Georgia*. By that time, the federal government's use of profiles, particularly the airport drug courier profile, over the course of the previous decade had introduced profiling to federal courts and presented legal issues attendant thereto in a number of cases.[24] As a general matter, courts frequently recognized the drug courier profile as a distinct law enforcement tool, although attitudes toward the practice were hardly uniform.[25]

Some courts praised the use of the drug courier profile as a valuable law enforcement tool. In *United States v. Rico,* for example, in evaluating the appropriateness of an airport search, the United States Court of Appeals for the Second Circuit spoke in favorable terms of the law enforcement agents who routinely employed profiles in attempting to deal with the drug traffic at airports: "[n]o doubt the cumulative experience of the special agents in the surveillance details at the airports must give rise to a kind of institutional expertness that can be summed into a check list of recurrent traits of conduct found in narcotics couriers."[26] A Maryland state court was even more effusive in its praise of the use of a drug courier profile in the case before it: "Far from being unreasonable, the investigative behavior in the case was a model of both thoroughness and restraint. Had they done other than they did, the police would have been derelict and the scourge upon our society that is the drug traffic would have gone unabated."[27] Moreover, DEA agent Markonni was recognized for his contribution in creating and using the profile by more than one court;[28] the work of other DEA agents also seemed to find an admiring or receptive audience with the courts.[29]

However, some courts expressed more skepticism about the use of the drug courier profile. The components of the drug courier profile prompted one court to write that, "[c]areful review of those characteristics causes this Court serious concern that the use of such profile, without more, could result in the interrogation of honest law-abiding citizens as easily as it could the apprehension of criminals."[30] Judge Oakes, of the United States Court of Appeals for the Second Circuit, was more critical. Dissenting in another case in which the defendant challenged (unsuccessfully) the validity of an airport search involving the use of the drug courier profile, Judge Oakes wrote,

The question in today's case is whether we will now expand the
Terry-Adams exception to a course of organized police conduct
practiced by the Drug Enforcement Administration at airports
across the country, not simply an individual police officer per-
ceiving that a crime is about to be or has been committed. This
case is just one of many [. . .] arising out of a DEA program in
operation in more than twenty United States airports. [. . .]

What has happened, I fear, is that this court, in a series of
cases which have usually involved a very active DEA agent, has
put its stamp of approval on a system of law enforcement,
without the full appreciation of its overall impact and implications. [. . .]

If airports can support special police conduct, why not other
public places[,] bus terminals, railroad stations, subway stops,
restaurants, bars? If Agent Gerard Whitmore and DEA agents in
general, why not any other officer "trained" to observe "suspicious conduct"? Once the dam is broken, a flood is likely to
occur. Anthony Amsterdam has perceptively warned against
the "perversion" of stop-and-frisk or similar limited-purpose
police actions into general search warrants, putting, in James
Otis's words, "the liberty of every man in the hands of every
petty officer."[31]

Thus, profiling at the end of the 1970s was a practice recognized by the courts, and, while it would be an exaggeration
to describe the lower court opinions as engaged in a raging
debate on the subject of profiling, the varied opinions had
produced a wide range of attitudes about the practice, both
positive and negative. Such was the legal landscape as the
Supreme Court approached the *Mendenhall* and *Reid* cases
at the end of the October 1979 term.

The Supreme Court Steps In

The *Mendenhall* Case

The Supreme Court first confronted a challenge to a stop
and search conducted pursuant to the drug courier profile in
United States v. Mendenhall. That case, however, turned out
to be something of a false start. In that case, Sylvia Mendenhall was stopped and searched by DEA agents at the Detroit
Metropolitan airport as a result of which she was found to

be carrying heroin and eventually convicted of smuggling narcotics. She sought to suppress evidence obtained during the search by challenging the stop and search as a violation of her Fourth Amendment rights.

Testimony at the trial in that case established that Mendenhall had been stopped because she met a number of the characteristics associated with the drug courier profile.[32] That prompted DEA agents to approach her for questioning, upon which they discovered that she had used an alias in purchasing her airline ticket, further arousing their suspicion. They asked her to accompany them to a DEA office at the airport, which she did. They also asked her if she would consent to a search of her person. She balked at first, but then submitted to the search, and two packets of heroin were found in the search.[33]

The trial court found that the profile characteristics in that case established the reasonable suspicion necessary to justify the stop and search and denied Mendenhall's motion to suppress the heroin found during the search, but the Sixth Circuit Court of Appeals reversed. The Supreme Court took the case, with an opportunity to provide some guidance on if and when the drug courier profile was a constitutionally permissible law enforcement technique.[34]

Unfortunately, the Court never got that far, because a majority of the Justices, in two separate opinions, found that Mendenhall had consented to the stop and search. *Mendenhall* actually produced a number of opinions that went in a variety of directions. The opinion for the Court, a plurality opinion written by Justice Stewart and joined by one other justice, found that, although the initial stop of Mendenhall had resulted from the use of the drug courier profile, Mendenhall had consented to the stop, and thus the stop and search did not raise any issues under the Fourth Amendment.[35]

Justice Powell authored a concurring opinion, joined in by two other justices, which also refused to treat the stop of Mendenhall as a seizure sufficient to trigger the Fourth Amendment because the issue had not been raised in the courts below. Justice Powell's concurrence, however, went further. He found that, even assuming a stop for purposes of the Fourth Amendment took place, the stop was justified under the rationale set forth in the decision in *Terry* because the DEA agents had a reasonable suspicion that Mendenhall was engaging in criminal activity. Powell briefly discussed the DEA's use of the drug courier profile, characterizing it as "a highly specialized law enforcement operation designed to combat the serious societal threat posed by narcotics distribution." However, for Powell, what was critical to the decision to stop Mendenhall and others in her situation was not the profile *per se,* but the ability of law enforcement to "perceive and articulate meaning in given conduct which would be wholly innocent to the untrained observer," and he further concluded that "the careful and commendable police work that led to the criminal conviction in this case satisfies the requirements of the Fourth Amendment."[36]

Finally, Justice White dissented, in an opinion joined by three other justices, arguing that Mendenhall had been subjected to a seizure for purposes of the Fourth Amendment and that the grounds offered to justify the stop—factors found in the drug courier profile—did not amount to reasonable suspicion that criminal activity was afoot because much of the conduct was otherwise innocent behavior. The dissent did not, however, use the occasion to engage in a meaningful discussion of the general validity of profiling as a practice.[37]

Altogether, the three opinions in *Mendenhall* cannot be said to constitute a careful or in-depth consideration of the practice of profiling, though some have argued that the five-member majority represented in Justice Stewart's lead opinion and Justice Powell's concurrence appeared to give tacit approval to the use of the drug courier profile by DEA agents.[38] Doubt was cast on even that assessment three months later when the Court issued its decision in *Reid v. Georgia.*

The Decision in *Reid*

In *Reid,* an agent of the DEA employing the drug courier profile stopped Tommy Reid and a companion at the Atlanta airport. The factors cited by the agent prompting the stop were that the two men had arrived from Fort Lauderdale, a "source city" for cocaine; they arrived early in the day when law enforcement presence is believed to be less; Reid and his companion appeared to attempt to conceal the fact that they were traveling together; and the only luggage the two men had were shoulder bags. In the course of the stop, the agents asked Reid and his companion to accompany them to an office where they could be searched. Although they at first indicated they would go with the agents, Reid suddenly bolted and tried to run away, but in doing so he abandoned a shoulder bag he was carrying. The DEA agent found cocaine in the bag and arrested Reid, who was later charged with drug possession. Before trial, a lower state court granted a defense motion to suppress the cocaine found as the result of an illegal seizure. The Georgia Court of Appeals, however, reversed that decision.[39]

On appeal from the Georgia Court of Appeals, the case presented a critical (indeed, perhaps the *central*) issue concerning profiling in about as direct a way as one can imagine: whether an investigatory stop by police could be justified for purposes of the Fourth Amendment, solely based on the fact that "the petitioner, 'in a number of respects, fit a "profile" of drug couriers compiled by the [DEA].'"[40] The Georgia Court of Appeals held the investigatory stop permissible, based solely on the Supreme Court's decision in *Terry*.[41]

Unlike Sylvia Mendenhall's equivocal effort to cooperate with the DEA, Reid's mad dash out of the airport precluded any argument that he had consented to the stop and search, and thus the issue of the constitutionality of the stop and search was joined. Unfortunately, for those hoping that the Court would take the opportunity to engage in a meaningful discussion of the drug courier profile and answer a number of the legal issues that had arisen about drug courier profiles in the preceding decade, what followed was a disappointment, for the Court's opinion did not clarify matters regarding the use of the drug courier profile.

In a brief *per curiam* opinion, the Court declined the opportunity to discuss at any length what is entailed by the use of a profile, whether it is a legitimate (or illegitimate) technique of law enforcement, or when, if ever, it can be used. Instead, the Court essentially ignored it as a law enforcement technique. The Court briefly described the "drug courier profile" as a "somewhat informal compilation of characteristics believed to be typical of persons unlawfully carrying narcotics."[42] After listing the four components of the profile that the lower court had relied upon to justify the stop, the Court concluded that "the [DEA] agent could not as a matter of law have reasonably suspected the petitioner of criminal activity on the basis of these observed characteristics."[43] Although the Court noted that most of the circumstances relied upon "describe a very large category of presumably innocent travelers," it did not use that fact or assessment to criticize profiling generally or to set parameters for the appropriate use of the practice under the Fourth Amendment. Instead, the profile was simply irrelevant to the Court's discussion. The Court ruled that law enforcement officials, as in any case involving a *Terry* stop, must have a reasonable and articulable basis for suspicion, which the Court found was not present based on the facts before it in the case.[44]

It has been suggested that a majority of the Court in *Mendenhall* gave a nod of approval to the use of drug courier profiles and *Reid* represents a retreat from that approval,[45] but actually that is not at all clear, because without a fuller discussion of profiling as a distinct law enforcement technique in either case, it is difficult to say what, if anything, the Justices liked and what they did not like about drug courier profiles. What *is* clear from the decision in *Reid* is that reliance on the profile was not enough by itself to justify an investigatory stop; in that regard, the Court's holding in *Reid* essentially followed what had been the prevailing law enunciated in the lower federal courts before the Court's decision.[46] Equally important, however, the use of the drug courier profile was a non-issue for the Court.

This was the lesson lower federal courts and law enforcement took from *Reid* concerning the use of profiles. Law enforcement continued to use profiling, especially the drug courier profile, with one result being that the number of cases in which such investigatory stops were at issue in the lower federal courts over the next decade increased significantly.[47] Lower federal courts, evaluating claims that Fourth Amendment rights had been violated on a case-by-case basis, looked for something more than the use of a profile in judging the validity of an investigatory stop. There are some decisions in which the lower courts appeared to try to come to grips with profiling as a practice,[48] but the decision in *Reid* appears not to have stirred any deep consideration of or debate about the practice of profiling as its own separate or unique law enforcement technique.[49]

Some lower courts expressed disappointment with the failure of the Supreme Court to provide more guidance in the area. One court, for example, lamented "the Supreme Court's refusal to issue a clear statement on the use of the profile and the facially inconsistent results reached in the case-by-case treatment of the issue, both in the Supreme Court and most lower courts."[50] Another court decried "the uncertainty created by decisions of the Supreme Court" regarding the use of profiles.[51] One study of the use of drug courier profiles, published a couple of years after the Supreme Court decisions, summarized the effect in the lower federal courts of the Supreme Court's decisions in *Mendenhall* and *Reid* as follows:

> Immediately after *Mendenhall* and *Reid* confusion abounded among the lower courts. Not only did the Supreme Court decline the opportunity presented in those cases to invalidate the drug courier profile . . . but it also left unanswered questions certain to arise with greater frequency following its decisions. For example, at what point during a profile stop does a seizure occur? And what circumstances justify a determination that an airline traveler has consented to a further intrusion or a search?
>
> Whether commentators viewed *Mendenhall* and *Reid* as "conflicting" or as "exacerbating the 'state of morass'" currently surrounding fourth amendment law, two things seemed clear.

First, lower courts generally upheld investigatory stops following the decisions, and, second, the courts no longer dwelled on
profile characteristics and the concept of reasonable suspicion.
Furthermore, the courts addressed the question whether the
facts known to DEA agents at the moment of the initial encounter constituted reasonable suspicion in rather summary fashion.[52]

Confusion reigned in the lower courts, trial and appellate,
which, because such courts must, as a general rule, hear
and decide the cases brought before them—as opposed to
the Supreme Court, which has discretion as to which cases
it will hear—could not avoid the cases involving questionable stops and searches by officials using the airport drug
courier profile. Nonetheless, despite the uncertainty engen-
dered by its decisions in *Mendenhall* and *Reid,* the Supreme
Court showed no appetite for dealing with the drug courier
profile as a separate or distinct law enforcement technique.
A few years after *Reid,* in *Royer v. Florida,* a stop pursuant to
the drug courier profile once again produced a search that
uncovered drugs, which the defendant tried to have ex-
cluded from his trial. In that case, the majority barely mentioned the use of the profile, and the case turned on two
separate issues: whether the defendant had initially been
seized within the meaning of the Fourth Amendment and
whether he had consented to the search of his luggage. Justice Marshall's majority opinion briefly discussed the investigative stops on less-than-probable cause allowed by *Terry*
but not in the context of the use of drug courier profiles.
Nonetheless, the *Royer* case produced what remains the
longest discussion of profiling as a concept and separate
law enforcement practice by a member of the Court, this in
a dissent by Justice Rehnquist:

> As one DEA agent explained: "basically it's a number of charac-
> teristics which we attribute or which we believe can be used to
> pick out drug couriers . . . we begin to see a pattern in these
> characteristics and began using them to pick out individuals we
> suspected as narcotic couriers without any prior information."
> [. . .] In fact, the function of the "profile" has been somewhat
> overplayed. Certainly, a law enforcement officer can rely on his

own experience in detection and prevention of crime. Likewise, in training police officers, instruction focuses on what has been learned through the collective experience of law enforcers. The "drug courier profile" is an example of such instruction. It is not intended to provide a mathematical formula or automatically establish ground rules for a belief that criminal activity is afoot. By the same reasoning, however, simply because those characteristics are accumulated in a "profile," they are not to be given less weight in assessing whether a suspicion is well founded. While each case will turn on its own facts, sheer logic dictates that where certain characteristics repeatedly are found among drug smugglers, the existence of those characteristics in a particular case is to be considered accordingly in determining whether there are grounds to believe that further investigation is appropriate.[53]

Not surprisingly, Justice Rehnquist's dissent, representing one Justice's view of profiling, did not solve anything or lead to different treatment of the practice in the lower courts. At the end of the decade, the Court took one last look at profiling.

The *Sokolow* Decision

The United States Supreme Court returned to the practice of profiling nearly a decade after *Mendenhall* and *Reid* in *United States v. Sokolow*,[54] and while the Court's analysis is somewhat more developed in the *Sokolow* decision, as opposed to the brief *per curiam* opinion in *Reid,* the overall thrust of the opinion is to the same effect as in the earlier decision.[55]

As described by Chief Justice Rehnquist in his opinion for the Court majority, the relevant facts are as follows. Andrew Sokolow and a companion were stopped by Drug Enforcement Administration agents, shortly after they got off a commercial airline flight that landed at Honolulu National Airport. At the time of the stop, the DEA agents knew a few things about Sokolow and his trip that matched an airport drug courier profile and that they claimed aroused their suspicions and prompted the stop. For one thing, Sokolow, who was dressed in a black jumpsuit and gold jewelry, had paid for the two round-trip tickets costing $2,100 in cash from a roll of twenty dollar bills totaling $4,000. His original destination was Miami with stopovers in Denver and Los Angeles; Sokolow and his companion stayed for only forty-eight hours in Miami, despite the fact that a round-trip from Honolulu to Miami takes twenty hours. Rounding out the facts DEA agents believed they knew that prompted the stop, Sokolow traveled under his mother's maiden name (Kray), and gave as his telephone number a number that was listed in yet another name that matched neither Sokolow nor Kray; Sokolow and his companion checked none of their luggage, and Sokolow appeared nervous when approached by DEA agents.[56]

Sokolow refused to consent to DEA's requests to search his luggage, but with the help of drug-sniffing dogs, the DEA agents obtained search warrants and found "several suspicious documents indicating [Sokolow's] involvement in drug trafficking" in his shoulder bag and 1,063 grams of cocaine in another piece of his carry-on luggage. Sokolow was charged with possession of cocaine with intent to distribute. After an initial motion to suppress was denied, Sokolow entered a conditional plea of guilty, reserving the right to challenge the initial stop further. At issue once again was a stop and search based on the use of a drug courier profile.

The United States Court of Appeals for the Ninth Circuit reversed the trial court and, in a 2 to 1 decision, ruled the initial stop of Sokolow was unconstitutional. But the Ninth Circuit did more than that. In one of the few extensive discussions of profiling found in lower courts after the Court's decision in *Reid,* the Ninth Circuit held that the use of a profile warranted a different analysis than the Court had set forth in *Terry,* or at least a variation on that analysis. The court stated that "The drug courier profile, if used as a measure of reasonable suspicion, operates in a different manner than did the officer's trained evaluation that warranted the stop in *Terry.*"[57] The court distinguished between two categories of characteristics found in profiles: those, such as using an alias and acting evasively, that were, by themselves, fairly strong indicia of ongoing criminal activity; and "probabilistic" personal characteristics, such as manner of attire, travel to a source city, and appearing nervous, that may be further evidence of criminal activity but may also simply be innocent conduct. The court held that to satisfy the Fourth Amendment, a stop and search using a profile must contain at least one or more element found in the first category and cannot be based solely on "probabilistic" factors.[58]

The Department of Justice appealed and the case made its way to the Supreme Court, as the Court "granted certiorari to review the decision of the Court of Appeals . . . because of the serious implications for the enforcement of the federal narcotics laws."[59]

The Supreme Court reversed the Ninth Circuit and upheld the stop and search. The Court, as it had in *Reid,* adhered closely to the analysis set forth in *Terry v. Ohio.* The majority of the Court ruled that an investigatory stop by the DEA agents did not violate the Fourth Amendment as long as the agents were able to identify and articulate facts or factors from which one could determine that a "reasonable suspicion" existed that "criminal activity was afoot" based on a consideration of the totality of the circumstances. "The officer," insisted Chief Justice Rehnquist, echoing *Terry,* "must be able to articulate something more than an "inchoate and unparticularized suspicion or 'hunch.'"[60] Based on the facts before it, the Court majority found that the agents had demonstrated the necessary "reasonable suspicion":

> Paying $2,100 in cash for two airplane tickets is out of the ordinary, and it is even more out of the ordinary to pay that sum from a roll of $20 bills containing nearly twice that amount of cash. Most business travelers, we feel confident, purchase airline tickets by credit card or check so as to have a record for tax purposes, and few vacationers carry with them thousands of dollars in $20 bills. We also think the agents had a reasonable ground to believe that respondent was traveling under an alias; the evidence was by no means conclusive, but it was sufficient to warrant consideration. While a trip from Honolulu to Miami, standing alone, is not a cause for any sort of suspicion, here

there was more; surely few residents of Honolulu travel from
the city for hours to spend 48 hours in Miami during the month
of July. Any one of those factors is not by itself proof of any illegal conduct and is quite consistent with innocent travel. But we
think taken together they amount to reasonable suspicion.[61]

One difference between the Court's approach in *Sokolow*
upholding the conduct of the DEA agents, compared to *Reid*
when the stop and search were held not to pass constitutional muster, was simply that this time around, the Court
decided to connect the dots, so to speak, and to draw inferences of suspicious conduct from otherwise innocent behavior (or at least to allow law enforcement to draw such inferences), when considering the facts in total.

What did not change was the Court's casual treatment of
the drug courier profile. That Sokolow was stopped using a
profile was clear; one might have expected that fact, coupled
with the passage just quoted, to have ushered in support for
the use of profiles or at least an extended discussion of the
pros and cons of the practice and recognition of profiling as
a separate and unique law enforcement tactic, especially
given that the use of a profile was of critical importance to
the analysis of the Ninth Circuit that the Court was reviewing, and that the lower court had gone so far as to carve out
a special test to measure the constitutionality of stops and
searches that are the product of the use of profiles.

Nonetheless, the Court's majority opinion contains neither an endorsement nor criticism of profiling, nor even a
meaningful discussion of the practice. Indeed, in contrast to
the view of profiling as a unique law enforcement technique
and the centrality of that consideration to the court's analysis found in the Ninth Circuit decision, the majority
opinion's consideration of profiling was very limited, essentially a paragraph in length, and responding to an argument
by Sokolow that the use of a profile had deprived some or
all of the facts surrounding his stop of any significance. The
Court rejected the argument, stating briefly:

We do not agree with respondent that our analysis is somehow
changed by the agent's belief that his behavior was consistent

with one of the DEA's "drug courier profiles.". . . A court sitting
to determine the existence of a reasonable suspicion must require the agent to articulate the factors leading to that conclusion, but the fact that these factors might be set forth in a "profile" does not somehow detract from their evidentiary
significance as seen by a trained agent.[62]

The use of a profile did not by itself disprove or argue
against the determination that there was reasonable suspicion that criminal activity was occurring. But neither did the
Court accord use of the profile, or the fact that Sokolow had
matched some of the factors, any significance. Rather,
under the Court's analysis, to determine whether a particular stop and search comports with the Fourth Amendment,
law enforcement officers, in accordance with *Terry,* had to
describe specific facts showing why they concluded that
there might be criminal activity afoot. That the object of the
stop and search matched some of the factors in a drug
courier profile neither added to nor detracted from the analysis. In short, as the Court majority saw it, the use of a profile by law enforcement to determine whom to stop and
search is essentially irrelevant.

Not every member of the Court was as unconcerned or
blasé about the practice of profiling as the majority opinion
reflects. Justice Thurgood Marshall tried to raise a more direct consideration of profiling in his dissenting opinion, in
which Justice William Brennan joined.

In part, Marshall's dissenting opinion harkened back to
the approach of the Court in *Reid,* in which the Court objected to the use of ostensibly innocent conduct and facts
to provoke a stop and search. Justice Marshall viewed the
consideration that Sokolow took a brief trip to a resort city
for which he brought only carry-on luggage as insufficient
to justify a stop, since it "describe[s] a very large category
of presumably innocent travelers."[63] Marshall went further, discounting the significance of the fact that Sokolow
paid for his tickets in cash, stating that this indicated "no
imminent or ongoing criminal activity."[64] He added,
"[t]hat Sokolow embarked from Miami, 'a source city of il-

legal drugs' is no more suggestive of illegality; thousands of innocent persons travel from 'source cities' every day."[65] Furthermore, "[t]hat Sokolow had his phone listed in another person's name also does not support the majority's assertion that the DEA agents reasonably believed Sokolow was using an alias; it is commonplace to have one's phone registered in the name of a roommate, which, it later turned out, was precisely what Sokolow had done."[66]

Notwithstanding the foregoing, however, Marshall was also upset with more than simply the majority's treatment of the facts surrounding Sokolow's stop and arrest; Marshall was as concerned with the manner in which the DEA agents carried out their responsibilities as with what they claimed to find. Unlike the approach reflected in the majority opinion, Marshall did not consider the use of a profile by the DEA agents to be insignificant or irrelevant. Marshall protested that "[i]t is highly significant that the DEA agents stopped Sokolow because he matched one of the DEA's 'profiles' of a paradigmatic drug courier."[67] Marshall continued:

> In my view, a law enforcement officer's mechanistic application of a formula of personal behavioral traits in deciding whom to detain can only dull the officer's ability and determination to make sensitive and fact-specific inferences in "light of his experience," particularly in ambiguous or borderline cases. Reflexive reliance on a profile of drug courier characteristics runs a far greater risk than does ordinary, case-by-case police work of subjecting innocent individuals to unwarranted police harassment and detention.[68]

He protested as well the majority's dismissing any consideration of the practice of profiling: "In asserting that it is not 'somehow' relevant that the agents who stopped Sokolow somehow did so in reliance on a prefabricated profile of criminal characteristics, [. . .] the majority thus ducks serious issues relating to a questionable law enforcement practice, to address the validity of which we granted certiorari in this case."[69]

TABLE 3 The United States Supreme Court and the Drug Courier Profile

NAME OF CASE	YEAR	DISCUSSION OF PROFILING
United States v. Mendenhall	1980	Justice Stewart, in a plurality opinion for the Court, found that, although Mendenhall had been stopped on account of the drug courier profile, she had consented to the stop, and thus the case did not raise any Fourth Amendment concerns. Justice Powell authored a concurrence that also avoided the Fourth Amendment issues but which emphasized the importance of law enforcement officers' training and perceptive powers. Finally, Justice White, with three others, dissented but did not engage in a sustained discussion of profiling as a practice.
Reid v. Georgia	1980	In a *per curiam* opinion, the Court concluded that the DEA agent could not have reasonably concluded that criminal activity was afoot, based simply on the four characteristics mentioned at trial, and thus did not have a reasonable and articulable basis for suspicion. The Court avoided any meaningful discussion of the practice of profiling.
Royer v. Florida	1983	Justice Marshall's majority opinion hardly mentioned profiling, though Justice Rehnquist's dissent stressed the significance of officers' accumulated instruction, experience, and intuition, and he explained that certain patterns should not be discounted simply because they are one part of a profile
United States v. Sokolow	1989	Justice Rehnquist, for the majority, found this search acceptable, but again emphasized that law enforcement officers must have more than a "hunch." The Court did not conclude that the invocation of the profile was in itself talismanic, nor did it conclude that conformity to such characteristics created grounds for "reasonable suspicion." An agent might rely on the profile, but she would still need to be able to articulate the particular causes of her suspicion, and the courts would have to review the totality of circumstances and decide whether the standard had been met on a case-by-case basis.

(continued)

TABLE 3 *(continued)*

NAME OF CASE	YEAR	DISCUSSION OF PROFILING
Illinois v. Wardlow	1999	Justice Stevens alludes to racial profiling in a dissent in this case, finding that minorities have many good reasons to fear—and thus avoid—contact with the police.
Atwater v. City of Lago Vista	2001	Dissenting, Justice O'Connor mentions the "recent debacle over racial profiling" and rejects the "unbounded discretion" afforded to the police by the majority's ruling.

The Court's Missed Opportunity

Sokolow is the last time the United States Supreme Court made any effort to deal with a stop in which the use of a profile in law enforcement's decision to make the stop was at issue. Even as the debate about racial profiling intensified, the Court did not return to a consideration of the practice. Indeed, even acknowledgment of the debate over profiling or racial profiling has been rare. Mention of profiling—this time racial profiling—is found in an opinion by Justice Stevens in a case from the October 1999 term, *Illinois v. Wardlow*.[70] In *Wardlow,* the Court ruled that an investigatory stop based essentially on the person's attempting to run away from law enforcement was justified under the Fourth Amendment, relying heavily in its decision on, among other cases, the decision in *Sokolow*. In an opinion dissenting in part from the majority opinion, Justice Stevens objected,

> Among some citizens, particularly minorities and those residing in high crime areas, there is also the possibility that the fleeing person is entirely innocent, but, with or without justification, believes that contact with the police can itself be dangerous, apart from any criminal activity associated with the officer's sudden presence. For such a person, unprovoked flight is neither "aberrant" nor "abnormal." Moreover, these concerns and fears are known to the police officers themselves, and are validated by law enforcement investigations into their own practices.[71]

In support of that last point, Justice Stevens alluded to the New Jersey Attorney General's investigation into racial profiling as well as an investigation by the Massachusetts Attorney General into police practices in that state.[72]

Even more pointed a reference to racial profiling is found in a case from the October 2000 term, *Atwater v. City of Lago Vista*,[73] again in a dissent. In *Atwater*, the Court ruled that there was no constitutional bar to a custodial arrest for a minor traffic offense, even when the underlying offense could not, by itself, be punished by imprisonment. Dissenting, Justice O'Connor objected to the "unbounded discretion" the Court's decision gave to police officers and supported her argument with the observation that "as the recent debate over racial profiling demonstrates all too clearly, a relatively minor traffic infraction may serve as an excuse for stopping and harassing an individual."[74] One recent study suggests that the Court majority in *Atwater* may also have been influenced by the specter of racial profiling even if the Court's opinion does not say so expressly.[75]

But those two references—Justice Stevens' in *Wardlow* and Justice O'Connor's in *Atwater*—appear to be the only references to the profiling debate by members of the Supreme Court over the last decade. And, like Justice Rehnquist's treatment of profiling in his dissent in the *Royer* case and Justice Marshall's unsuccessful effort in his dissent in *Sokolow* to persuade his brethren to address profiling directly, they represent only the isolated views of individual justices and are not in any way either binding or authoritative, nor do they present a fully developed consideration of the practice by the full Court.

As reflected first in *Reid* and later *Sokolow*, what is most significant about the Supreme Court's treatment of profiling is the Court's refusal to give it any special attention or consideration as a unique or distinct law enforcement technique. This is particularly significant in the period after *Sokolow*, as the appropriateness of profiling, and especially racial profiling, became such a visible public question. The present Supreme Court is not a group that appears shy or reluctant about getting involved in the pressing issues of the day.[76] Therefore, it is somewhat surprising that the Court has not directly and completely addressed the practice of profiling, either in its initial forays into the area or, more particularly since *Sokolow,* even though the interpretation of the decision by lower courts, especially state courts, has been spotty and uneven,[77] and especially as racial profiling has become perhaps the central law enforcement issue of the day.

Precisely *why* the Court has avoided addressing profiling in more considered terms, despite many opportunities to do so and the urging of some like Justice Marshall and many lower court judges and legal commentators, and what that failure says about profiling is unclear.[78] There are at least two significant consequences, however, of the Court's failure to step more fully into the breach. For one thing, as noted above in the discussion of the reaction of the lower federal courts to the *Mendenhall* and *Reid* decisions, the Supreme Court's treatment of profiling has, at best, left many questions unanswered and arguably has muddied the already murky waters of certain aspects of Fourth Amendment law.[79] It seems, at least in hindsight, that the *Reid* and *Sokolow* cases present something of a missed opportunity; it is at least possible that, had the Court dealt with profiling as a distinct law enforcement practice as it at least twice had the opportunity to do, and as Justice Marshall urged in his *Sokolow* dissent, the Court may have helped clarify concepts and issues that are currently very much the subject of debate.

Second, and perhaps equally important, one significant result of the Court's hands-off approach to profiling has been to divorce or at least distance the Court (and all of the other lower courts that are required to follow the Court's direction on these issues) from the public debate over racial profiling that flared in the mid-to-late 1990s. And that phenomenon was exacerbated by the Court's treatment of what became the central issue in the larger public debate, the issue of race. We return to the Court's treatment of race in Chapter 5.

CHAPTER 3

From the Drug Courier Profile to Racial Profiling on the Highways

*We must remember that the extent of any privilege of search and seizure
without warrant which we sustain, the officers interpret
and apply themselves and will push to the limit.*[1]

After the development and use of the drug courier profile at
airports, the next critical step in the evolution of racial profiling was the extension of that practice to the nation's
highways and the development and use of drug courier
profiles to search for drugs on the highways. Although used
primarily at airports, there was nothing about the drug
courier profile that limited its use to a particular venue or
type of travel. A similar profile to detect drug traffickers had
been developed for use on trains (although in one case, the

informal profile used by train personnel, as described by the court, consisted only of the suspect's purchase of a one-way rail ticket for a trip from Los Angeles to New York and his handling the heavy suitcases himself rather than checking them with railroad personnel).[2] Therefore, it was perhaps logical, if not inevitable, that a profile to catch drug runners was developed for the nation's highways.

Operation Pipeline

The War on Drugs begun under the Nixon administration waned a bit under the Carter administration, whose major contribution to the debate about drug enforcement was to raise the prospect of decriminalizing the use of marijuana. The War on Drugs, however, was rejuvenated again in the first term of the presidency of Ronald Reagan. And, like their counterparts in the Nixon administration, those responsible for developing strategies for aggressive enforcement of the drug laws in the Reagan administration sought to expand the various tools—such as laws allowing forfeiture of property, and use of wiretaps and preventive detention—available for the task.[3] That was also to include the extension of the drug courier profile to the nation's highways.

In 1982, the Reagan administration created the South Florida Drug Task Force, under the direction of Vice-President George H.W. Bush, to deal with what appeared to be the alarming rise of drug smuggling in south Florida, particularly cocaine coming into and moving through Miami. The success of the Task Force's various initiatives is subject to debate, but one effect of the intensification of the drug interdiction efforts was to spur state and local officials to get more involved in the effort to arrest those involved in the drug trade. Aggressive efforts to stop the transportation of drugs along the roadways began in a number of states. One state law enforcement unit that became actively involved was the Florida Highway Patrol.[4]

Beginning in about 1983 or 1984, Florida Highway Patrol officers began to stop motorists in unprecedented numbers in an effort to find smugglers of illegal drugs to Florida and other parts of the United States. Part of that effort involved development of a list of "common characteristics of drug couriers"—or, in other words, a drug courier profile—to guide officers in deciding which drivers to stop. While it does not appear that any one person played as prominent a role in development of the highway profile as DEA agent Paul Markonni did for the airport profile, Florida state trooper Robert L. Vogel, Jr. has sometimes been described as being central to the adaptation of the drug courier profile to highway travel. In the early 1980s, Vogel patrolled a stretch of I-95 near Daytona Beach. Vogel's success in using highway stops to catch drug traffickers earned him numerous law enforcement awards and recognition in the media, including a flattering portrait by the television newsmagazine, *60 Minutes*. Vogel became something of a celebrity (he was eventually elected sheriff) and his influence was felt beyond the Florida state line, reaching Washington, D.C.[5]

By 1985, use of a drug courier profile on highways had stretched to other states, including Georgia and New Mexico, and the DEA had begun to develop a program, "Operation Pipeline," to spread Vogel's "gospel" across the United States by funding and training local law enforcement officers in the use of the profile to stop drug traffic on the nation's highways. Ultimately, Operation Pipeline came to approximately forty-eight states and that or a similar program (sometimes operating under names such as "Operation Valkyrie" or "Operation Nighthawk") was employed by over 300 state and local law enforcement agencies in programs in a broad range of communities, from small municipalities to large cities and states.[6]

Kissing Many Frogs to Capture a Few Princes: The Anatomy of a Highway Stop

At least as first conceived, the drug courier profile in connection with stops along the highway operated essentially as follows.[7] Troopers parked at watch points along the highway, from which they would observe drivers in the flow of traffic. Initially, troopers looked for the factors or character-istics drawn from the profile that would indicate that a driver or his passengers might be transporting drugs, fac-tors that would presumably create sufficient "reasonable suspicion" that criminal activity might be afoot to justify a stop under the reasoning of cases such as *Terry v. Ohio* and *United States v. Sokolow.* However, as a practical matter, translating a *Terry*-type stop to a moving vehicle proved problematic. To begin with, the observation of objective characteristics sufficient to create reasonable suspicion that a crime was afoot was much more difficult when watching moving vehicles, some traveling at great speeds, than in the setting in which the stops occurred in *Terry* and *Sokolow.*[8] Compounding the problem is that, as a practical matter, stopping someone on the highway is much more intrusive than stopping someone on the street or at an airport. It is one thing to stop someone for questioning in a face-to-face encounter on the street or in an airport, particularly when there is not yet evidence sufficient to create probable cause that a crime has been committed, but only the lesser indica-tion of a "reasonable suspicion" that something illegal might be underway. It is another, and as a practical matter more intrusive, thing to conduct the same type of investiga-tive stop on a highway when cars are racing by.

Thus, after a few instances in which courts upbraided Trooper Vogel or his men for being too zealous and for vio-lating drivers' constitutional rights, Vogel changed tactics. Stops would no longer be "investigative stops" based on the type of "reasonable suspicion" required by *Terry, Reid,* and *Sokolow.* Rather, drivers would be stopped for viola-tions of the motor vehicle laws, very often minor viola-tions. These could range from speeding, to weaving, to fail-ing to signal when switching lanes to even more minor infractions.[9]

A trooper's observation of a traffic violation was gener-ally enough to create probable cause to stop or arrest the driver for the motor vehicle offense. Once the trooper stopped the driver, he would ask to see the driver's license and registration, examining the car and driver as he waited for and inspected the documents. He would also engage the driver, often politely, in conversation: Where was the driver headed? Who was he going to see? What was the person's address or phone number? If the driver could not answer such questions or was uncertain or hesitant in answering, that might well give the officer cause for suspicion.

If the trooper still suspected that the driver was up to no good, he asked the person to allow him to search the car. As often as not, the driver consented. If no consent was forthcoming, stopping a driver for a motor vehicle violation made other options available to the trooper. A check of the driver's license and registration might turn up information (for example, that the car was stolen) that created probable cause to arrest the driver for something more serious than the initial traffic violation. Also, in the course of looking into the car to talk to the driver, a trooper might observe drugs (or other evidence of a more serious crime) if they were in "plain view"[10]; there was also a corollary "plain smell" exception to the warrant requirement. Drugs might also be found in a pat-down of the defendant for the protection of the officer as allowed in *Terry* or as part of a search incident to the arrest for the motor vehicle violation, which, under lenient Fourth Amendment principles developed by the Supreme Court in the 1970s and 1980s, allowed the officer to search not only the driver and any passengers but the entire interior of the car, including the glove compartment and any containers in the car (although not the trunk).[11] If all that failed, the trooper could still advise the driver that, unless he consented to a search, the trooper would arrange for a drug-sniffing dog to inspect the car, a step that could take hours; that was often enough to compel consent to search. Moreover, under appropriate circumstances, the trooper could ask the driver and the other passengers to get out of the car and separate them. This could be done either as a safety measure or to give the trooper an opportunity to speak to the occupants of the car separately to test the veracity of their responses to the officer's questions.[12]

Of course, the concern of these drug interdiction units was not traffic or road safety; it was catching those involved in the drug trade. In that regard, using a motor vehicle violation as the basis of a stop and search to look for drugs was, in the vernacular, a "pretextual" stop; that is, the driver was really being pulled over for reasons unrelated to any traffic offense. In fact, troopers waiting by the side of the highway attempting to find drug couriers frequently parked their cars perpendicular to the highway, positioning that made it easier to see a car's driver and occupants, but that rendered radar to detect speeding ineffective. Indeed, testimony by state troopers elicited in a legal challenge to highway stops in New Jersey revealed that if troopers saw a car whose occupants they suspected may be transporting drugs but who were not violating any motor vehicle laws, they would follow the driver for a period of time. Eventually, the driver's constant checking in the rear view mirror to see whether the police were still right behind him would cause the driver to weave, a violation of the motor vehicle code and grounds for a stop.[13]

If the trooper found drugs or other evidence of more serious crimes, he then had probable cause to arrest the driver for the more serious criminal offense. If the search of the driver and the car turned up nothing, more often than not the trooper allowed the driver to proceed on his way, only occasionally writing a ticket. Sometimes the trooper wrote just enough tickets to lend credibility to the ruse that he was, in fact, on the highway looking only for traffic violations. Troopers were also trained in *how* to write tickets for the minor traffic violations, if they chose to do so, so as not to invite trouble in case the traffic stop was later challenged. The drug courier profile circulated for use among troopers for the New Jersey State Police who participated in Operation Pipeline beginning in 1986 included a list of possible motor vehicle offenses that could be used to stop drivers and closed with the following admonitions: "Do not form a pattern on your stops. Do not write the same summonses on all the vehicle stops you make. This will form a pattern and can latter [*sic*] be used as a defense in court."[14]

Fundamental to this approach was the idea that troopers would stop many drivers, including many innocent ones, in their search for those involved in the drug trade. Volume was key. Gary Webb, who investigated Operation Pipeline for the California Legislature, quoted a California Highway Patrol sergeant who summarized the essence of the program as follows: "It's sheer numbers. Our guys make a lot of stops. You've got to kiss a lot of frogs before you find a prince." One Ohio state trooper testified in a case that he had personally made 786 stops in one year; he made some of the stops for no reason other than to keep in practice.[15]

The Significance of the Pretextual Traffic Stop

The decision to change tactics from trying to justify stops on the highway based on reasonable suspicion that a crime was occurring to predicating the stop on the observation of a violation of the motor vehicle code has been characterized as a "slight" adjustment in the practice.[16] In truth, that decision has enormous significance for the development of racial profiling and warrants a few more words.

To begin with, reliance on a violation of the motor vehicle laws to initiate a stop and possible search greatly expanded the possible number of persons detained for further observations. Motor vehicle laws cover a breathtakingly broad range of behavior and conditions. As an example, attached to the drug courier profile distributed to New Jersey State Troopers was a list of "statutes commonly used on drug interdiction stops." It was a list of seventeen separate offenses, ranging in seriousness from speeding and driving while intoxicated to the improper display of license plates and the "failure to display inspection approval."[17] New Jersey's motor vehicle code is hardly unique in its breadth and reach. As Professor David Harris summarizes the effect of "the comprehensive scope of state traffic codes": "These codes regulate the details of driving in ways both big and small, obvious and arcane. In the most literal sense, no driver can avoid violating *some* traffic law during a short drive, even with the most careful attention."[18]

But the large number of violations and broad range of behavior that can provide the basis for a stop under the motor vehicle code are only half the story. Not only do drivers regularly violate the motor vehicle codes, but judicial scrutiny of those stops is for the most part extremely limited. Recall that for an investigative stop to pass constitutional muster under the standard established in *Terry v. Ohio,* the law enforcement official must be able to articulate a basis for a "reasonable suspicion" that the person has committed or is about to commit a crime. However, in contrast, the test for whether a traffic stop comports with the Fourth Amendment where a law enforcement official has actually *witnessed* a violation of the motor vehicle code is much less difficult to meet.

At the time Operation Pipeline got started, the governing law in most of the twelve federal circuits upheld those stops as consistent with the Fourth Amendment's insistence on reasonable searches and seizures as long as the officer *could* have stopped the car, regardless of the officer's actual reason for stopping the car: that is, regardless of whether the officer's concern in making the stop was actually traffic safety, a search for drugs, or something else. This turned into nothing more than a question of whether the officer had credibly testified that he saw the driver commit a violation—*any* violation—of the motor vehicle code. As one court phrased the "could have" test:

> When an officer observes a traffic offense—however minor—he has probable cause to stop the driver of the vehicle. . . . [T]his otherwise valid stop does not become unreasonable merely because the officer has intuitive suspicions that the occupants of the car are engaged in some sort of criminal activity. . . . [T]hat stop remains valid even if the officer would have ignored the traffic violation but for his other suspicions.[19]

A minority of circuits followed a slightly different test, known as the "would have" test. The question in those circuits was not whether the officer *could* have stopped the vehicle but whether a reasonable officer *would* have stopped the vehicle for that violation under the circumstances. That is a somewhat more stringent inquiry than the "could have" test, but not much more stringent. The inquiry still did not turn upon the subjective intent of the officer making the stop in question, whether the officer was concerned with traffic safety or finding drugs. It simply asked whether under standard police practices, a reasonable officer usually would have stopped a vehicle for that kind of violation, whether that was the type of offense for which troopers usually pulled drivers over.

Perhaps ironically, one of the circuits that followed the minority "would have" test was the Eleventh Circuit, which includes Florida, and the leading case establishing that as the standard to follow in the circuit involved a traffic stop by Trooper Vogel in which the court was critical of Vogel's methods. The facts of the case, *United States v. Smith,*[20] are interesting and instructive, at least as to the nature of traffic stops using a drug courier profile.

In *Smith,* Vogel and a fellow trooper stopped a driver for weaving, and a subsequent search of the car turned up drugs. In the face of a subsequent challenge to the stop and search, Vogel did not deny that he had pulled over the car because he suspected the driver was transporting drugs. That fact, however, did not doom the stop and search. Rather, it was the fact that he pulled the driver over for "weaving" when the driver crossed the white line in the road briefly after Vogel, who had been following in his patrol car for a period of time, flashed his lights at the driver. That very brief swerve, the court ruled, was a typical response to being followed by the police and not enough to constitute a violation of the motor vehicle code. Nor was Vogel successful in arguing that "reasonable suspicion" under the *Terry* test existed to justify the stop. Vogel stopped the driver because he and a passenger were young, driving an out-of-state car at 3 A.M., driving cautiously, and they refused to look at Vogel when he pulled up next to them. The court was unimpressed:

> Trooper Vogel stopped the car because the appellants matched a few nondistinguishing characteristics contained in a drug courier profile and, additionally, because Vogel was bothered by

the way the driver of the car chose not to look at him. Vogel's suspicions therefore was not the result of "reasonable inferences" from "unusual conduct," . . . but was instead a classic example of those "inarticulate hunches" that are insufficient to justify a seizure under the fourth amendment.

That Trooper Vogel's "hunch" about the appellants proved correct is perhaps a tribute to his policeman's intuition, but it is not sufficient to justify, *ex post facto,* a seizure that was not objectively reasonable at its inception.[21]

The opinion in *Smith* tells us much about Vogel's methods, but it should not be read as suggesting that traffic stops, even under the "would have" test, were usually struck down, for the opinion in *Smith* represents a level of scrutiny that was rare, even under the somewhat more rigorous "would have" test.[22] In any event, eventually, the United States Supreme Court resolved the split in the circuits by adopting the more deferential "could have" test in *Whren v. United States.*[23]

Both the "could have" and "would have" tests are extremely deferential to law enforcement (the "could have" test somewhat more deferential) and make it much more difficult for a driver to challenge a traffic stop as violation of his rights under the Fourth Amendment. As we saw in our discussion of the treatment of the airport drug courier profile in the courts, one can debate (and some have debated) whether the Court's decisions in *Mendenhall* and *Reid* watered down the "reasonable suspicion" test established for investigative stops in *Terry.* Even so, there are *some* teeth to the "reasonable suspicion" test, *some* oversight by the courts as to whether a particular investigative stop as the result of a profile (or otherwise) overstepped the bounds established by the Fourth Amendment. In fact, the reason cited for why Vogel changed tactics (from purely investigative stops to stops based on a violation of the motor vehicle code) was precisely to get away from the "reasonable suspicion" test. The same is difficult to say for traffic stops based on a violation of the motor vehicle code, for which any challenge to the stop is defeated simply by a showing that a violation, even a minor one, took place, regardless of whether the stop was a pretext to look for drugs or other crimes. Moreover, once a driver has been stopped for violating the motor vehicle code, the full panoply of search options, summarized above, becomes available.[24]

This development has prompted a large amount of criticism and concern in some circles. "A reasonable suspicion requirement prevents the state from stopping individuals based merely upon whims, hunches, suspicions and prejudices [. . .]," one commentator has written, "[and] [j]udicial sanction of pretextual traffic stops threatens this limited protection." And another scholar similarly summarized the state of affairs in this areas as follows: "Fairly read, *Whren* [that is, adoption of the "could have" test] says that any traffic violation can support a stop, no matter what the real reason for it is; this makes any citizen fair game for a stop, almost any time, anywhere, virtually at the whim of the police."[25]

The Highway Profile vs. the Airport Profile

Adaptation of the drug courier profile from the airport to the highway and the accompanying change in methodology are important for another reason related to the development of racial profiling. Just as the airport profile represented a step away from the skyjacker profile, so, too, the drug courier profile used on the highways goes even further down that path and away from profiling's original moorings.

Other than the fact that it is based to some extent on past observations and experience, the highway profile bore almost no relationship to profiling as originally conceived. It was not only pro-active rather than re-active, but it was no longer dependent in any way on any particular scientific expertise or the work of elite teams. Everyone—certainly everyone in the highway drug interdiction units—was now a profiler. Moreover, the original aim of profiling to be as precise as possible in detection efforts so as to pick out the criminal suspect who had otherwise eluded capture as the metaphorical needle in the haystack was replaced by a blunderbuss approach in which police stopped many, many drivers for offenses they would often if not usually ignore in the hopes of catching a few carrying illegal drugs. This evolution is of more than academic interest, moreover, for in those changes—in the wide range of suspects now implicated and the lack of precision in the methods used—are the seeds for what would eventually come to be called "racial profiling."

The Characteristics of the Highway Profile

What were the characteristics listed in the highway drug courier profile? As with the airport drug courier profile, answers to that question vary although perhaps not to as great an extent. As we have seen, stating with any certainty the precise characteristics of the airport drug profile is difficult because it was essentially an unwritten profile that could (and did) vary widely from airport to airport, region to region, even DEA agent to DEA agent, and court cases testing the constitutionality of various stops under the "reasonable suspicion" test produced a wide, and often contradictory, range of testimony by DEA agents and other law enforcement officials as to the factors considered in any individual case.[26]

The precise characteristics of the highway drug profile are also somewhat difficult to state with absolute certainty for some of the same reasons, but also because of the unique nature of the traffic stop used to stop and investigate further. Because the highway stops were essentially based on violations of the motor vehicle laws and judicial scrutiny of the stops turns not on the characteristics of the profile that prompted the stop but simply on whether the law enforcement official had actually witnessed a traffic violation, we often (although not always) lack testimony and findings in court opinions as to what factors actually prompted the initial stop. Also, as noted above, despite the fact that Operation Pipeline trained state and local law enforcement in

the techniques to be used in catching drug couriers, highway profiles like the airport drug profiles, were administered in a variety of settings and jurisdictions by different
law enforcement agencies, thus inviting adaptations and
changes as needed. Indeed, Trooper Vogel testified in a
number of cases that he used his own profile, which was different than the one used by the Florida State Police.[27]

Nonetheless, the core characteristics of the highway profile are somewhat accessible because, unlike the airport
drug courier profile, the highway profile (or at least some of
them) existed in written form. A 1999 study of Operation
Pipeline commissioned by the California Legislature looked
not only at the program in California but in other states as
well and found that "[t]he indicators are virtually identical
in every state involved in the Pipeline program . . . and they
have remained largely unchanged since they were first
compiled in the early 1980s."[28] The following description of
the highway drug courier profile comes from a number of
sources, including the profile used in New Jersey, a written
profile distributed by the DEA in Miami, the California
study, court testimony, and a few other sources.[29] The profiles contained a great many characteristics thought appropriate for consideration, hardly surprising given the aim of
stopping many drivers in the search for the few carrying
drugs. Those characteristics can be broken down into a
number of different categories.

- *Exteriors:* One category of characteristics were things that
  could be observed on and from the exterior of the car.
  This category included out-of-state license plates (especially license plates from certain states such as Florida,
  New York, Texas, Maryland, and New Jersey) or plates
  that indicated the vehicle was a rental car, tinted or
  blacked-out windows, numerous radio antennas, a police
  decal in the window, and air shocks on the car.
- *Interiors:* Another category of factors focused on items
  that law enforcement might observe in the interior of the
  car. Among the interior identifiers that signaled possible

drugs were cell phones, firearms, fireworks, tools on the floor, maps especially with "source" cities circled (law enforcement officers in Florida were alerted to look for maps with northern cities circled), fast food wrappers, ledgers, newspapers (which might indicate where the person has traveled), large amounts of cash either in bags or the driver's pants pockets, motel or gas receipts, address books or lists of phone numbers, scanners or radar detectors (sometimes listed in the profile as "fuzz busters"), portable radios, a solitary key in the ignition, very little luggage or new luggage, duct tape, plastic garbage bags, and, of course, drugs or drug paraphernalia such as joints in the ashtray, baggies filled with marijuana, and scales. Also considered red flags were odors, such as the smell of marijuana, or items used to mask odors, such as aerosol cans or air fresheners, particularly the ones shaped like pine trees or leaves, to which law enforcement gave the nickname "felony forests."[30]

- *"Deviant characteristics of narcotics couriers"*: In addition to physical items that could be observed, the profile listed types of conduct or behavior that might indicate suspicious or illegal behavior. This includes two or more cars driving in tandem, a passenger asleep in the back of the car, the driver's nervousness when he spots the police car, the driver's failure to look at the police car when the officer pulls next to him, the driver's taking an inordinately long time to pull over, and when the police officer does pull him over, the person's exiting the car and coming toward the police car rather than waiting for the police officer to come to him, and the driver's trying to engage the officer in "friendly dialog" [*sic*].

As a general matter, what marks the highway profiles is the sheer number of items (most of which alone seem purely innocent), that law enforcement were trained to recognize as indicating that a car and its occupants are carrying drugs. Some of the red flags contradicted other red flags, although there were fewer such instances than was the case with airport profiles as we discussed earlier. Thus, some profiles alerted law enforcement officials to be on the lookout for certain types of cars, but the list of suspect vehicles included large cars with large trunks, intermediate-size cars and small cars. Similarly, bumper stickers were factors to be considered, not only "deadhead" and ACLU stickers but also bumper stickers with messages warning *against* the use of drugs. Finally on this score, troopers were not only told to watch out for erratic driving behavior, which is understandable since such driving might logically indicate drug or alcohol use, but also, perhaps ironically, for drivers whose driving was marked by "scrupulous obedience to traffic laws."

Putting the "Race" into Racial Profiling

The concept of "racial profiling" is indicative of how race— easily the most contentious and significant feature of the larger debate—has been coupled with profiling in the public mind. "Racial profiling," in fact, seems to have become synonymous with its antecedent, to the point where when one imagines a law enforcement officer engaging in profiling practices, one assumes that racial considerations are being not just used, but abused. As a practical matter, the real problem with using pretextual traffic stops to catch drug dealers, one leading scholar has argued, is not that the use of motor vehicle violations and the limited judicial scrutiny of those stops allow police to go after everyone all of the time, or even that they allow random stops and searches. Rather, the problem is that the breadth of the power afforded to law enforcement using pretextual traffic stops enables them to target certain groups, in this case, minorities.[31] To assess that statement, one must answer a question: Did law enforcement officials implementing the highway drug courier profile consider race a factor? They clearly did, despite denials (sometimes vehement) by law enforcement officials. Indeed, the only real question is how much of a factor race played and continues to play in the decision to stop motorists.

Travel the information superhighway to the website of the DEA, and one finds the following assurance in the DEA's general description of Operation Pipeline: "Although Operation Pipeline relies in part on training officers to use characteristics to determine potential drug traffickers, it is important to understand that the program does not advocate such profiling by race or ethnic background."[32] Other law enforcement officials also insisted that they instructed their charges that use of race or ethnicity in trying to determine who might be carrying drugs was improper or illegal.[33]

Yet the same DEA material and many other DEA reports and publications make clear that by the 1980s and 1990s, one important, if not the *most* important, focus of the DEA was the international nature of the illegal drug traffic and the extent to which illegal drugs were brought into this country from foreign countries. Drug cartels from Colombia, such as the infamous Cali and Medelin cartels, were one important source but hardly the only groups to attract the attention of the DEA. The DEA traced various drugs to different ethnic groups. In one report, for example, the DEA identified Thai, Chinese and Nigerian groups as "deeply entrenched" in smuggling heroin from Southeast Asia and the groups responsible for heroin as coming from Southwest Asia, including "Afghanistan, Greece, Lebanon, Pakistan, India and Turkey"; in addition, Colombians, Jamaicans, Dominicans, Puerto Ricans and Cubans were described as responsible for cocaine trafficking.[34]

But the DEA was not focused only on foreign nationals operating overseas; they were also concerned with persons and groups, including United States citizens, operating within the United States. Thus, one study of the source of illegal drugs described a complex and extensive distribution system for cocaine featuring many groups from a number of countries, such as Colombia and Mexico, but also domestic groups as well: "Distribution groups [for cocaine] were comprised chiefly of the African-American street gangs and the ethnic Cuban, Dominican, Haitian, Jamaican, Mexican, and Puerto Rican criminal groups that controlled cocaine and crack sales at the retail level. Gangs, including the Crips, Bloods, and Dominican gangs as well as Jamaican posses, were primarily responsible for widespread cocaine and crack cocaine-related violence." The DEA was not alone in linking certain racial and ethnic groups with certain drugs. The website for the White House Drug Czar, the Office of National Drug Control Policy, does the same, identifying, for example, Mexican nationals with heroin traffic in Denver and African Americans with crack cocaine in Trenton, New Jersey.[35]

Perhaps, as one leading scholar has it, the DEA was sending mixed messages; on the other hand, perhaps the message was not as ambiguous as that would suggest. As one New Jersey Deputy Attorney General, complaining of the influence of the DEA on state practices, said in a memorandum to superiors: "Once a motor vehicle is stopped for a motor vehicle violation, the DEA, through its training materials and intelligence information, make it very clear that certain racial or ethnic groups are more likely than other groups to be engaged in illegal activity."[36]

In any event, given the DEA's focus and training on the racial and ethnic groups responsible for the drug trade, it is hardly surprising that the highway drug courier profiles included racial and ethnic characteristics of the drivers, as well as the physical features of the cars and behavioral factors. In the highway profile distributed in New Jersey, for example, troopers were instructed about a fourth category, this one focused on the occupants of the vehicle. "Identifiers" regarding the occupants included:

- "fatigue" from extended driving
- "greasy hair"
- dirty clothing
- "shorts in the winter" and "pastel clothing"
- occupants that do not "fit the vehicle."
- "Colombian males"
- "Hispanic males"
- "Hispanic Male and a Black Male Together"

- "Hispanic Male and Female Posing as a Couple"

Or, the list concluded, "any combination of sexes or races."
The DEA profile from Miami similarly listed:

- "Colombian Males, 25–30 years"
- "Black Males, 20–50 years"
- "White Males, 20–30 years"

And a "Criminal Intelligence Report" in Maryland also contained a profile identifying African Americans as persons to stop on the highway.[37]

Statements by police officers also attest to the fact that race was a factor in the profiles they used. Indeed, some testimony or statements suggest that race was more than just one of a large number of factors on a profile. The testimony of New Jersey state troopers in *State of New Jersey v. Soto*,[38] a wide-ranging challenge to traffic stops in New Jersey, illustrates the point. Despite the fact that senior law enforcement officials argued that they told troopers that race could *not* lawfully be a component of a highway drug courier profile, two troopers testified that, as part of their training, they were taught to look for black drivers, especially if they were driving cars with Florida license plates, even if that training was implicit rather than explicit. One exchange in the testimony went as follows:

Q: What was the profile training that you received at that in-service training?

A: Well, in addition to of course, to our general knowledge that we received in the academy? During this block of instruction? It pretty much said of, um, it was pretty much conveyed to us the likelihood of who would be transporting and couriering drugs.

Q: When you talked about the likelihood of who would be transporting and couriering drugs. Was there a nationality or a race component to that teaching?

A: Yes.

Q: Okay. What was that nationality? What was the race of these people supposedly couriering drugs?

A: Okay, we spoke of um, black males, between the ages of 20 and 30. We spoke of Colombians, Hispanic. We also spoke of Latino women. . . .

What is stated now was you have a vested interest in looking for specific individuals, specific races, specific nationalities aside from you know the probable cause and to effect a drug related arrest.[39]

At least in New Jersey, the use of race as an identifier in the War on Drugs became part of the "culture" of the state police. One internal memorandum described the message sent to young troopers:

The State Police have plenty of documentation to say that a Trooper should not engage in selective prosecution. However, when you leave the academy you are assigned a coach and his job is to teach you how to get ahead. Trooper after Trooper has testified that the coach taught them how to profile minorities. The coaches also teach this to minority Troopers. . . . It's not written, it's practiced. . . . Not all Troopers engage in profiling. However, there is a perception that to get ahead you must make "good arrests." There are arrests where guns, drugs or money are recovered. The perception among young Troopers is that you are more likely to make a good arrest if you stop minorities. This is what they are taught by their coach, enforced by first-line supervisors and tacitly approved by upper management. . . . It was clearly reflected in the latest press release where they had a disproportional number of minorities being arrested. They justified this by saying that they had a high conviction rate. Again, the attitude is that the end justifies the means.[40]

Another internal law enforcement memorandum dated shortly after the one just quoted summarized the state of affairs this way:

Racial profiling exists as part of the culture. There is no written policy on it, but you are taught that if you see "Johnnies" [the nickname Troopers gave to minority drivers] in a "good" car, they "don't belong" and should be stopped and investigated. This also applies to minorities in old cars. The assumption is made that minorities are drug dealers, and cops are encouraged to stop them and toss their cars.[41]

It should be noted that more information about and insight into practices in New Jersey are available because a number of events—including a successful state court challenge to the practice of targeting minority drivers and a notorious incident in which minority drivers were fired upon by troopers in the course of a "routine" traffic stop—have led to unusual access to and scrutiny of documents and testimony by troopers and their superiors. But it would be a mistake to think this problem was limited to New Jersey.

Indeed, by the mid-1990s, it was evident that the targeting of minority drivers was a nationwide problem. In New Mexico, a training tape used by the state police showed mock stops and arrests in which all of the persons stopped were Hispanic. And, in a case from Michigan, a law enforcement officer testified that the defendants "fit a profile" due to the fact that they were three young black males in a car; he added that he repeatedly considered a driver's race to be a factor in the profile. After one of the persons arrested filed suit, police officers in a town in Ohio confirmed that there was an informal group of police officers who called themselves the "Special Nigger Arrest Team" and who specifically targeted minorities for traffic stops and arrests. In Avon, Connecticut, the supervising sergeant of the local police department instructed officers working under him to stop cars driven by persons "who do not appear to have business in Avon"; he made it clear that cars carrying a large number of blacks or Hispanics fell within that category. Once the sergeant's instructions came to light, "other officers and former officers admitted that 'top Avon police officials have long tolerated a practice of targeting blacks and Hispanics' who drive through Connecticut." Similar statements by other police officers lend credence to the argument that police around the country were being taught or encouraged to single out racial minorities in the search for illegal drugs. One assessment of racial profiling contended that police were more likely not only to stop minority drivers, but also to pressure minorities to consent to searches

and that minority drivers were more likely than white drivers to consent to searches. [42]

The Profiling Data

Even without express admissions that race was considered
in administering the profiles, and notwithstanding denials
by law enforcement officials that troopers were taught to
consider a driver's race, strong circumstantial empirical evidence also suggested that race was a factor and an important one. Thus, the report by the California legislature on
Operation Pipeline noted that, based on the data provided
by the California Highway Patrol, "between 80% and 90% of
all motorists arrested by Pipeline units since 1991 have
been members of minority groups. Only 10% have been
white." And the author of the report did not believe that pattern was based on different driving habits or the actions of
a few rogue cops:

> This program has been conducted with the support of CHP
> management. Individual officers involved in these operations
> and training programs have been carrying out what they per-
> ceived to be the policy of the CHP, the Department of Justice,
> and the Deukmejian and Wilson Administrations. [. . .] While
> CHP has a strong official policy against racial profiling and un-
> warranted traffic stops, it appears that some of these activities
> were unofficially tolerated and, at lower supervisory levels,
> even encouraged.[43]

Studies in other states also produced evidence that minority drivers were subjected to traffic stops in far greater
proportions to white drivers. For example, an investigation
by reporters for the *Orlando Sentinel* of 1,084 stops made
between 1989 and 1992 by members of Sheriff Robert
Vogel's drug squad revealed that 70% of the drivers stopped
on I-95 and 80% of those searched were either black or Hispanic. Moreover, once stopped, police encounters with minority drivers lasted an average of twelve minutes, with
white drivers, just five minutes. Nor did it appear that the
stops were based on a concern for traffic safety, as less than

1% of the drivers stopped received traffic tickets. Based on the evidence they reviewed, the reporters concluded that "Volusia County Sheriff Bob Vogel's drug squad uses skin color to decide whom to stop and search for cash on Interstate 95."[44]

However, the most widely noted quantitative data to date has been the work of John Lamberth, a professor and past-chair of the Department of Psychology at Temple University, gathered as a result of lawsuits in Maryland and New Jersey alleging racial profiling along a stretch of Interstate highway I-95 in the respective states.[45] In published testimony prepared for litigation in Maryland, Lamberth found that, in fact, race appeared to dramatically affect trooper discretion in a particular Maryland corridor of I-95.[46] Lamberth, employing techniques in Maryland similar to those he used in New Jersey and Virginia, used data that had been collected by the ACLU from January 1995 to September 1996.[47] Lamberth helped design the ACLU assigned-rider project during a 12-month period.[48] The researchers rode up and down I-95, and were given specific guidance as to how to (1) count the over-all numbers of cars that passed them (2) determine the number of potential traffic violators among these cars (3) classify the race of the driver.[49] The results of the survey were instructive. Over 5,000 cars were included, and consistent with David Harris' contentions about the ease of finding violations, the coders determined that about 93% of the drivers were in violation of some traffic law and, thus, could be stopped.[50] Of the drivers, slightly more than 17% were African-Americans, and 74.7% were Caucasians (apparently, in the other cases, race could not be confidently determined).[51] During this same study period the Maryland police reported 823 motorist stops in this I-95 stretch.[52] Of these, nearly 73% of those stopped were African-American (and another 7% were Hispanic or members of other racial minorities). Only about 20% of those stopped were Caucasian.[53]

Interestingly, these data were very similar to Lamberth's findings about the southern stretch of the New Jersey Turnpike prepared in connection with *State of New Jersey v. Soto*.[54]

In New Jersey, 98% of the drivers committed offenses that could subject them to a stop, and 15% of the drivers were black.[55] Yet the percentages of trooper stops were remarkably similar to the Maryland stops, with a substantial majority of those stopped being black, and a minority, white.[56]

Before turning to the matter of finding contraband after the stops, two other findings support Lamberth's contention that, with respect to stops, race looms large in this stretch of I-95.[57] First, Lamberth notes that, according to Maryland State Police data, nearly 64% of the stops statewide involve whites (in contrast to 20% on the selected I-95 strip).[58] Second, stops by race were not randomly distributed among troopers patrolling the studied area.[59] With the exception of one trooper who stopped blacks at close to the percentage of black drivers in the study area, nine of the remaining thirteen troopers who made over ten searches during the study period stopped 75% or more blacks.[60] Two of the troopers stopped over 90% minorities.[61]

There is one omission in these data—namely, specifics regarding the efficacy of the stops.[62] Did the stop yield contraband and lead to an arrest? Lamberth reports that about 30% of the stops did lead to an arrest of the driver, but this means that in 70% of the stops no arrest was made.[63] Intuitively, this strongly suggests that, since blacks are being stopped at dramatically higher rates than the actual proportion of black drivers to white drivers, many blacks are being subjected to unnecessary police stops because of their race.

These data, however, are not without their problems. These data alone do not indict police practices, for perhaps the police were responding to higher rates by blacks of the "underlying" felony, and thus the greater percentage of stops (recall that pretextual stops are permissible).[64] The problem with this argument, say Lamberth and others, is that of those searched after the stops (in Maryland, for example), the "hit" rate, the rate at which illegal substances were in fact found, is 28.4% for blacks, and 28.8% for whites. Blacks were stopped at a substantially greater rate than their numbers on the highway would suggest, and yet the rate of successful searches for contraband was the same as whites.[65] What this means—and we will return to this argument later—is that there are many "false positives" in police searches. A "false positive" in this context represents an individual singled out by the police, who is, in fact, not guilty. Whites and blacks have high false positive rates, but since blacks are disproportionately stopped, they suffer from false attribution of culpability at a rate far greater than their percentage on the highway would justify.[66]

Moreover, it should be emphasized that, as far as could be determined from Lamberth's testimony, questions remain about the specific data on the stretch of I-95 he examined. First, he does not provide the "find" data for this stretch; it is quite correct to suggest that in light of the general data about the disproportional rate of minority stops, and the statewide data, many minorities on this stretch are probably also being subjected to unnecessary stops. Nonetheless, data about the percentage of "finds" for his study group would be valuable. Second, it would be helpful to know more about what is found in the productive stops and about the specifics (i.e., quantity, type) of what is found. Of course, these matters would not justify racial selection, but they would still assist in assessing how much police "wisdom" should legitimately be weighed in the exercise of police discretion.[67]

Finally, the bottom line: the data suggest the fact that race looms large in some initial stop practices of police. Some defend this use of race in categories of crime in which there are differences in offending by race and in which the use of race, along with other variables, might increase the police likelihood of apprehending the guilty. Others suggest that it is not really race per se that is being used, but it is race plus other associated variables and/or just these variables which also "happen to be" associated with race.

Lamberth's studies were the most influential, widely circulated, and probably most systematic efforts to collect

data. They were not the only such efforts. Studies of stops
and arrests for motor vehicle violations in Philadelphia and
Illinois showed the same pattern of stops and searches
spread disproportionately according to the race of the
driver.[68] Indeed, such was the perception, at least in certain
circles, that police considered race to be a critical component of the drug courier profile that a portion of Interstate
95 in New York and New Jersey has come to be called
"White Man's Pass," and some drug dealers started using
white women to carry drugs in an effort to outsmart the police and circumvent the profiles.[69]

Racial Profiling: The Monster Awakens

As we have seen, the use of race in the airport drug profile
stayed under the radar screen (remarkably so, in hindsight).
It was not an issue in any of the cases in which the Supreme
Court confronted the practice and was rarely mentioned as
a factor, much less a concern, in the lower courts. Nor did
race as a factor in the airport profile attract much media
scrutiny or any sustained media attention.

The same cannot be said with regard to the highway drug
courier profile and the practice of stopping cars in an effort
to find drug traffickers. Indeed, shortly after Operation Pipeline and its local progeny were in full swing and continuing
throughout the 1990s, some people started to complain that
a disproportionate number of minority drivers were being
stopped and subjected to searches on the roads. The complaints came at first from minority drivers and criminal defense attorneys but eventually spread much further than
that. Slowly at first and somewhat sporadically, those complaints led to news stories and lawsuits challenging the
practice. In 1989, for example, an investigative report by a
local television station scrutinized the situation in New Jersey and produced evidence that minority drivers were indeed pulled over at a much greater rate than white drivers;
similar spurts of investigative journalism produced reports
in the Pittsburgh *Post-Gazette* and Orlando *Sentinel* in the

early 1990s. By the mid-1990s, complaints of police singling out minority drivers for traffic stops were made in a number of states, including many in the states of the South, such as Tennessee, Louisiana, North Carolina, Mississippi, and Georgia. Moreover, while the early press reports concerned themselves primarily with local law enforcement efforts and incidents, as the 1990s progressed, news reports in different cities and communities reported abuses in the system from around the country. In addition, lawyers, many representing groups or classes of motorists rather than individual drivers, filed lawsuits in a number of states including Colorado, New Jersey, Maryland, and Illinois, alleging that minorities were stopped and searched in disproportionate numbers.[70]

What emerged from the stories and statistics was a picture of a law enforcement practice that was much different than that suggested by the DEA's material on Operation Pipeline of a well-intentioned and effective weapon in the War on Drugs. It wasn't only that, as suggested by the studies of Lamberth and others, minority drivers were stopped at a far greater rate than whites, although that was problem enough. A basic problem was often also the conduct of the law enforcement officials once the stop was initiated.

Some stops involved humiliating treatment far beyond what is normally associated with an ordinary traffic stop. A few stories illustrate the point: An African American dentist from East Orange, New Jersey, who drove a BMW, was stopped for motor vehicle violations on the New Jersey Turnpike approximately one hundred times between 1984 and 1988 although he never received a ticket in connection with any of the stops. On some of the stops, police asked to search his trunk. Once, when he refused, the trooper took his license and registration back to the police car and forced him to wait fifteen to twenty minutes before returning them and letting him proceed. The dentist learned, he later said, that it was better to consent to the search than risk being late for his patients. Another African American driver, a college professor who lived in New Jersey but taught a course at a college in Massachusetts every Friday, was stopped on his trips to Massachusetts week after week. Two African American men were stopped, detained for two hours, and searched by four troopers and a police dog after police arrested them on the grounds that the air freshener hanging from their rear-view mirror violated the law. And after two African American college students were stopped, police essentially took apart their car in an unsuccessful search for drugs. As the police were leaving, with car parts removed and the students' belongings left lying about, one officer handed the students a screwdriver, telling them, "You are going to need this."[71] Of course, many African American drivers and passengers find the frequent stops based on minor or non-existent violations of traffic laws humiliating *per se,* without any extra indignities added.[72]

Unfortunately, other stops involved police conduct that went far beyond humiliation, conduct that to some extent recalled some of the worst excesses of the treatment of African Americans at the hands of police from the modern civil rights movement. Among the most widely publicized incidents were the following:

• In the spring of 1992, Robert Wilkins and his family were traveling back to Washington, D.C. from Chicago where they had attended a funeral. As they drove through Maryland in a pouring rain with his cousin driving, a Maryland state trooper who claimed that they were speeding stopped them. Before writing a ticket, the trooper asked permission to search the car but the family refused, prompting the trooper to remark that "if you have nothing to hide, then what is the problem?" The family continued to refuse the request to search the car. Wilkins, a lawyer in the public defender's office in Washington, D.C., pointed out to the trooper that he could not search the car without probable cause and asked the trooper the reason for the request to search the car. Wilkins also told the trooper that the family was on their way home from a funeral in Chicago and offered to show the trooper proof in the form of an obituary, but the trooper refused the offer and continued to ask for permission to search the car. Ultimately, when the family refused to relent on the request to search the car, the trooper made them wait while he arranged to have a narcotics-sniffing dog brought to the site. Once the dog was brought to the site, the trooper made the family wait outside the car in the rain for more than a half an hour while the dog sniffed around the car. The trooper failed to find any drugs but issued a ticket for speeding before allowing Wilkins and his family to leave.

- In August, 1998, Sergeant First Class Rossano Gerald, a decorated veteran from the Gulf War, was driving in Oklahoma with his twelve-year old son. Gerald was stopped twice in a span of thirty minutes, once by a local police officer and then by Oklahoma state troopers. During the second stop, which lasted two and a half hours, the troopers kept Gerald and his son in a hot car with the windows up and no air conditioning and warned them that they would be attacked by a police dog if they tried to escape, while the troopers searched Gerald's car. The incident left Gerald's son in tears.

- In April of 1998, New Jersey state troopers stopped a minivan carrying four African American high school students, on their way to North Carolina for basketball tryouts, for speeding on the New Jersey Turnpike. When the minivan began rolling back, the troopers fired eleven shots at the four men, who were unarmed, seriously wounding three of them. After the shooting, the troopers brought in drug-sniffing dogs in an effort to find drugs so that the shootings might appear more justified, but no drugs were found, only basketball equipment and a Bible. Two of the troopers were charged with attempted murder and aggravated assault for their actions in the incident after the case brought national attention to the practice of racial profiling, but the trial judge dismissed those charges, scolding the prosecutors for being overzealous and accusing them, by those charges, of trying to take the political heat off of administration officials, such as

Governor Christine Todd Whitman and former Attorney
General and then-New Jersey Supreme Court Justice Peter
Verniero, both of whom had come under mounting criticism as revelations about racial profiling by the New Jersey state troopers came to light. After almost four years of
maneuvering, and as more and more information was becoming available that state officials at the highest levels
had known about racial profiling but not said anything,
the troopers worked out a plea agreement whereby they
pled guilty to charges for which they received probation.[73]

Certainly, not every stop and search involved such outra-
geous behavior, nor do we have evidence that most stops
featured such police conduct. These data are anecdotal, but
nonetheless, stories like these touched a nerve and influenced the debate over the use of race as a factor in the drug
courier profile and in decisions to pull drivers over for
motor vehicle violations. Recall that the first news stories,
particularly the aggressive forays into investigative journalism in places like New Jersey and Florida, focused largely on
the disproportionate number of minority drivers stopped
and searched and that media attention to the practice became nationwide around 1998; that incident on the New
Jersey Turnpike, in which troopers shot at four unarmed
young men, is generally identified as the event that turned
racial profiling into a nationwide story.

For opponents of the drug courier profile programs,
such incidents suggested, if they did not compel the belief,
that something even more insidious was going on than application by law enforcement of a carefully thought-out
drug courier profile. And, conversely, for proponents of the
highway drug courier profile and programs such as Operation Pipeline, such stories made it more difficult to argue
that the fact that those programs resulted in a disproportionate number of stops, searches, and arrests of minority
drivers was an unintentional and unavoidable by-product
of a racially neutral and effective law enforcement technique. But most important, such incidents also brought a

tremendous amount of attention to what would come to be called "racial profiling" to catch drug traffickers. Ultimately, in the debate over the use of race as a factor by law enforcement, profiling as a separate and distinct law enforcement technique got lost in the battle.

CHAPTER 4

The Debate over Racial Profiling

In the previous chapter we explored in some detail the development of the drug courier profile and the use of pretextual traffic stops to further the search for drugs. However, those two developments did more than simply add new weapons to the law enforcement arsenal. They also triggered a vigorous public debate over the practices and strongly influenced and altered the evolution of the concept of racial profiling. It is these developments—the terms of the public debate and the evolution of the concept—that are the subject of this chapter.

Pros and Cons: The Debate over Racial Profiling

The highway drug courier profile and pretextual traffic stops, particularly when used to stop minority drivers in disproportionate numbers, generated a debate over appropriate law enforcement techniques and provided a new theater for America's continuing battle over race. What came to be called "racial profiling" was, depending on the speaker's politics, either a benefit of or another of the many policy mistakes in the nation's War on Drugs.[1] The debate began slowly at first, but, by the late 1990s, it was perhaps the most prominent and important debate in law enforcement after the death penalty. We will summarize some of the basic arguments both against and in support of racial profiling in highway stops. (The terms of the debate changed significantly again after the terrorist attacks on New York City and Washington, D.C., on September 11, 2001, and we will treat these new issues separately in a later chapter.)

The Critics

Critics of what has come to be called "racial profiling" have made numerous arguments. There are, to be sure, the same policy arguments that were brought to bear against airport drug courier profiles: that the highway stops (and the profiles that led to them) were over-inclusive and roped in too many innocent drivers; that the profiles relied too much on generalized information and did not treat individuals as autonomous beings; that the precise contents and contours of the profiles varied and were unclear, and that there was little statistical evidence that they worked.[2] But the most frequently articulated and most forcefully asserted criticisms turned not on simply on straightforward public policy debates but on issues that went to the heart of the freedoms protected by the Constitution.

On one level, the highway drug courier profiles and pre-textual traffic stops have been criticized as undermining the fundamental premises and protections of the Fourth Amendment's ban on unreasonable searches and seizures. The Fourth Amendment serves at least two purposes. First, it makes certain that a person is not subjected to investigation and prosecution by law enforcement unless there is particularized suspicion that the person has done something wrong. In a related vein, it serves to curb the discretion given to law enforcement, particularly police, a concern that certainly pre-dated the current furor over racial profiling.[3]

The highway drug courier profile and pretextual traffic stops to implement it, critics maintain, defeat both purposes of the Fourth Amendment. People are stopped and searched for drugs without any legitimate reason, let alone solid proof, to believe that they are carrying them. And, the argument continues, because the mechanism for effecting this stop and search is usually a minor violation of the motor vehicle code—a code, as noted above, that reaches so broadly that it is likely that almost every driver violates some provision at some time—police have effectively been given the power to stop anyone, anytime. As described by one critic of the tactic:

> [I]f a police officer wants to stop someone for questioning and perhaps a search, but has no constitutional grounds for doing so, he need only wait until the individual gets into his car, follow him until he inevitably violates one of the myriad traffic regulations that rule the road, and use that infraction as a pretext for a stop.[4]

And another scholar has articulated the argument as follows:

> Given that nearly all motorists commit some traffic offense, even on short trips, the base-line expectation of an ordinary traffic offender is that his liberty and privacy will go undisturbed. Permitting an officer standardless discretion to determine which of the many traffic offenders to single out, stop, and subject to the indignity of a request to search runs afoul of an Amendment designed to prevent placing "the liberty of every man in the hands of every petty officer."[5]

Finally, and along the same lines, another commentator, critical of the use of pretextual traffic stops, has written, "A reasonable suspicion requirement prevents the state from stopping individuals based merely upon whims, hunches, suspicions and prejudices. [. . .] Judicial sanction of pretextual traffic stops threatens this limited protection." And another critic objected "an individual can lose all Fourth Amendment protections against arbitrary seizures and searches when he or she gets behind the wheel of a car."[6]

This concern for the protections provided by the Fourth Amendment constitutes a serious argument that merits consideration although as such the criticism has been largely the province of criminal defense lawyers and constitutional and criminal procedure theorists. As we have seen, the argument that stopping a driver for a violation of the motor vehicle laws in order to investigate further for drugs, with or without the use of the highway drug courier profile, violates the Fourth Amendment has not persuaded many courts. Indeed, this argument against the drug courier profile and pretextual stops is usually aimed as much at court opinions, particularly the Supreme Court's decision in *Whren* (we will discuss *Whren* below and at greater length in the next chapter) as at local or state law enforcement officials

Therefore, and perhaps more importantly, criticism of highway drug profiles and pretextual stops also operates at another level. Concern for protections embodied in the Fourth Amendment is, at least to some extent, more abstract than real, for, as we also noted earlier, the problem has not generally been couched in terms of the police randomly stopping everyone. Rather, that criticism, without more, omits the critical element of race. What has galvanized and propelled the debate is the impact of those practices on minority drivers and their passengers.

For critics, the use of highway drug profiles and pretextual traffic stops in disproportionate numbers against minority drivers and their passengers is only another, and the latest, manifestation of the problem of racial discrimination in law enforcement that has plagued America for much of the last century, if not longer. It is, in some regard, a more modern manifestation of the "legacy of slavery." Responding to comments by the head of the State Police in New Jersey that seemed to endorse the practice, an African American minister complained "What he has done, by his language, has made every minority a suspect for drugs. Therefore troopers on the New Jersey Turnpike stop minorities randomly not because they've broken any law. Not because they're driving crazy on the turnpike. Simply because they are a minority. That's wrong, it's illegal and it needs to stop."[7] And the New Jersey chapter of the American Civil Liberties Union, at the height of the controversy concerning actions of New Jersey State Troopers, declared that "Racial profiling was born of slavery, raised by segregation, and has matured under pervasive, patently-false stereotypes of minorities, especially African-Americans and Latinos."[8]

Some opponents of the practice argue that many white Americans view being stopped by police on the highway for a minor violation to allow them to search for drugs as a minor and relatively infrequent inconvenience; for African Americans, Latinos, and other minorities, however, such practices are frequent and occur against a backdrop of discriminatory treatment. As Ira Glasser, executive director of the American Civil Liberties Union, expressed the sentiment: "Racial profiling on our highways has long been a secret from most Americans, and from virtually all white Americans. But it's never been a secret to its victims. There seems to be almost no one of color who has not been victimized by this practice or who does not know somebody close to them who has."[9] For those who thought that progress has been made to rid the criminal justice system of racially discriminatory treatment, stopping minority drivers is seen as a very unfortunate step backwards; for those more skeptical and pessimistic about racial equality in law enforcement, racial profiling is just more of the same. In fact, pretextual traffic stops, argues a leading critic, may represent an even more egregious instance of racially discriminatory treatment: "Stopping disproportionate numbers of black drivers because some small percentage are criminals means that skin color is being used as evidence of wrongdoing. In effect, blackness itself has been criminalized."[10]

Adding fuel to this criticism are claims that the rationale for the highway drug profiles and pretextual stops is fundamentally flawed in its basic premises and not even effective. Relying upon the studies done by John Lamberth and others, critics maintain that African American drivers are no more likely to commit traffic offenses than white drivers, thus making clear that the traffic stops are for a purpose other than highway safety. What is worse, as we have seen, is that the vast majority of drivers whom law enforcement stop are innocent, and that stopping minority drivers fails to turn up drugs more often than stopping white drivers. Critics of the practice of targeting minority drivers described what has been called the "circularity" argument: even if drugs are found more often with minority drivers, that only happens because law enforcement efforts are focused on minority drivers. Thus, the drug courier profile could be a self-fulfilling prophesy, falsely creating a statistical basis that can be used to justify later stops. "Racial stereotypes influence police to arrest minorities," wrote one commentator, "thereby creating the arrest statistics to justify the criminal stereotype. Police officers defend their conduct by citing statistics showing higher crime and arrest rates among minorities. This tends to perpetuate the fallacy and generate more unbalanced arrest patterns."[11] Even if it could be proven that minority drivers are more likely to commit traffic offenses, it has been argued, that still does not mean that police have not used race in deciding whom to stop and, just as important, feeding the perception in the minority community and elsewhere that race is indeed a critical factor in the decision to stop.[12]

But, critics maintain, it is not simply that singling out minority drivers for stops is ineffective or based on mistaken factual premises. The effects of the practice are much worse. For one thing, singling out minorities for special treatment by police breeds, as we saw in the last chapter, contempt for law and actually undermines efforts at law enforcement. "Racially targeted traffic stops," a leading critic has written, "cause deep cynicism among blacks about the fairness and legitimacy of law enforcement and courts." One scholar described the deleterious effects of the double standard that is at the heart of racial profiling:

> First, they undermine law enforcement itself, because they breed resentment and alienation among minorities and the poor. People who see the criminal justice system as fundamentally unfair will be less likely to cooperate with police, to testify as witnesses, to serve on juries, and to convict guilty defendants when they do serve. In addition, people who have lost respect for the law's legitimacy are more likely to break the law themselves. Legitimacy is one of the law's most powerful tools, and when the law forfeits its legitimacy, its only alternative is to rely on brute force.[13]

Another opponent of racial profiling took this argument further, reasoning that singling out members of the minority community by law enforcement undermined a number of values generally embraced by conservatives—effective law enforcement being one, in addition to the ideal of color-blindness often invoked in the argument against affirmative action—and thus racial profiling should be rejected by conservatives as well as liberals:

> Many black people report that, when they see the police pulling over a car with a black driver or searching a black kid on the street, they don't ask: "What did that guy do?" They instead wonder: "Why is that cop harassing that guy?" The stigma of lawbreaking is weakened. Conservatives—usually the ones arguing for attaching more, not less, stigma to law breakers—ought to grasp this intuitively.[14]

Critics also point to a second effect of stopping minority drivers in disproportionate numbers. In reaction to some of the more humiliating aspects described in the previous chapter that often accompanied such traffic stops, many critics pointed out that unwarranted traffic stops aimed at minority motorists create or, worse, reinforce, feelings of humiliation or inferior status among members of the minority community. "For many blacks, the emotional cost is profound," wrote one prominent critic of pretextual stops, who went on to describe the psychological effects felt by one African American who believed that she had been unfairly singled out because of her race:

> Karen Brank missed work and experienced depression. For some time afterwards, she felt a wave of fear wash over her every time she saw a police car in her rearview mirror. In that one brief encounter, her entire sense of herself—her job, the fact that she is a mother and an educated, law-abiding person working on a master's degree—was stripped away.[15]

Others expressed similar if not identical feelings. Don Jackson is a former police officer who, like a lot of minority police officers, was subjected to traffic stops due to his race when he was not wearing his uniform. Following one stop in which his attempt to challenge the officers' reason for stopping him resulted in his being beaten and thrown through a window, Jackson commented that "We have learned that there are cars we are not supposed to drive, streets we are not supposed to walk. We may still be stopped and asked 'Where are you going, boy?' whether we are in a Mercedes or a Volkswagen." According to Jackson, such treatment at the hands of the police serves to remind African Americans of their "second-class citizenship."[16] Another minority driver—an account executive at a media company who had been repeatedly pulled over by police—who was stopped, interrogated, and threatened with a ticket for not wearing a seat belt after leaving the home of a friend in an upper-class neighborhood, similarly felt great anger at his treatment, resentment that lasted months: "I think he saw a black male in that neighborhood and he was suspicious. [. . .] [W]e just constantly get harassed. So we just feel like we can't go nowhere without being bothered." An African American police officer counseled his son that he, too, could expect to be subjected to such treatment notwithstanding the fact that his father was a veteran police officer: "[If] you're black, you're out in the neighborhood, it's a fact of life that you are going to be stopped." An African American firefighter, upon discovering that his stopping to talk to a resident of a subdivision prompted an investigation by local police, had new vanity license plates created that read "SUSPECT." The legal director of the Illinois chapter of the ACLU stated the predicament for minority drivers even more dramatically: "It's the equivalent of traveling in a totalitarian state where you are routinely stopped for searches. It's like a tax for driving on the highway."[17] Indeed, in part because of the psychological toll taken by the repeated practice of stopping minority drivers in disproportionate numbers, some critics of the highway drug courier profile and pretextual stops argued that the practice should be outlawed even if it were shown to be an accurate measure of criminality and likely to lead to more arrests of persons carrying drugs.[18]

Responding to the Critics: The Defenders

Proponents of the use of the drug courier profile and pretextual traffic stops have replied to their critics in a number of ways. The response of high-ranking officials in New Jersey to the various media stories, complaints, and lawsuits accusing the state police officers of singling out minority drivers is instructive and worth spelling out even if it falls short of a defense of racial profiling *per se*. New Jersey state officials at the highest levels first vehemently denied that they were doing anything wrong before their own internal investigation eventually led them to accept the evidence and negotiate a Consent Decree with the United States Department of Justice to stop the practice.

For much of the time that accusations were made in the media and in lawsuits that New Jersey state troopers were unfairly singling out minority drivers for stops, high-ranking New Jersey officials, including the Governor and the Attorney General, simply denied that was happening. The denials, emphatic and public, persisted even after a state court, based in part on testimony of former state troopers, found that the State Police did in fact engage in such a practice, after the shooting incident of the four high-schoolers on their way to basketball tryouts, and after the United States Department of Justice began an investigation into police practices in the state. "It is difficult for me to believe that despite a clear official policy prohibiting racial profiling and repeated declarations requiring adherence to this policy, that troopers assigned to one station would continue to reject it," wrote Attorney General Peter Verniero to a representative of the Department of Justice investigating practices in New Jersey.[19]

But stories and accusations multiplied, and the emphatic denials became increasingly problematic. Even the New Jersey State Police Chief, Colonel Carl Williams, appeared to endorse the idea that focusing on members of the minority community was good police work because minorities were more responsible for the drug traffic. "Two weeks ago," Williams was quoted as saying in early 1999, "the President of the United States went to Mexico to talk to the President of Mexico about drugs. He didn't go to Ireland. He didn't go to England. Today, with this drug problem, the drug problem is cocaine or marijuana. It is most likely a minority group that's involved with that." Williams' remarks got him fired immediately, even though, ironically, Williams had in the same interview expressly condemned racial profiling. These comments also elicited from Governor Christie Todd Whitman yet another denial that New Jersey law enforcement personnel were focusing on minorities in attempting to deal with the drug problem; she dismissed such accusations as based only on "allegations" and not evidence.[20]

The April 1998 shooting of the four high-schoolers on the Turnpike prompted a number of investigations. Ultimately, in response to the public pressure, the Governor of New Jersey asked her Attorney General's Office to conduct its own investigation into the relevant police practices. The specially commissioned Task Force, in its April 1999 report, concluded that New Jersey State Police on the Turnpike had, in

fact, targeted minority drivers. The authors of the Interim
Report, who included Attorney General Peter Verniero, tried
to put their findings in as positive a light as possible, assur-
ing readers that "the great majority of state troopers are
honest, dedicated professionals who are committed to enforcing the laws fairly and impartially." Still, the Report concluded that "minority drivers have been treated differently
than non-minority motorists during the course of traffic
stops on the New Jersey Turnpike," and, while less than 1%
of all stops on the Turnpike resulted in searches, "minority
motorists are disproportionately subject to searches. . . . "[21]

The fallout from the Interim Report was huge. It brought
increasing criticism of, among others, Whitman and Attorney General Verniero. Verniero had it particularly rough. Just
before the Interim Report was released, he had been confirmed by the State Senate for a seat on the New Jersey Supreme Court; the contents of the Report had many in the
state, including some legislators, questioning not only his
conduct and testimony while a nominee for the seat but also
his fitness to remain on the bench. Whitman avoided more
criticism as she eventually left the governorship before her
term was up to become the head of the Environmental Protection Agency under George W. Bush, although the findings
of racial profiling and her handling of the situation became
an issue as she went through the confirmation process for
the federal post. Also coming back to haunt Whitman was a
photograph taken of her in 1996 "frisking" a suspect in the
course of the suspect's arrest. The suspect happened to be
African American and what might have seemed like an innocent photo opportunity to show her administration was
tough on crime at the time it was taken turned, a few years
later when the racial profiling debate was at its most intense,
into evidence that Whitman was insensitive to the issues
swirling around the racial profiling controversy. High-
ranking officials tried to deflect some of the criticism, accusing some troopers of keeping top officials in the dark by fal-
sifying arrest records. DEA also came in for some blame as
some in the Attorney General's Office argued that if in fact

minority drivers were stopped more frequently than non-minority motorists, New Jersey was only following the teachings of Operation Pipeline, which, as noted earlier, had long stressed the involvement of certain racial and ethnic groups in various aspects of the drug trade.[22]

Eventually, New Jersey agreed to enter into a Consent Decree with the Department of Justice to monitor and stop the use of race by law enforcement officers in New Jersey when making decisions on whom to stop on the highway.[23] Also important, the New Jersey Attorney General's Office, in an effort to deal with the public outcry, released to public view over seventy thousand pages of internal documents regarding police practices of stopping drivers on the New Jersey Turnpike. Those documents not only confirmed the findings of the Interim Report but suggested that many high-ranking officials, including governors and attorneys general dating back to the late 1980s, had been aware of the accusations and allegations regarding the targeting of minority motorists but had largely ignored the problem.[24]

New Jersey is not the only state where public officials responded to complaints of racial profiling, at least initially, by denying that the practice existed. Police officials in Colorado also denied that such practices took place even in the face of court rulings that they had; similarly, after Robert Wilkins brought suit for the conduct he and his family were subjected to, Maryland officials denied the practice until an internal memorandum made it clear that African Americans were included in a drug courier profile. Florida law enforcement officials also denied that they considered race in making stops, notwithstanding their own videotapes that provided strong evidence of disparate treatment. And, as noted above, the DEA insisted it instructed law enforcement personnel not to single out drivers because of their race or ethnicity despite the fact that it regularly broadcast that certain minorities were overwhelmingly represented in drug trafficking.[25] Some law enforcement officials did not go so far as to deny that racial profiling existed, but argued that it happened infrequently. Said one black police chief:

Not to say that it doesn't happen, but it's clearly not as serious or widespread as the publicity suggests. I get so tired of hearing that "Driving While Black" stuff. It's just to the point where it has no meaning. I drive while black—I'm black. I sleep while black too. It's victimology. Black people commit traffic violations. What are we supposed to say? People get a free pass because they're black?[26]

Of course, repeated denials that minority drivers are targeted are, to say the least, hardly a vigorous defense of the practice or of the use of the drug courier profile in general. Still the penchant to deny that police officers were targeting minority drivers is significant for at least two reasons. First, that the highest-ranking officials—in New Jersey and elsewhere—denied the problem until they could no longer credibly do so is itself significant. Secondly, it demonstrates how much the issue of race influenced, dominated, and also skewed, the debate.

Notwithstanding the frequent denials by law enforcement officials that anything special was going on, the use of the highway drug courier profile gained some defenders, even if it did result in more stops of minority drivers. One extended defense of highway stops of more minority drivers, presented by Heather McDonald, called racial profiling a "myth" and made a number of points in support of police efforts to catch those involved in the drug traffic. McDonald conceded that highway stops based solely on the race of the driver were improper, but dismissed such stops as the actions of a few rogue cops. If minority drivers were pulled over more often than non-minority drivers, she maintained, it was because young minority male drivers actually committed more traffic offenses than other groups driving on the highway. Beyond that, searches are proper, this argument went, if race is only one of many factors. And significant here, McDonald continued, is that minorities were involved in drug trafficking in much greater numbers than non-minorities. In fact, she argued, if police found drugs in the same percentage of stops for white drivers and black drivers who were searched, it demonstrated not disproportionate treatment of minorities but the fact that the police were successfully targeting drug dealers generally, regardless of race. The circularity argument (that biased stops and arrests created a false basis for future stops and arrests) was dismissed as "an insult to law enforcement and a prime example of the anti-police advocates' willingness to rewrite reality." The people most hurt by criticism of the use of drug profiles to catch those involved in the drug trade were those in the neighborhoods most affected by and infested with illegal drug traffic. McDonald also harshly criticized the April 1999 Interim Report of the New Jersey Attorney General for encouraging criticism of law enforcement.[27]

Probably the most frequent defense of racial profiling, then, has been that police are not racist but instead are just doing their job. If minorities are pulled over more often than non-minorities, the argument is made, it is only because they are more often involved in the drug trade, and that is effective police work. One law enforcement official denied that drug interdiction operations trained officers to recognize that race is a characteristic of drug couriers but continued,

> Those who purport to be shocked that ethnic groups are over-represented in the population arrested for drug courier activities must have been in a coma for the last twenty years. The fact is that ethnic groups control the majority of the drug trade in the United States. They also tend to hire as their underlings and couriers others of their same group. Why? Because these are the people they grew up with, feel comfortable around and because it's human nature.
>
> The truth is, if you work drug interdiction in this country, you will not arrest the same percentages of ethnic groups as represented in the U.S. general population. People may not like it but that is the reality.[28]

Another defender, sociologist Jackson Toby, likened the practice of using highway traffic stops in the War on Drugs to the "broken windows" theory of policing that appeared to work effectively in stopping crime in New York City in the 1990s. That theory reasoned that if police made efforts to stop minor crimes, such as evading fares on the subway or graffiti, they prevented more serious crime later. Toby argued that the same phenomenon was at work in the highway stops of drug traffickers: "People who violate major laws are probably inclined to violate minor ones, such as traffic regulations. Consequently, stopping motorists for traffic violations has led to the seizure of major shipments of illegal drugs to Newark or New York. . . . " That minorities are stopped in numbers disproportionate to their presence in the larger population is not necessarily evidence of racism: "[I]f drug traffickers are disproportionately black or Hispanic, the police don't have to be racist to stop many minority motorists; they simply have to be efficient in targeting potential drug traffickers." Some police made mistakes, but so do some doctors and some lawyers: "But the police deserve extra leeway for their mistakes because, unlike other professionals, they don't have the luxury of turning down unpleasant cases."[29]

Along similar lines, defenders have criticized the statistical studies upon which critics of racial profiling rely. Many argued that the statistical studies are flawed because they do not measure or compare the right things; for example, some argued that a comparison of minority drivers pulled over compared to the percentage of that minority group in the larger population was meaningless; the proper measurement was the number of minority drivers pulled over compared to the number of minority drivers who actually commit traffic violations:

> The problem with such studies is that they suggest there should be a correlation between a community's demographics and the people pulled over by the police—that the percentage of, say, African-Americans stopped should track the percentage of African-Americans living in the town. And if they don't parallel, then the police are guilty of racial discrimination. Nonsense. Any number of factors can skew the figures, and they have zip to do with discrimination. The number of women stopped by police will never track the demographic occurrence of women in a city's population. Neither will the number of people over the age of 65. Make that 35. The criminal census does not track the general census.[30]

Another defender argued that under the reasoning of the critics of racial profiling, police should stop and investigate sixty-year-old grandmothers in proportion to their numbers in the general population and that any difference in the numbers would indicate that the police are either "pro or anti Granny. Well—here is a newsflash: Grannies account for virtually none of the arrests for crack dealing. [. . .] Am I stereotyping grandmothers here? Of course! But the point is that there are many social causes that explain the action of the police that have nothing to do with bias."[31] Defenders also pointed out that police not only stopped blacks on the highways but whites in neighborhoods when their presence suggested criminal activity.

Some defenders accepted the critics' statistical studies but, viewing the glass as half full rather than half empty, saw in those studies evidence of solid police work. Bernard Parks, the Chief of Police in Los Angeles (who is African American), when asked his reaction to the fact that highway stops in Maryland turned up drugs in only three out of ten stops, responded,

> Three out of ten? That would get you into the Hall of Fame. That's a success story. At some point, someone figured out that the drugs are being delivered by males of this color driving these kinds of vehicles at this time of night. This isn't brain surgery. The profile didn't get invented for nothing.[32]

The comments of Chief Parks make clear that many people concede that race is a factor in racial profiling but still see it as good police work. As another law enforcement official remarked, "Of course we do racial profiling at the train station. If 20 people get off the train and 19 are white guys in suits and one is a black female, guess who gets followed? If racial profiling is intuition and experience, I guess we all racial-profile."[33] In fact, many police officers responded to the criticism leveled at racial profiling with the belief that they were being unfairly singled out for a practice that everyone does. As one journalist summarized it,

This is what a cop might tell you in a moment of reckless can-
dor: in crime fighting, race matters. When asked, most cops
will declare themselves colorblind. But watch them on the job
for several months and get them talking about the way that policing is really done, and the truth will emerge, the truth being
that cops, white and black, profile. Here's why, they say.
African-Americans commit a disproportionate percentage of
the types of crimes that draw the attention of the police. Blacks
make up 12 percent of the population, but accounted for 58
percent of all carjackers between 1992 and 1996. (Whites accounted for 19 percent.) Victim surveys—and most victims of
black criminals are black—indicate that blacks commit almost
50 percent of all robberies. Blacks and Hispanics are widely believed to be the blue-collar backbone of the country's heroin-
and cocaine-distribution networks. Black males between the
ages of 14 and 24 make up 1.1 percent of the country's population, yet commit more than 28 percent of its homicides. Reason, not racism, cops say, directs their attention. Cops, white
and black, know one other thing: they're not the only ones who
profile. Civilians profile all the time—when they buy a house, or
pick a school district, or walk down the street. Even civil rights
leaders profile.[34]

Indeed, in an ironic twist, in the same way that many of the
minority drivers who are stopped found the practice humiliating, many police officers found the criticism and accusations of racism demoralizing. One police officer from Maryland complained that when 95% of his arrests were of
"dirt-ball whites" on Maryland's Eastern Shore, he was a
star, but when he was assigned the highway patrol and he
started arresting blacks and recovering much larger
amounts of illegal drugs, "[s]uddenly I'm not the greatest
trooper in the world. I'm a racist. I'm locking up blacks, but
I can't help it. . . . I dream at night about arresting white
people for cocaine. I do. I try to think of innovative ways to
arrest white males. But the reality is different." [35] And in an
even more ironic twist, it has been suggested that insisting
on divorcing race from the list of valid considerations in police work might breed contempt for the law among law enforcement personnel (just as including race breeds contempt for the law for the critics of racial profiling):

Criminal enterprises are not equal opportunity employers. As Janet Landa's work on Asian commercial markets shows, where legal protections do not operate, ethnic bonds can serve as a substitute, a means by which market actors reduce the risk of cheating by those with whom they deal. The same idea applies to illegal enterprises. It follows that drug distribution networks and terrorist organizations, like Mafia families, are bound to have a racial or ethnic cast. The police, whether FBI agents looking for members of al Qaeda or local cops trying to break up a heroin ring, are bound to know what the relevant racial or ethnic cast is. If the law asks them to feign ignorance, the likely effect is not to reduce the role ethnicity plays in policing, but rather to reduce the respect the law enjoys among the police.[36]

Racial Profiling: The Birth of a Concept

Notwithstanding that criticism and concern that the highway drug courier profile was being used disproportionately against minority drivers began in the mid-1980s, it took a while for the practice to be called "racial profiling," at least in the larger public debate. And while news stories regarding the practice occasionally spoke in terms of profiles, with a racial component to the profile, there were only a few stories until the mid-1990s, the first appearing in late 1987, that used even the concept of a "racial profile" in a law enforcement context.[37] Indeed, throughout the 1980s and early 1990s, discussion of a "racial profile" in an article in the popular media was more likely to come about in the context of discussions of Affirmative Action in university admissions or residential patterns in low-income housing, and in those contexts to refer only to the number of minority students in a given student body or the occupants of a housing unit or neighborhood as opposed to a conscious government program.

That began to change in the mid-1990s, as news stories about stops and searches of minority drivers started to become more numerous. "Racial profiling" as a term describing a type of police conduct first appeared in the media in late 1994, and appears to have become an accepted shorthand phrase for stops and searches of minority drivers by 1995 or 1996.[38] Similarly "Driving While Black" also began to get currency in popular media and discourse by 1995.[39] It should be noted that, before becoming part of the national lexicon, both terms are likely to have been in somewhat wider circulation among specific groups, such as defense attorneys and their clients, and the people most directly affected by the practices.[40] Nonetheless, "racial profiling" as a term and, more importantly, a concept that furthered the public debate over a specific law enforcement technique did not get wide circulation until the mid-1990s.

Two more things of great significance happened to the concept of racial profiling in the mid- to late 1990s. First, stories about (and hence attention to) the practice of stops and searches of minority motorists on the highways increased dramatically. Even in the early 1990s, media coverage of the practice was limited, notwithstanding those occasional articles or presentations that claimed or attempted to be an in-depth look at the practice. For most of the 1990s, half a dozen to a dozen stories a year was all the attention the practice could muster. A search on Westlaw, for example, turned up fewer than a dozen stories mentioning racial profiling in 1995 and a little more than two dozen such stories in 1996 and 1997, with most of the stories appearing in media in the Northeastern part of the country.

Media coverage picked up dramatically in 1998, however. The first and most prominent catalyst that year was the shooting on the New Jersey Turnpike of four high school students by New Jersey state troopers in the spring. Other stories discussing racial profiling also garnered considerable media coverage and attention, including the recommendations of a civil rights task force commissioned by the Clinton administration that included further investigation into the practice. In addition, attention was also drawn to the experiences of a number of prominent athletes and celebrities—including Olympic medallist Al Joyner and film star Wesley Snipes—who were also the subject of such stops.[41] By 1998, the number of articles in the popular media men-

tioning racial profiling numbered a couple hundred and expanded to more than a thousand articles each year in 1999,
2000, and 2001.[42]

Moreover, not only were more stories about racial profiling making their way into the media, but local stories began
to get national attention. We have already discussed the instance of the shooting of the high schoolers on the New Jersey Turnpike, which was reported around the country.[43] But
it was also true of stories that previously might not have gotten much coverage outside of the communities involved,
such as the discovery in 1998 of a 1993 memorandum written by the chief of police in predominantly white Trumbell,
Connecticut. In that memorandum, the police chief, in response to a string of burglaries, wrote

> one form of deterrence might be to develop a sense of proclivity
> toward the type of persons and vehicles usually involved in these
> crimes. [. . .] [N]ot only is it our obligation to enforce the motor
> vehicle laws, but in doing so we are provided with a profile of our
> community and those who travel within its boundaries.

The memorandum, not surprisingly, prompted accusations
by leaders of Connecticut's minority community that police
were engaged in racial profiling and an investigation by a
local FBI office. What is surprising, or at least significant, is
that the story received press coverage in media outlets far
beyond Trumbull.[44] Of course, this was not the first time
that a newspaper article in one city or community discussed incidents in other cities or states; the articles from
the Pittsburgh *Post-Gazette* in 1991 brought together stories
from other cities and states, for example. But initial coverage in the late 1980s and 1990s was, generally speaking,
limited to events in the local community. The extraterrito-
rial coverage of such incidents became increasingly common after racial profiling was reported more often following
the shootings on the New Jersey Turnpike.

Second, and equally important, if not more so, is that the
definition and understanding of racial profiling changed.
Even in the 1980s and early to mid-1990s, discussion of the

disproportionate stops of minority drivers often, though not always, discussed the use of race in connection with or as part of a profile developed by law enforcement in its effort to stop the drug trade. By the end of the 1990s, that changed and a broader conception of racial profiling took hold. For example, in the 1999 report prepared by the New Jersey Attorney General's office admitting that minority motorists were unfairly singled out, the authors, after due consideration of narrower formulations, adopted a very broad definition of racial profiling:

> To some extent, divergent opinions about racial profiling within and outside the law enforcement community depend on definitions. We choose to define racial profiling broadly to encompass any actions taken by a state trooper during a traffic stop that is based upon racial or ethnic stereotypes and that has the effect of treating minority motorists differently than non-minority motorists.[45]

Others went even further. One prominent critic defined racial profiling to encompass "any stop, search or arrest of a person based in whole or in part on the race of the suspect, except where police are acting on a racial description of the perpetrator of a crime." A defender of racial profiling similarly offered a broad formulation, "Put simply, racial profiling is when law enforcement agencies, or officers within agencies, focus their attention and enforcement onto particular racial or ethnic groups."[46]

Indeed, as it became more and more a subject of national debate, racial profiling was like a genie let out of the bottle. Eventually, just about every law enforcement action about which a speaker was critical that appeared to be based on a consideration of race was called "racial profiling." Thus, the term was applied to the shooting of an unarmed African immigrant in New York City, application of the death penalty to an African American prisoner in Texas, and the unsuccessful prosecution of an Asian American on espionage charges stemming from his work at the Los Alamos, New Mexico, nuclear laboratories. Indeed, accusations of racial profiling were also leveled extra-species, when a police dog in a Pennsylvania community attacked an African American child and was accused of racial profiling in so doing. After a two month investigation, the dog was cleared of the accusation of racial profiling.[47] This is so even though none of the incidents involved either a highway stop or, as far as the evidence was presented, a profile of any sort. "Racial profiling" came to mean "racial discrimination." It even had application outside the law enforcement context, as reflected in protests, and even some lawsuits, in Washington, D.C. and other cities when the refusal of pizza franchises to deliver pizzas to minority communities in which its drivers were being victimized by robberies and worse was attacked as racial profiling, as was the refusal of cab drivers to pick up minority passengers.[48]

Is Racial Profiling Really Profiling?

Throughout our discussion, we have traced development of profiling as a law enforcement technique from criminal profiling through the airport drug courier profile to the highway drug courier profile. With racial profiling moving even further away from profiling as practiced by the FBI Behavioral Science Unit and essentially becoming synonymous with racial discrimination in some respects, the movement away from the original manner of criminal profiling is complete. Far from a carefully considered, essentially *reactive* law enforcement technique based on past experience and data, practiced by a scientifically trained elite in connection with select crimes, racial profiling as commonly understood and debated has ceased to have anything at all to do with the use of profiles as a unique law enforcement technique.

How did it happen that racial profiling came to be synonymous with racial discrimination? This change was not inevitable but is perhaps not surprising, at least not when viewed in hindsight. Part of the reason for this development, perhaps a large part, comes from the media culture that has marked America over the last decade or so: the development of a sound-bite culture. When the most important speeches, from State of the Union addresses to major policy initiatives, are reduced to 30-second (or shorter) snippets on the evening news, the ground was laid for racial profiling to become a shorthand phrase for a whole host of practices, including but not limited to those involving the use of profiles, that appeared to feature racially discriminatory treatment.

This development has been assisted by the responses of the various arms of the government involved. When high-ranking law enforcement officials and politicians chose to deny that race was involved in the decision to stop motorists in the search for drugs, at least until the evidence that race *was* involved became overwhelming, they passed on the opportunity to define the term as part of a more meaningful debate in which the value, if any, of profiling as a law enforcement technique could be considered, in part by avoiding any discussion as to what extent race was considered in such stops (As the sole reason for the stop? As one factor among many? Based on historical evidence regarding past practices or an officer's gut reaction based on bias?). The same is true of the response of the courts, where the only issue was whether law enforcement had actually witnessed a violation of the motor vehicle code. Nor, in the end, did either the Congress or any of the state legislatures embark upon or insist on a meaningful consideration of what exactly profiling entailed and what role, if any, race could play in that practice.

CHAPTER 5

The Supreme Court and the Issue of Race

Having sketched the development by law enforcement of the use of drug courier profiles and pretextual traffic stops in Chapter 3, and having looked at the vigorous debate that was thus generated in the last chapter, we turn now to what role, if any, the courts played in the development of those law enforcement practices and the larger public debate.

Race and Profiling

The role that consideration of race in criminal justice issues has played and should play has generated a huge literature, particularly with regard to the type of Fourth Amendment issues relevant to the current public debate concerning profiling. As is true for many of the rights guaranteed by the Bill of Rights, development of most of the rights associated with the criminal justice system guaranteed by the Fourth, Fifth, and Sixth Amendments has taken place in the twentieth century. And in many cases, including many landmark cases, the struggle for racial justice has played a prominent role in the development of those rights. As one scholar has described the work of the Supreme Court in this area,

> It is almost commonplace by now that much of the Court's criminal jurisprudence during the middle part of [the twentieth] century was a form of race jurisprudence, prompted largely by the treatment of black suspects and black defendants in the South. The Court's concern with race relations served as the unspoken subtext of many of its significant criminal procedure decisions. [. . .][1]

For those reasons, one might expect the Supreme Court to play a central role in the debate over racial profiling, particularly, as previously noted, as race has become a critical, perhaps *the* critical issue, in the debate. But such is not the case. In fact, the opposite is true: the Court has essentially ducked the issue of race in the context of the current debate over racial profiling.

The Court has not yet dealt specifically with racial profiling, at least expressly so, in that the Court has not specifically considered the use by law enforcement of an actual profile in which race was one among many factors. None of the Court's cases that dealt specifically with a profile—*Mendenhall, Reid,* or *Sokolow,* for example—raised the issue of race at all. But that is not to say that the Court's current treatment of race in the context of the Fourth Amendment does not affect the issues surrounding racial profiling. Moreover, just as the Court has refused to treat the use of profiles as a separate law enforcement technique (as we noted in our discussion of *Mendenhall, Reid,* and *Sokolow*), it has even more directly refused to consider claims of racial bias or targeting of minorities in assessing Fourth Amendment claims, even as, ironically, the larger public debate has placed the issue of race at the heart of the controversy over profiling. The Court's decisions in this area as well have served, even more than the decisions in *Mendenhall, Reid,* and *Sokolow,* essentially to write the Court out of the current public debate over profiling. We begin with a brief overview of the relevant decisions, starting again with *Terry v. Ohio.*

The Issue of Race in Some of the Early Decisions

In setting up the ground rules that legitimate investigatory stops in certain circumstances, the Supreme Court in *Terry v. Ohio,* never really dealt with the race of the defendants and what impact, if any, that had on the decision to make the stop at issue in the case. Most significant, nowhere in the decision did the Court mention the race of the petition- ers/defendants—who were African American—nor did their race appear to influence the Court's ruling, at least as ex- pressed in Chief Justice Warren's majority opinion.

It now appears, however, that race played an important role in the decision of Detective McFadden in that case to make the investigatory stop at issue, and, more broadly, race was an important, if essentially unmentioned, subtext in the case. To begin with, the case came to the Court against a backdrop not only of rising crime rates but also fol- lowing summers in which race riots plagued many American inner cities and only a few months after publica- tion of the Kerner Report, prepared by the National Advisory Commission on Civil Disorder set up by President Johnson following the riots in Detroit the previous summer, which warned of the problems of race in American society.[2] As An- thony Thompson has recently demonstrated, those repre- senting the defendants, who were African American, in *Terry* tried to introduce the issue of race into the case. More- over, Thompson has argued, the actual decision to stop makes most sense if one assumes that the detective who made the stop had, in fact, considered the defendants' race in the decision to stop and question them.[3] Finally on this point, two groups—the National Association for the Ad- vancement of Colored People Legal Defense and Education Fund and the Americans for Effective Law Enforcement— filed briefs as *amicus curiae,* raising the issue of race. In counter-arguments that foreshadowed some of the arguments later made regarding racial profiling, the NAACP argued against allowing stops by police on less than probable cause because African Americans were much more frequently subjected to such stops and frisks than whites; the stops were based largely on racial prejudice by the police, and that practice was a significant cause of friction between law enforcement and members of minority communities. AELE countered the NAACP argument by claiming that any disparate impact of stops and frisks was due to the fact that minorities committed more crime, not to police prejudice.[4]

Nonetheless, in its opinion the Court essentially ignored the race issue, relegating to a single sentence and accompanying footnote the observation that "minority groups, particularly Negroes, frequently complain" of "wholesale harassment by certain elements of the police community," and recognition of the fact that frequent frisks of youths and other members of minority groups "cannot help but be a severely exacerbating factor in police-community tensions."[5] Moreover, in language that might have been an ironic foreboding of the later public debate about racial profiling, the Court justified in race-neutral terms what on the facts of the case might well have been viewed as a racially motivated stop by relying on and stressing the more than thirty years experience and the resulting expertise of the detective making the stop: "It would have been poor police work indeed for an officer of 30 years experience in the detection of thievery from stores in the same neighborhood to have failed to investigate this behavior further."[6]

The treatment of the issue of race in *Terry* is significant for two reasons. First, as Adina Schwartz has pointed out, in its discussion, albeit very brief, of the issue, the Court appears to accept the factual argument made by the Legal Defense Fund—that investigatory stops and frisks would, or at least could, be used to harass minorities—but nonetheless rejects what the Legal Defense Fund argued strongly should follow from that observation: that such stops should be strictly limited by being allowed only upon a showing of probable cause. Second, in its reliance on police expertise to justify the new category of stops, Schwartz continues, the Court undercut consideration of other possibly improper motives: "[O]nce an officer advances a nonracial justification for a decision to stop or frisk, courts have tended not to ask whether race was in fact the sole basis for the decision." Anthony Thompson has expressed a similar point somewhat differently, "In stripping away race from the case and substituting the officer-as-expert narrative, the Court in *Terry* essentially created a conceptual construct: an officer who was unaffected by considerations of race and who could be trusted even in a race-laden case like *Terry* to be acting on the basis of legitimate indicia of criminal activity. Such an officer could be trusted with the expanded powers conferred by the *Terry* opinion, notwithstanding the dire warnings of the Legal Defense Fund."[7]

Brignoni-Pierce and Martinez-Fuerte

Shortly after the decision in *Terry*, in two cases involving stops at the border to apprehend illegal immigrants, the Court appeared receptive to the use of race by law enforcement as at least one factor justifying a decision to make an investigatory stop. In *United States v. Brignoni-Pierce*, the Court ruled unconstitutional a stop, made by a roving patrol of the United States Border Patrol, that was based *solely* on the fact that the persons in the car that was stopped were of Mexican ancestry. In its ruling, however, the Court suggested that Mexican ancestry could be one factor that law enforcement might permissibly use to make a decision as to whom to stop:

> In this case the officers relied on a single factor to justify stopping the respondent's car: the apparent Mexican ancestry of the occupants. We cannot conclude that this furnished reasonable grounds to believe that the three occupants were aliens. . . . Even if [the officers] saw enough to think that the occupants were of Mexican descent, this factor alone would justify neither a reasonable belief that they were aliens or that the car concealed other aliens who were illegally in this country. . . . The

likelihood that any given person of Mexican ancestry is an alien
is high enough to make Mexican appearance a relevant factor,
but standing alone it does not justify stopping all Mexican-
Americans to ask if they are aliens.[8]

A year later, the Court's comfort level with the use of race
to justify a stop at the border was strengthened in *United
States v. Martinez-Fuerte*. In that case, involving brief stops
for questioning at a border checkpoint, as opposed to a roving patrol, the Court held that stops based "largely" on the
basis of apparent Mexican ancestry of the person stopped
passed constitutional muster, in part because the Court
found that the "intrusion [in such stops] is sufficiently minimal that no particularized reason need exist to justify it."[9]

Of course, neither case expressly dealt with profiles, and
stops at the border are not necessarily based on formal profiles, although they may be. Such stops are, however, sufficiently akin to at least some of the practices that have come
today to be labeled racial profiling that, had the Court continued to develop that line of analysis, it would have been
short work to apply the principles set forth in those cases to
the debate about racial profiling (or perhaps, as the debate
over racial profiling heated up, to reconsider those principles). Instead, the Court went in the opposite direction, developing jurisprudence in a line of cases that essentially
made race irrelevant to any analysis under the Fourth
Amendment.

Say Whren

We return to the Supreme Court's 1996 decision in *Whren v.
United States*.[10] As we discussed earlier, *Whren* was important in resolving a conflict in the federal circuit courts as to
what standard to use in judging the constitutional validity of
traffic stops, choosing the very deferential "could have" test
over the slightly less deferential "would have" test.[11] The
Court's decision in *Whren*, however, is just as important—
and indeed has drawn most attention—for its treatment of
the issue of race,[12] for the decision is both emblematic of

the basic thrust of the Court's current guiding principles on the intersection of race and the Fourth Amendment and important in its own right in the debate over racial profiling.

At issue in *Whren* was the stop of a vehicle for a traffic violation that resulted in the arrest of the defendants on drug charges after the police spotted two bags of cocaine in the vehicle during the traffic stop. The defendants, who were African American, argued, among other things, that the stop violated their Fourth Amendment rights because the initial stop had been a pretext, and, just as important if not more so, the decision to stop the vehicle had been based on the race of its occupants (the defendants)

In a unanimous opinion, the Court rejected the argument. Although the Court conceded that selective enforcement of the law based on considerations of race was prohibited by the Constitution, it ruled that in considering whether a stop was warranted under the Fourth Amendment, the only question was whether there was objectively enough evidence that the officer had witnessed a violation of the motor vehicle code in order to justify the stop. A court could not consider the actual motives of the law enforcement officers in making the stop even if the officers were motivated by the race of the suspects. Any redress for a racially motivated stop would have to come under the Equal Protection Clause of the Fourteenth Amendment in a separate lawsuit, not as a Fourth Amendment challenge to the stop in the criminal case.[13] Under the Court's reasoning in *Whren,* as a number of commentators have pointed out, race is irrelevant to any issues raised under the Fourth Amendment.[14]

Of course, it must be noted that, in so ruling, *Whren* did not create new law, as the Court went to some lengths to point out. A refusal to consider race as a relevant factor in Fourth Amendment challenges, even when the defendants had pressed the issue before the Court, had been the hallmark of the Supreme Court for more than a decade before the decision in *Whren.*[15] *Whren* was, perhaps, the culmination of that line of cases, if only because of how central the objection to a racially motivated stop was to the defendants' argument. Indeed, what marks *Whren,* one scholar has noted, is not that the Court rejected any consideration of race in considering the issues before it but how unanimous and unqualified that determination is in the Court's opinion.[16]

The Problems with *Whren*

The decision has drawn harsh criticism, including some who question the Court's suggestion that challenges to racially motivated stops be litigated separately under the Equal Protection Clause. On this latter point, commentators note both practical and doctrinal or philosophical problems. From a practical standpoint, Equal Protection challenges to race-based pretextual traffic stops present a number of problems. To begin with, it is not at all clear that the remedy for such an equal protection claim would include the exclusion of evidence the way a violation of Fourth Amendment rights does, a remedy that is often critical to defending a criminal action. Thus, someone caught with drugs as a result of a racially discriminatory traffic stop may find his only recourse is in a civil suit following conviction. Those who are stopped and found with drugs or other contraband make very unappealing plaintiffs in later civil suits, particularly if they are suing from a prison cell; indeed, recognition of this fact was for years a central underpinning of arguments favoring the exclusionary rule over civil lawsuits as the appropriate remedy in other types of cases involving challenges to police conduct based on the Fourth and Fifth Amendments. Even for innocent motorists who are stopped because of their race and are not carrying drugs, civil litigation can prove to be an expensive, time-consuming process *if* they can find a lawyer willing to take the case.

Even in cases in which a violation of the plaintiff's rights is clear, juries may consider the amount of damages appropriate to compensate such illegal action to be very small, further discouraging prospective plaintiffs. Challenges under the Equal Protection Clause are also difficult because the Court's jurisprudence in this area requires that plaintiffs demonstrate not just racially disparate impact but that the police were motivated by racial animus as well, a much more difficult burden of proof. Moreover, a plaintiff would have to prove that, regardless of whether other stops were motivated by racial animus, the police acted with racial animus directed toward *him*. Finally, it has been argued that the Court's directing victims of discriminatory treatment to the Equal Protection Clause again undermines the protections that the Fourth Amendment is supposed to supply. As David Sklansky put it, "Equal protection doctrine treats claims of inequitable policing the same as any other claim of inequity; it gives no special recognition to the special reasons to insist on evenhanded law enforcement, or to the distinctive concerns with arbitrariness underlying the Fourth Amendment."[17]

The problem with using the Equal Protection Clause to challenge racial profiling is illustrated by *Brown v. City of Oneonta*.[18] In that case, an elderly woman was assaulted from behind. All she saw of her assailant were his hands and forearm; she also thought her attacker was male and young from the way in which he bolted out of the room and that he had cut himself in the scuffle. That was the information she gave the police, who began searching in the upstate New York college town that had very few African American residents, either as permanent residents or students at the local State University of New York campus. Using that information, the police proceeded to question every African American male student in the community in an effort to identify the assailant. When that did not lead to the assailant, they questioned every other African American man in the local community that they could find. A number of African American residents of Oneonta who were stopped and questioned brought a civil rights class action on behalf of all black residents of the town, alleging that the manner in which the town police had conducted the investigation— with its *carte blanche* approach of questioning most of the black residents of the town—violated their civil rights.[19]

The situation in *Brown* is not, strictly speaking, a case of racial profiling. Neither was a profile used nor was race used as a proxy drawn from past incidents from which an inference of criminality was drawn. Race was one component in a description of the attacker, although a very limited description. *Brown* falls somewhere in the gray area between cases in which race is part of the description of a known suspect (cases which even the harshest critics of racial profiling do not usually describe as racial profiling) and those cases in which race alone is the deciding factor driving law enforcement actions. Still, there are aspects of the police investigation that are disturbing and raise issues similar to criticisms frequently leveled at racial profiling, among them that the investigation subjected large numbers of innocent persons to humiliating stops and questioning, that the investigation was largely ineffective in finding the assailant, and that it is unlikely that the police would have adopted the same approach had the assailant been white.[20] Indeed although the facts in *Brown* are striking, similar sweeps by police targeting large numbers of particular ethnic or racial groups are, while perhaps not everyday occurrences, also not unprecedented.[21] That the *Brown* case is frequently cited as an example of racial profiling reflects the tendency of critics, discussed in the previous chapter, to label any improper use of race as an instance of racial profiling.

In any event, in that case both the lower and appellate courts dismissed those portions of the plaintiffs' complaint alleging that the Equal Protection Clause was violated by the manner in which the police conducted their investigation. Foremost, the Court rejected arguments by the plaintiffs that the police's stopping and questioning black men in town had violated their rights under the Equal Protection Clause. The Court of Appeals refused to find the type of invidious intentional discrimination necessary to prevail under the Equal Protection Clause. The Court found that the Oneonta Police did not have a policy of routinely singling out African American residents in investigating violent crime. Rather, the Court found that the plaintiffs were questioned because race was one factor among others—in-cluding age and gender—given to the police by the victim. Ironically, the Court did allow to stand allegations that stops of certain of the plaintiffs violated their rights under the Fourth Amendment, because there was not sufficient evidence to establish the "reasonable suspicion" needed for such stops under the rationale in *Terry*. [22]

Brown is thus somewhat ironic in that it flips the analysis in *Whren* by being more receptive to charges that the plaintiffs' Fourth Amendment rights were violated than that their rights under the Equal Protection Clause were after the Supreme Court suggested that such challenges were more appropriately brought under the latter constitutional provision. (It should be noted that none of the stops in *Brown* in-volved traffic stops in which the police had witnessed a vio-lation of some provision of the motor vehicle code.) But more than that, it also demonstrates somewhat the diffi-culty of bringing an Equal Protection challenge in these circumstances. The Court of Appeals gave the police quite a bit of leeway and allowed investigative stops of just about every young African American man in a predominantly white community based on a very limited description pro-vided by the victim.

Whren and Racial Profiling

While we will not enter the debate over whether *Whren* was correctly decided, for our purposes the case is important for a number of reasons. To begin with, there is the nature of the police conduct involved: an allegedly pretextual traffic stop, the real reason for which may have been the race of the occupants of the vehicle. As we discussed in the prior chapter, this was not the type of carefully drawn profile based on hard objective data that had originally been the heart of profiling. But, perhaps just as important, it is al-most the paradigmatic type of police conduct that has come to be associated with racial profiling at the center of the cur-rent debate. Moreover, the Court elected to hear and decide *Whren,* unlike *Sokolow* and *Reid,* at a time when the larger public debate was underway. *Whren* presented the Court with a golden opportunity to enter and contribute to the larger public debate in a meaningful way and to address the central issues involved.

Rather than becoming engaged, however, the effect of the decision in *Whren* was essentially to write the Court out of the debate. If the Court's approach in *Sokolow* and *Reid* can be described as a missed opportunity to clarify the appropriate role of profiling as a general law enforcement tactic, the Court's approach to the issue of race and such police practices under the Fourth Amendment in *Whren* represents something more (or less, depending on your perspective). Its reasoning on the central issue of race has made the Court essentially irrelevant in the larger public debate by not simply taking one position or another but failing fundamentally to address the key issues that have gripped the others involved in the debate.[23]

In addition, the Court's treatment of race in *Whren* somewhat mirrors for that crucial issue what its selection of the "could have" test did for police discretion generally. Recall the point made earlier[24] that, whether one thinks the "reasonable suspicion" test of *Terry* is strong or weak, adopting that test for pretextual traffic stops would require at least *some* level of scrutiny by an independent entity (i.e., the judiciary) of the decision to stop someone to search for drugs. Instead, the Court elected not to ask that question at all and in that way prevents or discourages legitimate inquiry into what many believe is a proper question—whether, in any given case, police have overstepped their bounds.

The same is true with regard to the issue of race. By refusing to consider an officer's motivation, the Court again undermines consideration of what has become, and by all rights *should* be, a critical issue. As Anthony Thompson aptly phrases it,

> The current status of ignoring race—or "declaring" race irrelevant—both drives the discussion underground and encourages courts to assume nonracial motives in instances where the facts suggest otherwise. Further, it "demonizes" the use of race and

predisposes courts against labeling a law enforcement officer a "racist." Under a system that acknowledges that race does play a role in the exercise of discretion, there is a beginning to the long and difficult process of dealing with and working through the issue.[25]

Indeed, Thompson's observation suggests that the Court has not only written itself out of the larger public debate but impeded that debate as well, even if unintentionally. For those who object to traffic stops based solely on the race of the driver but who might find some value in profiles that use race as one factor among many to be considered under the right circumstances, it is important to get a handle on exactly who is doing what and why; who are the police stopping and precisely why are they stopping them? The Court's treatment of the two central issues in cases involving pretextual stops prevents those factual issues—who is doing what and why—from being considered or at least it drives consideration of those issues elsewhere. In so doing, the opportunity is lost to determine exactly what is going on with what has come to be called racial profiling. Thus it is not surprising that many in the larger public debate talk past each other, with critics frequently assuming that every stop is based solely or mostly on the driver's race and defenders assuming that that is never the case.

The Road Less Traveled

We have considered at some length the treatment of the important issues by the Supreme Court because it is not only the highest court in the federal system but, as such, usually directly influences how issues are treated by the lower courts, either (as with federal courts) establishing a precedent that must be followed or, even in the absence of a mandatory precedent, providing a persuasive articulation of basic principles. It is worth taking a moment then to consider *State of New Jersey v. Soto*,[26] decided a few months before *Whren*, coming out of a court at the other end of the structural spectrum, a state trial court.

Soto was a case in which a number of defendants joined together to challenge what they alleged was the practice of the New Jersey State Troopers to target minority motorists in the search for drugs. At issue in *Soto,* as in *Whren,* was whether law enforcement officers had made the decisions to stop based on the race of the driver and the occupants of the car. And, like *Whren,* the defendants in *Soto* brought their challenge in the context of motions to suppress evidence found as a result of the traffic stops.

To decide the motions, the trial judge, the Honorable Robert Francis, held a hearing and accepted into evidence a large amount of statistical material concerning how the New Jersey State Police conducted traffic stops on the New Jersey Turnpike. The court also heard testimony from former state troopers "about [their] having been trained and coached to make race-based profile stops."[27]

Judge Francis granted the motions to suppress. As part of its reasoning the court noted "police may not stop a motorist based on race or any other invidious classification."[28] The court also explained that the standard to be applied is an objective one, not a search for the motivation of the police officers,[29] essentially the same standard used by the Supreme Court in *Whren* to dismiss consideration of the defendants' arguments there. But in *Soto,* unlike *Whren,* the court considered evidence of institutional racism and sustained the defendants' challenge, based largely, although not exclusively, on the statistical evidence concerning police stops and arrests presented during the hearing. In so doing, the court employed language that was not only critical of the New Jersey State Police but that went to the heart of the debate over racial profiling:

> [W]here objective evidence establishes "that a police agency has embarked upon an officially sanctioned or *de facto* policy of targeting minorities for investigation and arrest," any evidence seized will be suppressed to deter future insolence in office by those charged with enforcement of the law and to maintain judicial integrity.[30]

Moreover, relying in part upon evidence "that the State Police hierarchy allowed, condoned, cultivated and tolerated discrimination between 1988 and 1991 in its crusade to rid New Jersey of the scourge of drugs,"[31] the court concluded its opinion as follows:

> Here, defendants have proven at least a *de facto* policy on the part of the State Police out of the Moorestown Station of targeting blacks for investigation and arrest between April 1988 and May 1991, both south of exit 3 and between exits 1 and 7A of the Turnpike. . . . The discretion devolved upon general road troopers to stop any car they want as long as Title 39 [that is, the section of the New Jersey criminal code that sets out motor vehicle offenses] is used evinces a selection process that is susceptible of abuse. The utter failure of the State Police hierarchy to monitor and control a crackdown program like DITU or investigate the many claims of institutional discrimination manifests its indifference if not acceptance . . . The eradication of illegal drugs from our State is an obviously worthy goal, but not at the expense of individual rights. . . . [32]

It should be noted that, strictly as a matter of legal doctrine, *Soto* did not differ from *Whren*.[33] As discussed above, both cases recognized the constitutional problems with using race as a basis to stop a motorist, and both claimed to apply an objective standard to assess the conduct of law enforcement as opposed to looking for the officers' subjective motivations.[34] And yet, it would be difficult to find two more different approaches, in terms of language, analysis and result, to the same problem or set of allegations than those taken in *Whren* and *Soto*. Moreover, there is something ironic in this.

At first glance, it may make some sense, given the public furor over racial profiling, that a local state court would be more alert and responsive to allegations of racial profiling, particularly in a state like New Jersey that has become something of a focal point in the controversy. But the New Jersey state court's greater sensitivity to concerns of racial justice than that of the Supreme Court turns on its head the model for enforcement of constitutional rights that we had become used to in the last half-century, most notably in connection with the landmark decision in *Brown v. Board of Education* and the implementation of the relief ordered by that decision but elsewhere as well, where plaintiffs in local communities looked for vindication to sometimes distant federal courts and often the Supreme Court in Washington, in the face of more direct resistance closer to home.[35] And perhaps that twist, as much as anything else, speaks volumes about the approach of the judiciary in general, and the Supreme Court in particular, to the issues raised by racial profiling.

In the Lower Courts

For better or worse, while *Soto* may have had some influence on how New Jersey has dealt with the racial profiling controversy, for the rest of the nation the approach embodied in the Supreme Court's decision in *Whren* appears, not surprisingly, to have had the broader impact.[36] Before we examine the treatment of race and profiling in the lower courts, it is important to put the *Whren* decision in context so that we understand but do not overstate the importance of *Whren*.

First, it would be a mistake to view *Whren* as representing a sea change that introduced a refusal to consider the racial motivations of law enforcement into a world in which courts had previously aggressively scrutinized and prohibited such motivations. For one thing, as noted, in refusing to consider the racial motivations of law enforcement, *Whren* is properly viewed not as a beginning but as the culmination of a line of cases that began more than a decade earlier. Even in those cases in which the Court had considered the extent to which race played a role in the decision to stop someone, the Court had not been unmistakably hostile to the idea. After all, the Court's decision in *Martinez-Feurte* held that race can be one factor among others in the decision to make a stop. With regard to the use of highway drug courier profiles and pretextual traffic stops by law enforcement, the importance of *Whren* lies not only, or even primarily, in the Court's foreclosing consideration of the subjective motivation of law enforcement in considering Fourth Amendment challenges inasmuch as the Court had been taking that direction before the decision. The striking thing about the *Whren* decision with regard to the larger public debate over racial profiling is that the Court had a golden opportunity to address what was becoming the central issue in the use of profiles by law enforcement, and the Court, again, simply ducked the issue.

Second, while the Court's decision in *Whren* to prohibit considerations of racial motivation in cases involving pretextual traffic stops is significant, it is also important not to make too large a distinction between consideration of race in cases involving the highway drug courier profile and in cases that preceded *Whren* involving use of the airport drug courier profiles, where the "reasonable suspicion" test of *Terry* applied. In practice, those cases were nearly as unreceptive to challenges that stops were racially motivated as those involving pretextual traffic stops. As one commentator, analyzing airport drug courier profile stops before the decision in *Whren,* has noted, the "reasonable suspicion" test is sufficiently broad to "permit almost any conduct to be evidence of suspicion. Law enforcement officers can determine whom to stop based on arbitrary criteria and then justify the stops later with almost any rationale." This, too, works to prevent consideration of an officer's racial motivation, although not as directly or perhaps quite as completely as the outright prohibition in *Whren:*

> The reasonable articulable suspicion standard creates a situation in which the issue of race is obscured by many other factors which comprise the totality of circumstances. Because courts use so many other factors indicative of suspicion to determine the reasonableness of the articulated suspicion, the race factor receives little or no judicial scrutiny.[37]

And therefore it is not surprising that, as noted in our discussion of the development of the airport profile, the use of race did not provoke significant comment or become an issue of any public visibility or attention in connection with the airport drug courier profile, particularly when compared to what happened with regard to stops on the highway.

This is not to say that every lower court, which does not enjoy the Supreme Court's luxury of being able to pick and choose which cases it will hear, has shown, or will show, the same insensitivity to profiling as a concept or to its racial component that is reflected in the Supreme Court decisions. In one lower court case involving a highway stop, decided prior to *Whren,* the court found that the defendant had been subjected to a pretextual traffic stop using a profile in which race had played a key role (along with the fact that the defendant was from out of state) and granted the defendant's motion to suppress evidence found as a result of the stop. The court did not condemn all stops based on the use of profiles but did hold that "profile stops may not be predicated on unconstitutional discrimination based on race, ethnicity or state of residence." The court found that the stop at issue violated the defendant's Fourth Amendment right to be free of unreasonable seizure, Fourteenth Amendment right to the equal protection of the laws, and First Amendment right to travel. The case also produced some curious testimony by the police officer, who denied that race played any role in the decision to stop but, apparently trying unsuccessfully to persuade the court that he had *not* used a profile in deciding to stop the defendant, admitted that the initial stop had been a pretext so that he could use a profile to tell whether the driver was carrying drugs.[38]

Similar sentiments can be found in cases after *Whren* as well. "Racial profiling by law enforcement officials is an odious practice that often unfairly burdens people of color," noted one court in *dicta,* although the court in that case also upheld the stop at issue, finding that the decision to stop the defendant was not impermissibly based on race. And in another case, this one involving a stop of a car at the California border to search for illegal immigrants, the court held that a person's Hispanic appearance was not a proper factor for the Border Patrol to consider in deciding whether to make the stop, at least in areas where large segments of the population were Hispanic. In its opinion, in which the court relied in part on both *Sokolow* and *Wardlow,* the court discussed sympathetically the impact that such law enforcement practices can have on minority populations and questioned the current validity of the Supreme Court's invitation to law enforcement in *Martinez-Fuerte* to use race as a factor in deciding whether to make a stop, as based on outdated and invalid demographic information.[39] Indeed, in a number of cases, lower courts have been critical of stops made solely on the basis of the suspect's race, although, again, sometimes they expressed that concern in situations where the court did not find a race-based decision to stop.[40]

But courts have also demonstrated and articulated high levels of tolerance for, bordering on insensitivity to, the *racial* component of profiling. Thus, in an early case in which the court found that a stop made pursuant to an airport drug courier profile failed to establish "reasonable suspicion," the court found that race had played a critical role in the decision to stop the defendant. Yet the fact that race had been a key factor received no criticism and little attention.[41] Even more striking, and typical, are the sentiments expressed by the Eighth Circuit in a frequently cited case:

> Facts are not to be ignored simply because they may be unpleasant—and the unpleasant fact in this case is that [the DEA agent] had knowledge, based upon his own experience and upon the intelligence reports he had received from the Los Angeles authorities, that young male members of the black Los Angeles gangs were flooding the Kansas City area with cocaine. To that extent, then, race, when coupled with the other factors [the agent] relied upon, was a factor in the decision to approach and ultimately detain [the suspect]. We wish it were otherwise, but we take the facts as they are presented to us, not as we would like them to be.[42]

Equally curious, and occasionally unsettling, is another approach found in the lower court decisions in which the court denounced consideration of race in the decision to

stop and search the defendant but then ignored or dis-
counted evidence that the stop or search at issue in the case
was racially motivated. Thus, in one case, at issue was a
stop and search based on the fact that the defendant, a well-
dressed Hispanic male traveling in the first-class compartment of a train, appeared nervous when, after leaving the
train, he was approached and questioned by a DEA agent
and would not consent to a search of the trunk of his car. In
its opinion, the court appeared to go further than the Supreme Court has gone and refused to allow *any* consideration by law enforcement of a suspect's race to play a role in
the decision to make a stop. However, the court did not in-
validate the stop in that case although it was undoubtedly
based, at least in part, on the defendant's race. Instead, the
court simply took that factor out of its consideration of
whether there was reasonable suspicion sufficient to justify
the stop as if the racial component had never existed.[43]
Similarly, in a case involving the forfeiture of funds following an illegal search, the court found that the evidence presented by the plaintiff "substantiate[d] . . . claims that . . .
[agents] make investigative decisions on the basis of race"
as a general proposition but refused to find that the stop involving the plaintiff was racially motivated.[44]

Most often, however, it appears that courts simply discuss the facts surrounding the stop, giving significant defer-
ence to law enforcement and disregarding the race of the
suspect without any significant consideration or discussion
of whether law enforcement agents had used a profile or
considered race as a factor in deciding whether to make the
stop. A case decided shortly after *Sokolow* illustrates the approach. In *United States v. Williams,*[45] Judge Nathaniel Jones
in dramatic language criticized the use of race in the decision to detain the defendant based on his fitting many of
the characteristics of the drug courier profile used by police
officers in the case, concluding,

> I cannot come away from this case without feeling deeply trou-
> bled: troubled that this Nation's citizens are receiving disparate
> treatment at the hands of police officers primarily on the basis

of race, troubled that such unequal racial treatment is considered increasingly appropriate by trial courts, and most troubled by this court's conclusion that such race-based treatment is entirely unobjectionable as a legal matter. It is undoubtedly tragic when a significant number of black Americans fear that they are presumptively under suspicion of criminal activity in the eyes of the law merely because of their race. Infinitely more tragic is the strong possibility that their fear may be justified.[46]

But Judge Jones' remarks come in a dissent. Nowhere did the majority opinion mention either the fact that a profile was used in the decision to detain the suspect, or the race of the suspect, although it did discuss other factors, and despite the fact that, according to Judge Jones, the lower court acknowledged that the defendant's race was one of the factors used in the profile employed and played a role in the decision to detain.[47] In short, in *Williams* as in many other cases, both profiling and any racial component are irrelevant to the analysis and provoke no discussion at all. And in so doing, the courts are doing exactly what the Supreme Court has instructed them to do.

Whither State v. Soto?

Is there, then, nothing to be said for *Soto* and the approach suggested in that case? One critical question regarding the decision in *Soto* is whether it represents a one-time aberration or whether it will prove to be something of a harbinger, at least when combined with other more recent events. The decision did have some influence, though in ways outside of and separate from formal litigation. Whether or not the decision prompted or encouraged additional legal challenges to racial profiling is difficult to state with precision, although it can at least be inferred.

It certainly facilitated some of the challenges that have followed—at least in New Jersey. Before *Soto,* a few other state courts in New Jersey had issued decisions invalidating arrests made on the basis of a profile where consideration of the suspect's race was involved, although not in language and with findings as strong as *Soto.*[48] However, the extensive statistical information taken into evidence by the court in *Soto* and the findings of the court with regard to the complicity of the State Police hierarchy, along with similar findings in the Attorney General's 1999 *Interim Report* on racial profiling, have been held sufficient to present a "colorable basis" to demonstrate a formal policy of racial profiling. Indeed, in one subsequent case, a New Jersey appellate court found that the defendants in that case had met the burden of establishing the police had "an officially sanctioned or *de facto* policy of selective enforcement against minorities" based essentially on the finding in *Soto* of the existence of a *de facto* policy of targeting minorities by the State Police and the lack of evidence that there had been any changes in that policy.[49]

Since *Soto,* the New Jersey Supreme Court has twice addressed challenges to profiling and the results, perhaps not surprisingly, were mixed. One case decided in January 2002, *State v. Stovall,*[50] involved a challenge to a stop and search for drugs made on the basis of an airport drug courier profile. Some expected the court to use the case to fully examine the practice of profiling.[51] The final decision by the New Jersey Supreme Court, however, simply applied the existing law as set out in cases such as *Reid* and *Sokolow.* The decision in *Stovall* did not overturn *Soto* or even criticize the earlier decision. But, like the Supreme Court's treatment of cases involving racial profiling, the New Jersey Supreme Court passed on the opportunity to stake out new grounds using state constitutional law.

A few weeks later, however, the New Jersey Supreme Court did take a significant step in a case involving a pretextual traffic stop. In *State v. Carty,* the New Jersey Supreme Court ruled that even when a driver pulled over for violating a provision of the motor vehicle code consents to a search, law enforcement officers still need a "reasonable suspicion" to search the vehicle. The Court based its holding on Article I, paragraph 7, of the New Jersey Constitution, not the Fourth Amendment to the United States Constitution. In so ruling, the Court accepted the criticisms of many opponents of pretextual traffic stops that the breadth of motor vehicle violations makes everyone subject to such stops, as well as psychological studies that suggested that consent in such situations is often not freely given. Moreover, the Court cited and relied upon the 1999 *Interim Report* on racial profiling by the Attorney General as well as reports issued by the monitor assigned to supervise compliance by the State with the Consent Decree entered with the Department of Justice, although the Court did not engage in a discussion of racial profiling *per se*.[52] The decision in *Carty* does not eliminate pretextual traffic stops altogether; there is nothing in the Court's decision, for example, to suggest that a search incident to arrest would be unconstitutional or one in which contraband is found "in plain view" would be unconstitutional. Still, by greatly limiting consent searches, the Court took a big step toward curbing some of the abuses associated with pretextual traffic stops. Reports of the decision in the media also treated it as a significant statement in the ongoing debate over racial profiling.[53]

The Civil Cases

So far, we have focused primarily on criminal law cases in which the challenge to the use of a profile has come from a defendant in a criminal case facing criminal charges as a result of evidence of contraband found during the search by law enforcement officers. There is, however, another avenue to challenge the use of a profile or racial profiling: a civil lawsuit. In a civil lawsuit, the goal of the plaintiff is not to avoid or reverse a conviction of the criminal laws; rather, plaintiffs in such lawsuits generally seek either monetary damages to compensate for the wrong suffered (the illegal stop and search) or injunctive relief to prevent reoccurrences of the illegal conduct or both. Civil litigation to challenge racial profiling has been resorted to much less often than challenges to a stop based on a profile or pretextual stop in criminal cases, and many lawsuits, as this book goes to press, have not been resolved. Still, they warrant some consideration.

As with criminal cases, the civil cases present a mixed picture. Some civil cases succeeded in their challenges to racial profiling, with a few civil cases, as in some criminal cases, containing statements critical of racial profiling. "Racial profiling of any kind is anathema to our criminal justice system because it eviscerates the core integrity that is necessary to operate that system effectively in our diverse democracy," wrote one court in approving a settlement in a case brought by a Hispanic police trainee in which complaints of racial profiling were a significant part of a larger set of allegations of employment discrimination and a hostile work environment.[54] The court in that case approved the settlement but only after making certain that the settlement agreement required significant steps by the police force to eliminate its illegal conduct. Those steps included the town's adoption of a formal policy banning racial profiling and ticket quotas for police officers and requiring police to keep records of the race of all persons they stop.[55]

Other plaintiffs in civil cases challenging racial profiling also had some significant successes. Recall Robert Wilkins who, along with his family, was stopped on the Maryland Turnpike as he was returning from a family funeral in Chicago. Wilkins brought suit against the Maryland State Police. In the litigation, Wilkins was represented by the local chapter of the American Civil Liberties Union, which brought suit on behalf of Wilkins, his family, and other similarly situated minority drivers. Maryland initially contested the case aggressively. But the ACLU gathered the statistical evidence, compiled by John Lamberth, of how frequently minority drivers were stopped compared to their white counterparts and discovered a memorandum in the files of the Maryland State Police containing a profile used by police targeting minority drivers. Eventually, the parties settled the lawsuit with Maryland agreeing to adopt a formal policy banning racial profiling, instituting training for its officers, and monitoring the racial impact of stops on the Maryland highways. Maryland also paid Wilkins monetary damages. Similarly, a lawsuit brought on behalf of four hundred drivers alleging that they had been improperly stopped because of racial profiling in Eagle County, Colorado, produced a settlement involving payment of more than $800,000 in damages and an agreement by the police that they would no longer stop any driver without "objective reasonable suspicion" that the person had done something wrong.[56]

But not all plaintiffs were as successful and there have been some notable failures in civil suits challenging racial profiling as well. For example, a widely publicized lawsuit brought against the Illinois State Police challenging alleged targeting of minority drivers was ultimately dismissed, as were a number of challenges to the actions of the state police under the direction of Florida's Sheriff Vogel. The latter fact was a source of some pride for Vogel, who commented, "I've been investigated by just about everyone—the FBI, the Justice Department, the NAACP, the ACLU—and they haven't been able to win a solitary case. This whole thing is something that drug lawyers grabbed ahold of to try to beat some arrests by dragging race into it."[57]

Plaintiffs in civil challenges to racial profiling face obstacles both legal and practical. With regard to the practical problems, as we noted in our discussion of the Supreme Court's invitation to use the Equal Protection Clause to combat racially motivated stops, persons subjected to racial profiling who have been found with drugs or other contraband make decidedly unappealing plaintiffs. Even those who have been improperly stopped and were found not to be carrying drugs learn that the monetary damages for such a wrongful stop are often minimal and not worth the time and expense of litigation. That problem can be solved if plaintiffs bring class action suits on behalf of persons similarly situated. Sometimes that tactic succeeds, as it did in the Eagle County, Colorado, suit and the Wilkins suit. But courts are not always receptive to the idea that broad groups of persons are sufficiently similarly situated to constitute a class.

A different problem confronts plaintiffs seeking injunctive relief to remedy future conduct by police in addition to or in lieu of monetary damages. In order to bring any suit, a plaintiff must have "standing." Standing is a complex topic, but the basic point is that the plaintiff must be the proper person to be complaining of the defendant's conduct. This is generally expressed as a requirement that the plaintiff have suffered an actual injury caused by the conduct that is the subject of the lawsuit.[58] When a plaintiff is suing for monetary damages for a past stop alleged to be illegal, standing does not present much of a problem. But if a plaintiff is suing for injunctive relief to stop *future* illegal stops and searches, the law requires the plaintiff to demonstrate that he or she is likely to suffer a similar harm—that is, will be subjected to another illegal stop and search—in the future. At some level, this issue resembles one of the key debates about racial profiling—whether it is a broad-based, systemic problem or isolated and infrequent incidents by a few rogue cops and, thus, not representative of general police work. It is not surprising that courts have gone both ways on the issue. Some have accepted the argument that if a plaintiff is once the victim of an illegal stop and search due to racial profiling, he or she will likely be stopped again. Other courts have been more skeptical of the claim and have dismissed lawsuits for precisely that reason.[59]

In sum, civil suits by private citizens to challenge racial profiling have produced a mixed result. It appears that such challenges get a somewhat more receptive audience than challenges in the context of a criminal prosecution, but that assessment is made primarily on the basis of a small number of cases and, in any event, might reflect more the problems faced by criminal defendants than a prospect for sure success by civil plaintiffs. While some have argued that recent decisions reflect a trend suggesting that the courts are receptive to such civil challenges, other students and commentators are more pessimistic regarding whether true reform lies with civil suits brought by private parties.[60] In either case, the limited number of civil challenges may have unintended consequences impeding efforts at broader reform. One commentator has argued that the reluctance of those "innocent drivers" (that is, those not found carrying drugs) subjected to discriminatory traffic stops to complain and bring litigation to redress the problem has given the impression that the highway stops are much more effective than they really are since the cases then receiving most attention involve those in which the person complaining has been caught with illegal drugs.[61]

The Department of Justice

Mention must be made of another avenue for civil challenges to the practice of racial profiling: investigations and lawsuits brought by the Special Litigation section of the Department of Justice's Division of Civil Rights. That section investigates and sometimes litigates in a number of areas, including rights of juveniles and persons in mental health institutions and in prison. It also devotes significant attention to the conduct of law enforcement agencies. Among the areas of investigation in that latter area has been racial profiling.[62]

The Special Litigation section derives its authority from a number of statutes, including that portion of the Violent Crime Control and Law Enforcement Act of 1994 that addresses police misconduct and those portions of the Omnibus Crime Control and Safe Street Act of 1968 and Title VI of the Civil Rights Act of 1964 that outlaw discrimination. The DOJ does not act in response to individual or isolated complaints, but is authorized to investigate and attempt to remedy system-wide abuses in what are known as "pattern and practice" cases. Since the mid-1990s, DOJ has begun a number of investigations into allegations or concerns that minorities were being stopped disproportionately on the roads or highways in a number of states and local communities, including New Jersey and Maryland. While no case has yet been litigated to a decision, DOJ has managed to negotiate a number of consent decrees.[63]

New Jersey, for example, agreed to a fairly wide-ranging and detailed consent decree governing its problems with racial profiling. The decree touches upon a number of areas, including training both in the academy and after, the gathering of extensive data regarding highway stops and searches incident to stops (including why each stop and/or search is made and the facts involved in each stop and/or search), procedures to be followed in connection with stops, including "call-ins" to the communications center for each stop, and provisions to ensure that management in the State Police is aware of what is happening in connection with the stops and that the data being collected are reviewed by supervisors. It also contains provisions dealing with the handling and investigation of allegations of misconduct and, where appropriate, "disciplinary procedures." Two other sections of the consent decree deserve mention. One section imposes duties on the New Jersey Attorney General's Office, including the creation of an Office of State Police Affairs to ensure compliance with the consent decree. The other, entitled "Policy Requirements," includes a provision that bans the consideration of a person's race "in any fashion or to any degree" in any motor vehicle stop or law enforcement action attendant thereto, unless the trooper has been given a "suspect specific" description for a particular person that includes the person's race. Interestingly (and significantly), the consent decree applies to every motor vehicle stop, regardless of whether a profile is involved.[64]

Students and opponents of racial profiling have generally praised the efforts of the DOJ in these investigations and lawsuits,[65] although the number of actual cases so far is still so small that a reliable prediction of future success is hazardous. News reports tracking the reports of the monitor in New Jersey overseeing compliance with the consent decree show some progress in the effort to eliminate racial profiling. Indeed, one report issued in January 2002 stated that a review of 175 stops revealed that *all* racial profiling—that is, pretextual traffic stops—had disappeared. A report in June 2002 also showed a dramatic drop in the number of motorists asked to consent to a search of their vehicles. But reports also show minority drivers were still being stopped disproportionately compared to white drivers. As one would predict, the reported results drew different responses from opposite camps. In response to one report indicating that the number of drivers asked to consent to a search after a traffic stop had declined dramatically, leaders of the minority community expressed great satisfaction. But representatives of a police fraternal association drew a different message from the numbers: "These guys [i.e., the police] just don't think that it's worth doing the right thing if you're not going to get any level of support. The guys just can't justify going that extra yard." Some expressed concern over the fact that minority drivers are still stopped much more frequently than white drivers. As William Buckman, a lawyer who has played an important role in challenging racial profiling in New Jersey, concluded, "I fear we're going backwards here. The State Police have never attempted to eliminate the culture of profiling and biased policing these statistics reflect."[66]

It might be helpful at this point to summarize the evolution and meaning of profiling generally and racial profiling specifically and to review the changing contexts in which the concepts and terms have been employed. Table 4 traces this evolution and serves to mark critical developments:

TABLE 4. Timeline—the Evolution of Criminal Profiling

1800s: "Profiling" in detective fiction (Edgar Allan Poe and Sir Arthur Conan Doyle)

1940s and '50s: Dr. James A. Brussel constructs a profile for the "Mad Bomber" in New York City. Brussel's methods are successful, and he eventually works on the Boston Strangler case. Others begin to work in the same arena.

1962: Howard Teten, a student of Brussel's, moves to the Federal Bureau of Investigation and begins developing techniques for criminal profiling while working in the Behavioral Sciences Unit.

1968: United States Supreme Court decision in *Terry v. Ohio* upholds the "stop and frisk" practice despite the lack of probable cause for search or seizure; investigative stops are now constitutionally permissible so long as the law enforcement officer is able to articulate facts sufficient to demonstrate a "reasonable suspicion."

Presidential election year (Nixon, Humphrey, and Wallace); "War on Drugs" commences.

Creation of Federal Government Task Force to study airplane hijackings; "skyjacking" profile is created and employed in airports.

1973: Establishment of the Drug Enforcement Agency (DEA).

1974: Creation of the Drug Courier Profile.

1982: President Reagan establishes the South Florida Drug Task Force to combat the increasing amount of drug smuggling.

1985: DEA develops "Operation Pipeline," a program that ultimately spreads to forty-eight states. Agents borrow from the skyjacking profile model.

1994: "Racial profiling" first appears as a term in the media.

1995: "Driving While Black" enters the popular discourse.

1996: The Supreme Court decides *Whren v. United States*, resolving a circuit conflict and promoting the "could have" test over the "would have" test.

1998: Shooting of four high school students by New Jersey state troopers; media scrutiny increases dramatically.

2001: Terrorist attacks on the World Trade Center and Pentagon; profiling takes on a new and different significance.

The Court Steps Out

In assessing this state of affairs, one might argue that perhaps the Court has attempted to reach for the high ground and assume the proper role described for it by the late Alexander Bickel in his classic study, *The Least Dangerous Branch*. In that work, in defending judicial review against charges that it was "counter-majoritarian" and therefore frustrated the will of the people that is supposed to govern a democracy, Bickel described the role of judges as rising above the heat and passion of the moment to allow the application of a society's enduring principles to contemporary problems.[67]

The trouble with that analysis as applied to the racial profiling debate is that the Supreme Court, and the lower courts that are following its lead, do not appear to be elevating the debate but rather avoiding it. It is difficult to see what higher principle emerges from the Court's opinions on what has become one of the most fiercely debated issues in criminal justice and how, if at all, the Court has advanced the debate. Because of the nature of the conduct at issue—law enforcement personnel deciding to stop persons ultimately charged with a crime—the courts must

necessarily become involved. And indeed, the Court's refusal to engage in consideration of factors such as the racial
motivation of the law enforcement officers making the
stops has done nothing to reduce the number of cases
coming to the courts involving profiling in its narrow and
broader forms. Profiling generally, and racial profiling specifically, are simply not "political questions" that raise constitutional issues and problems the solution of which is
uniquely delegated to the other branches of government.
This is particularly so as the debate has raged at a time
when the Court has shown itself to be less and less receptive to competing visions of the scope of constitutional
rights by other branches of government.[68]

Of course, this observation about the approach of the
Court drawn from a series of disparate decisions over the
past decade (or more) is about the *role* (or, more accurately,
the *lack* of a role) the Court has chosen or is, in effect, playing in the larger public debate and not an assessment of how
the Court would or should rule if it does decide to address
the practice of racial profiling. Indeed, veteran Supreme
Court watchers like to be on the alert for the subtle (sometimes not so subtle) statements in cases that send a signal
that the Court wants or is about to address a given issue.[69] In
that regard, perhaps the recent allusions to racial profiling by
Justice Stevens in *Wardlow* and Justice O'Connor in *Atwater*[70]
signal that the Court is prepared, perhaps even looking, to
address racial profiling head-on. Of course to do so, the
Court will have to revisit *Whren* and the jurisprudential approach to race in a line of Fourth Amendment cases that cul-
minated in that case, either reversing that approach, modify-
ing it, or, in the face of widespread and passionate concern
about the interaction of race and profiling, affirming and further cementing the *Whren* approach.

And maybe, for those most concerned about racial profiling, the Court's silence or apathy on the issue is not a bad
thing. Perhaps this is not the time (or the Justices) for the
Court to decide to jump into the fray. We note that "within
hours" after the Court's decision in *Atwater* giving police a

free hand in making custodial arrests for minor traffic violations, a bill was circulating in the Texas legislature barring
such arrests.[71] If this Court is less sensitive to potential police abuses than the Texas legislature, perhaps it is just as
well, some may argue, that the Court has dropped out and
left it to the other players to grapple with the key issues.

In any event, the Court's hands-off approach is at least
curious and ultimately significant, given that the Court has,
at least for the last half-century, been in the forefront of issues related to police practices and race. Indeed, for at least
a part of that time the Court was arguably the leading voice
on issues of racial justice. And while some have come to
question whether some of the Court's landmark decisions,
most notably *Brown v. Board of Education,* were effective,[72]
or perhaps even counterproductive,[73] in achieving desegre-
gation, few have doubted the central role the Court has
played in addressing the key issues. Of course, the current
Court is a distant cousin to the Warren Court, as not only
Whren but cases in other areas such as Affirmative Action[74]
and civil rights[75] unmistakably reveal. But that makes it no
less noteworthy that the Court is not playing a significant
part in the larger public debate.

CHAPTER 6

The Costs and Benefits, September 11th and Racial Profiling's Future

"Grave threats to liberty often come in times of urgency, when constitutional rights seem too extravagant to endure." [1]

We began this book with a look at beginnings of criminal profiling, starting as the careful, scientifically based search for suspects in response to a limited set of usually heinous crimes. We then considered the classic literature on police practices generally, focusing on those aspects that dealt with the use by experienced police of information and intuition to identify suspects: the search for "symbolic assailants." Accepted police practices, the literature indicates, not only tolerate the use of such information (including race) to identify suspects but find no problem with and even encourage such practices. Then, against this background, we have traced the evolution of racial profiling from an outgrowth of criminal profiling through the development and use of progressively more proactive and less scientific and carefully thought-out tools, embodied first in the skyjacker profile, then in the airport drug courier profile, then in the drug courier profile on the nation's highways, until the concept of racial profiling had stretched so far as to be equated by many with outright racial discrimination.

And that conclusion or taint, if you will, seemed to be pushing the debate in favor of those opposing racial profiling. According to one assessment, "We had just reached a consensus on racial profiling. By September 10, 2001, virtually everyone, from Jesse Jackson to Al Gore to George W. Bush to John Ashcroft, agreed that racial profilng was bad." Indeed, this analysis continued,

> [t]he problem may be that before September 11 there was too much agreement on the issue, at least on the surface. Racial profiling continued to occur, as it does today, but since no public official would defend it, the game turned entirely on labeling. If a practice was successfully tagged as racial profiling, the cops lost: if not, they won.[2]

And the sentiment appears to have spread beyond that. As evidence of this, recall the debates in the primaries and general election for the presidency in 2000, where candidates crawled over each other to connect their rivals in some way with racial profiling.[3]

Still, if the past thirty years has taught us anything, it is that profiling generally, and racial profiling in particular, is a constantly evolving concept. In light of that, and having considered where we have been, we want to consider where society and law enforcement are going with racial profiling and to raise some of the questions that will confront this subject in the twenty-first century. We will address at some length two large issues: First, what conclusions, if any, are we confident in drawing about the costs and benefits of racial profiling? In particular, is there any legitimate role for race to play in profiling? Second, how, if at all, did the horrific terrorist attacks of September 11, 2001, affect the debate over profiling? Finally, we raise what we believe are additional questions and suggest areas for further research.

The Costs and Benefits of Racial Profiling

In the preceding pages we have, *inter alia,* traced the development of profiling as a concept and practice from criminal profiling through racial profiling to the point where racial profiling has become widely taken to mean the use of race and race alone in law enforcement decisions, almost always in an invidious way. Should it matter that racial profiling as a term or concept has changed so much that it is now essentially synonymous with racial discrimination? After all, it is hardly the first time social convention and usage have fundamentally changed the meaning of a word so that it bears little if any relation to the word's earlier or original meaning.[4] Let us suggest a few reasons why it should matter or at least why we might want to try to see whether there is a distinction worth preserving between a profile using race and racial profiling as discrimination.

Some Preliminary Questions

We need to return to some first principles. Profiling—the use by law enforcement of a number of factors, drawn from objective data in the historical record with sufficient probative value of potential criminal activity to warrant law enforcement attention or action—appears to be a much narrower type of specific conduct than what has garnered most of the popular reaction. It is also a more distinctive law enforcement technique than courts, or at least the United States Supreme Court, have been willing to recognize so far. Recognition of that fact raises other questions—most notably, as discussed elsewhere in this book, how effective profiling is at actually detecting criminal activity, and whether the practice is more effective and less subject to abuse in some settings as opposed to others. These issues should be part of the public debate.

If one accepts a narrower and more sophisticated conception of profiling, does the automatic equation of racial profiling with racial discrimination threaten to deprive law enforcement of a legitimate tool? Do we, to state it differently, risk throwing out the profiling baby with the bathwater of invidious discrimination? Is there a way to preserve racial profiling without having the practice become racial discrimination, or is that, as a practical matter, too tenuous or difficult a distinction to make?

Those questions are not easily answered, for the use of race as it relates to profiling raises additional questions that must be part of the debate. What exactly does it mean to present racial profiling as singling out a person for questioning because of the person's race? Does that mean race is the sole factor? Does that mean consideration of a suspect's race as one among many factors? In our own assessment of the costs and benefits of racial profiling, we adhere to the more sophisticated concept of profiling. We are not talking about stopping, searching, or profiling someone simply because of his or her race. We are instead talking about race as part of a profile in which other variables are also weighed. For the purposes of this section, we will assume that race can be part of a profile and assess costs and benefits with this in mind.

We are mindful that there is an important discussion here, one that we will begin without attempting to provide any definitive answer: Can race function in any profile without being the variable that necessarily trumps all others? Is a suspect's race as part of a carefully devised profile no different than other, neutral facts—such as whether a person has purchased airline tickets with cash to fly to a city associated with the drug trade or is traveling north from Florida in a rental car—that do not otherwise invite controversy? Or will race become the critical factor in the decision to stop a suspect?[5] Going further, as a practical matter, will race *always* become *the* critical factor on which the decision to make a stop is based? Is it possible, as a practical matter, to employ race as a factor in profiling without the practice turning into unchecked targeting of minorities that have historically been discriminated against?

On the other hand, is it possible, for that matter, realistically to wean police off considerations of race in the performance of their duties? If not, is the best cure to develop an objective "scientific" method of profiling to control considerations of race and to avoid abusive pretextual stops? In a recent study of police practices, including profiling, William Stuntz argues that it is unrealistic to believe that we *can* prevent or discourage police from considering race in deciding whom to stop. Stuntz would, therefore, shift the analysis from regulating *whom* police stop to *how* police conduct those stops, urging the development of "legal limits on the coercion— and rudeness—police inflict on suspects." Responding to the obvious question of how one would define "polite" police practices, Stuntz believes that the parameters of respectful policing would become obvious as it played out in the streets. Stuntz concedes that it might be difficult to articulate such standards in formal legal rules or doctrine but claims that they would become evident as the parties interacted and the relationships played them out, calling to mind Justice Potter Stewart's famous definition of pornography: "I know it when I see it."[6]

Thus, some may argue that using race as one factor in connection with a carefully devised programming of profiling, properly understood, should eliminate the worst aspects of what we have called "hunch policing" and pretextual stops in which a suspect's race provides all the motivation to stop someone to search for evidence of crimes for which there is no known evidence at the time of the stop. Or, conversely, perhaps the more sanitary view of "race as part of a profile, not race alone" is an illusory one. Perhaps whenever race enters a profile, it necessarily pushes all other variables aside.[7]

An Assessment of the Costs of Racial Profiling

That last issue—whether race can ever realistically be any-thing other than *the* critical factor in a profile—necessarily leads finally to what may be the most challenging questions, the ones most difficult to answer. Even if it is possible to devise an objective method of profiling such that consideration of race as one among many factors adds *something* reliable to law enforcement's decision whether to detain a suspect, are the psychological and societal costs of such profiling too high to justify the practice?

President George W. Bush framed one perspective on the issue during the 2000 presidential debates, "I can't imagine what it would be like to be singled out because of race and stopped and harassed. That's just plain wrong."[8] Singling out individuals for a package of variables, one of them being race, or falsely believing that race is the primary factor, may inflict pain and shame on the object of selection in other words. Indeed, the psychological harm of examples of "Driving While Black" (discussed in more detail in Chapter 4) are all too common, as the following summary suggests:

> One journalist who interviewed delegates to the 1996 Black Caucus convention reported that nearly every African-American he spoke with—doctors, lawyers, university professors—had been pulled over by police on a number of occasions without being charged with violating any traffic law.[9]

The cumulative effect of these stops, it is argued, is to dramatically lower blacks' assessments of the police in particular and the criminal justice system more generally.[10]

Emphasizing race in a criminal profile, then, has several very direct costs. It pains the person stopped, who believes that an inappropriate variable is being used—alone or in conjunction with others—to single out the subject. It leads to the stopping of many who perceive themselves as guilty of nothing other than having the particular attribute the police are sorting by—in this case race. Further, effectuating these stops based on a profile results in a vast number of "false positives." The pretextual traffic stop led to the detaining of a substantial number of minority citizens because of a belief that "race" was associated with criminogenic behavior, but in fact most persons were falsely stopped. (Recall the data we examined in Chapter 3. They were false positives.) And because of this, the persons stopped leave the encounter feeling more negative about the police and the criminal justice system, and their views become widely shared in their communities as well.

These are the costs, but it is important to note that arguments are advanced in defense of profiling as well. Some of these precede September 11th; others are the result of the events of that day and suggest that the cost/benefit balance shifted dramatically after that watershed day in American history. The pre-September 11th arguments turn on matters we have already examined—namely, whether profiling works. We have seen that the data seem to suggest that police decisions—at least on the Turnpike—lead to many stops of minorities that prove to be "false positives." We have also noted that questions can be raised about the limited data on which these studies rely.[11] Thus, scholars noting the disproportionate involvement of different minorities with particular crimes maintain that at least under some circumstances, profiling, in which race is one variable, continues to make sense.[12] False positives may be a price, but the argument is that the benefits in terms of identifying lawbreakers and confiscating contraband are worth what is seen as a relatively minor intrusion.

One response to this kind of claim is to simply deny any extra predictive power of using race in any police decision. Here we write not on a clean slate but on a cluttered one. The data, as noted, raise many questions about the efficacy of certain highway stops; they are not plentiful or determinative on the more generalizable questions about the efficacy of including racial variables. The proverbial jury is out on the empirical predictive value. One of the most important writers on the matter of race and crime, Professor Randall Kennedy of Harvard Law School begins by questioning whether the data support use of race in a profile. *But,* even more significantly, he goes on to note that even if race, when added to decision-making, increases the correctness of predictions, the price of using race is not worth the benefit because of the toll exacted on the many "false positives" and because of the unique role race played in our history.[13]

An aside is apposite here. One might question the feasibility of Kennedy's notion that race should never be used unless to identify a particular defendant, or in extraordinary circumstances. Kennedy himself recognizes the possibility that the police will continue to use race but will just no longer admit to it. His response is that in fact many cops will comply with a proscription on the use of race, and that when some cops do continue to use it, the system ought to "work harder to bring the actual conduct of officials in line with appropriate goals."[14] In contrast, Jerome Skolnick, who introduced the concept of the "symbolic assailant," has both supported Kennedy's wish for color-blind policing, and questioned its likelihood in the real world of policing. "But I expect," he wrote in a review of Kennedy's book,

> that in the real world of social and color stratification, disproportionate black criminality, and racism, it is inevitable that police will continue to use race as an indicator. . . . [I]f courts say that police cannot use race as an indicator, they won't report what they did, and will testify that what they saw was solely odd behavior.[15]

In this context, however, it is worth noting the comments of Professor Anthony Thompson from NYU Law School, who disagrees with Kennedy's goal of generally prohibiting consideration or discussion of race and offers an alternative to the burying of the race issue that Skolnick predicts:

> The current status of ignoring race—or "declaring" race irrelevant—both drives the discussion underground and encourages courts to assume the use of race and predisposes courts against labeling a law enforcement officer a "racist." Under a system that acknowledges that race does play a role in the exercise of discretion, there is a beginning of the long and difficult process of dealing with and working through the issue.[16]

To recap, some commentators argue for the inappropriateness and ineffectiveness of the use of race in a profile. On the other side, some suggest that including race may increase predictive power and that not to use race is to naively ignore differential crime rates among racial groups. Randall Kennedy argues that the data do not justify the use of race, but even if the data did legitimate the use of race, it still ought not be employed. It is, for Kennedy, simply wrong.

To this, some might object that a double standard is at work. It is true that we have in the past refused to allow consideration of the impact of race on a practice even when we were prepared to assume the truth of the facts asserted. For example, when the Civil Rights Act of 1964 outlawed discrimination in public accommodations, white hotel and restaurant owners were not allowed an exemption from the law on the grounds that serving African Americans would drive off the establishment's usual white customers even if that were true.[17] Indeed, many of those who have written on the subject of racially motivated pretextual traffic stops have described the humiliating effects of the practice on the persons being stopped and the African American community in general.[18] On the other hand, there have been settings, albeit limited ones, in which we have allowed objective considerations of race a role in decision-making; most notably Affirmative Action, at least until recent judicial decisions appear to be foreclosing that option as well.[19] Others respond, in a more pragmatic vein, that race *will* be used whether or not its use is formally banned, and therefore making its use explicit allows for more careful examination of how it is being employed and the implementation of restrictions to address the worst excesses.

The cost and benefits, then, are measured in terms of the yield that is obtained by allowing race to be a component in a profile. Related to this balancing are issues about whether race can be banned from the sorting processes police engage in and whether the cost of banning is greater than the benefits of making explicit "real" police decisions. Is the use of race as one among many factors in profiling a legitimate use of objective, historically based data or does its use—particularly in the criminal justice setting, in which race has too often played a pernicious and discriminatory role—impose costs too great to bear?

Profiling and the September 11th Attacks

On September 11, 2001, at least nineteen members of the terrorist organization Al-Qaeda hijacked four commercial airplanes and managed to crash three of the planes into the World Trade Center in New York City and into the Pentagon.[20] Those attacks plunged the country into an unconventional war of unknown duration and had profound repercussions for almost every facet of American life, at least in the months following the attacks. It is thus no surprise that it reinvigorated and in some ways reshaped the debate over racial profiling[21] as well. If the terms of the debate—particularly the ready equation of racial profiling with racial discrimination—were turning public sentiment against the practice by 2000, the September 11th attacks introduced a whole new set of considerations. In fact, it has been argued that the events of September 11th have made racial profiling an even-larger issue than it was before.[22]

First a word or two about how profiling was used or manifested itself after the attacks. It says a lot about profiling that, after September 11th, profiling took at least two forms, reflecting something of where profiling generally had traveled in the past three decades. For one thing, law enforcement created somewhat detailed and sophisticated profiles based on available information about the terrorists and those believed to be working with them. For example, the federal government created a "Hijacker Financial Profile" to track and cut off funding for terrorists and their activities, to further the goal of "[i]dentifying, tracking and dismantling the financial structure supporting terrorist groups . . . [to be able to] prevent future terrorist attacks."[23]

The profile covered four areas: an "Account Profile," a

"Transaction Profile," "International Activity," and a "Non-Financial Profile." The first category—dealing with the accounts opened by the terrorists at financial institutions—noted the following characteristics among others: Accounts were opened usually within 30 days of entry into the United States at branches of large, well-known banks, with cash or cash equivalents in the average range of $3,000 to $5,000 and were normal checking accounts with debit cards; the hijackers tended to open accounts in groups of three or four individuals and would often use the same address or telephone number for the various accounts; the account holder lacked a social security number.

The "Transactions" component was marked, *inter alia,* by the following: the accounts sent and received wire transfers of small amounts from and to foreign countries such as Saudi Arabia, the United Arab Emirate, and Germany; cash withdrawals were usually made by way of debit cards rather than checks, often in amounts that exceeded the limit of the debit card; hijackers made numerous inquiries of the account balances; there was no evidence of the types of usual or routine deposits or expenses one might expect, such as a deposit of payroll checks, rent payments, or auto payments; there was no normal monthly consistency regarding deposits or disbursements.

The "International Activity" facet of the profile notes the following: that three of the hijackers opened checking accounts at banks located in the UAE, and three continued to maintain bank accounts and credit cards in Germany after they arrived in this country; hijackers on all four flights purchased traveler's checks overseas and brought those checks to the United States where they were partially deposited into their United States accounts; one of the hijackers opened an account in the UAE in 1999 and gave power of attorney over the account to a person who had been wiring money to his German account.

Finally, the "Non-Financial" components included the following: that the hijackers were born in a Middle Eastern Country and ranged in age from early 20s to mid-30s; they had limited use of the English language and appointed one person as a spokesman for the group and wanted to deal with one person at the bank; they did not want to deal with women.

The "Hijacker Financial Profile" has some of the earmarks of the more carefully thought-out early profiles firmly grounded in historical data (in this case information about the known hijackers) such as the skyjacker profile. Profiling after September 11th, however, also took another form that looks, at least from the outside, more like the extreme kind of racial profiling, in which decisions of whom to investigate, whom to question, whom to suspect appear to be driven primarily—or perhaps even solely—by a person's race or ethnicity, specifically whether the person was Arab or Muslim. This was manifested in a number of ways and tactics, including decisions by law enforcement to detain and/or question large numbers of males of Arab or Muslim descent; strategies over whom to subject to extra scrutiny, particularly at airports; arguments (mostly from private citizens) that Arab or Muslim passengers should be taken off airplanes; and a seemingly nearly universal suspicion in the general population of anyone who appeared to be Arab or Muslim. "Flying While Arab," some warn, is joining "Driving While Black" as a new offense. It is this latter type of "racial profiling" that attracted the most attention and discussion in the immediate aftermath of the attacks.

Initial Responses to Profiling after September 11th

Discussion of the use of racial profiling in the War Against Terrorism emerged in newspapers and over the airwaves within a day or two of the attacks and continued[24] with many voices, if not most, wondering whether, as a nation, we have rushed too quickly to condemn racial profiling.[25] Many raised the issue of whether, had law enforcement employed racial profiling, the terrorist attacks could have been prevented; some simply insisted that racial profiling *would* have prevented the attacks although evidentiary support for that conclusion was lacking.

For others, what occurred on September 11th prompted more ambivalent feelings. Justice Sandra Day O'Connor, after visiting Ground Zero at the World Trade Center, noted, "We're likely to experience more restrictions on our personal freedom than has ever been the case in our country."[26] Yet she also quoted Margaret Thatcher, cautioning that "[w]here law ends, tyranny begins."[27] And, stressing the need for attorneys, she raised some interesting questions:

> First, can a society that prides itself on equality before the law, treat terrorists differently from ordinary criminals? And where do we draw the line between them? Second, at what point does the cost to civil liberties from legislation designed to prevent terrorism outweigh the added security that legislation provides?[28]

Ironically, ambivalent comments have also come from some unexpected corners. From then-New Jersey Attorney General John Farmer, for example, whose state has served as a focal point in the battle over racial profiling and whose state police are under a Department of Justice Consent Decree to stop the practice, come measured remarks that appear to stop short of a blanket rejection of racial profiling:

> Last week's events will put a lot of pressure on law enforcement to strike the proper balance between public safety and individual liberty. If you look at American history, liberties have always been calibrated based on the nature of the public threat we have experienced . . . . But I don't think it will come to a point where we will sacrifice our individual liberties to maintain public safety.[29]

Similarly, Floyd Abrams, who a few years earlier had served on a panel that advised against profiling on airlines based on factors such as race and national origin, said after the attacks on the World Trade Center and the Pentagon that the airline industry will be challenged to "walk a line that avoids simplistic ethnic profiling while still allowing common-sense law enforcement."[30] In addition, Abrams said:

> It would be a dereliction of duty to the American public to forget that the people who committed these terrible crimes all

spoke Arabic to each other . . . At the same time . . . we don't want to be in a position where we're pulling every Arab-American out of line for detailed strip-searches. At the same time, we have to protect ourselves.[31]

Such sentiments are not limited to those already on the public record regarding profiling. Commentator Michael Kinsley, in addressing the issue of whether racial profiling was among appropriate police practices in response to terrorist attacks, continued to reject racial profiling as applied to "pulling over black male drivers" but was open to consideration of whether "rational discrimination" was acceptable. Kinsley stopped short of endorsing blanket use of security measures based on a person's race or ethnicity, attempting to set a balancing test to prevent the use of generalizations as a vehicle for pure discrimination.[32] Another commentator suggested profiling based on race *and* religion, focusing efforts on those who are both Arab and Muslim but sparing the large numbers of Arabs who are Catholic, Jewish, and Protestant.[33] Many who expressed distress over attacks on Muslims around the country reflected their own ambivalence in news reports. "Those interviewed spoke of national ideals of color-blindness—but nearly in the same breath they said that for the sake of national safety, the police should single out Arab-looking men for questioning."[34]

For some, including some who would otherwise object to racial profiling, the events of September 11th appear to have provided an epiphany of sorts, prompting a realization that they engage in racial profiling of a type that they would otherwise criticize.[35] Some, including Stuart Taylor, a well-known legal commentator, continued to condemn racial profiling practices against African Americans in the strongest terms, but nonetheless argued in the aftermath of September 11th for an exception to a ban against racial profiling to allow use of heightened security measures against "Arab-looking" persons.[36]

Indeed, perhaps most interesting, and some measure of how the events of September 11th may be changing the debate, are comments and attitudes from members of the minority communities most often victimized by racial profiling prior to September 11th and whom, therefore, one would expect to be among racial profiling's harshest critics. In response to a reporter's questions about racial profiling in light of the terrorist attacks, one African American man noted that he has been a victim of racial profiling many times and knows "[I]t's wrong."[37] Yet he admitted to doing it himself; for example, if people of Middle Eastern descent got on a plane, he said, "I'd be nervous. It sickens me that I feel that way, but it's the real world."[38] A Hispanic man expressed a similar sentiment saying that he was absolutely against racial profiling but would be anxious in the airline scenario.[39]

Even some in the targeted groups spoke in defense of the practice. A prominent Arab American living in Chicago was receptive to the idea of *some* profiling directed against Arabs or Muslims: "Hey, I don't want to get hijacked, either, whether it's by an Arab or someone else."[40] And a law professor of Middle Eastern descent also thought that extra scrutiny on airplanes for Arabs and Muslims was warranted after September 11th. After describing some of the security measures she had to go through in Europe and the Middle East, she said:

> Despite the inconvenience to me, I believe this scrutiny is a defensible tactic for picking out potential problem passengers. Although I am not a terrorist, others do not necessarily know it. The airline security procedures I ran into also protect me from terrorism. [. . .]
>
> Arab-Americans like me want to be safe when we fly. Cooperating with security procedures, even when we suspect that we are getting more attention than our fellow citizens, makes sense. Does anyone really want a security official to hesitate before stopping a suspicious passenger out of fear of an accusation of bias?[41]

A couple of polls taken shortly after the attacks suggest that those sentiments are not isolated. A Gallup poll showed that 71% of African Americans and 63% of other "non-white" respondents would support special, more intensive security measures before boarding airplanes with Arabs, including U.S. citizens of Arab descent; a smaller majority of whites—57%—favored such a policy.[42] Nor does this appear to be a transient sentiment; a poll taken almost two months after the attacks showed even broader support for a federal program to investigate and question Arab Americans and foreign visitors from the Middle East.[43] Another poll reflected that 64% of African Americans and 56% of other "non-white" respondents would support a requirement that Arabs, including U.S. citizens of Arab descent, be required to carry special identification.[44] Indeed, a poll reported in the *Detroit Free Press* found that 61% of Arab Americans supported heightened security of persons with Middle Eastern features and accents.[45] These data are particularly interesting in that that they suggest a counterintuitive proposition: those who have been most subject to the abuses of racial profiling are most inclined to support the practice when *other* groups are the chosen focus.

This is not to say that everyone has embraced racial profiling as an acceptable tool to use in combating terrorism. On the one side there are charges that profiling "is pure racism and should not stand."[46] Congressman Robert Menendez of New Jersey, for example, objected to the idea of stopping more people of Middle Eastern background for questioning, comparing the practice to the internment of Japanese Americans during World War II. His colleague Rush Holt called for better policing rather than racial profiling: "Racial profiling is intellectually lazy. It's never good policing."[47] Indeed, some objected that racial profiling in the aftermath of September 11th was counter-productive to the effort to find actual terrorists: because the practice fell on and burdened most heavily members of those communities where terrorists might be hiding, it alienated those in the communities (most of whom had not and would not do anything wrong) who might be able to identify the true targets of any investigation. And noted criminal defense attorney and self-proclaimed civil libertarian Alan Dershowitz has recommended the use of national identification cards, partly as a substitute for racial profiling.[48]

Opposition to racial and ethnic profiling was also expressed, perhaps ironically but tellingly, by representatives of the federal government. In November 2001, Michael Chertoff, the third-highest ranking official of the Department of Justice, appeared before a Congressional panel to defend some of the actions and initiatives used by the Justice Department to ferret out terrorism and terrorists since the attacks. Following September 11th federal law enforcement officials had proposed and/or used a number of "new" tactics in the war on terrorism that raised serious questions for many, including some in Congress, about whether the civil liberties of innocent persons were unnecessarily threatened. Those new tactics included broad sweeps to detain and question individuals, wiretapping conversations between persons detained and their lawyers, and the proposed use of military tribunals to adjudicate charges brought against captured terrorists.[49] Chertoff vigorously defended those proposed tactics, even the proposed use of military tribunals that had attracted a considerable amount of criticism. Chertoff insisted, however, that no one in law enforcement was engaging in or would engage in racial or ethnic profiling against Arabs or Muslims. He did note, though, that decisions of whom to question and investigate were based on "characteristics like country of issuance of passport."[50] Of course, in this context, the distinction described by Chertoff might not be substantively different than ethnic profiling.[51]

Equally instructive is an absolutely fascinating exchange during a post-September 11th episode of the television series *60 Minutes*. On that program, Norman Mineta, the Secretary of Transportation who gained some small measure of fame for his aggressive order immediately after the crash at the World Trade Center that *all* in-flight domestic flights be grounded,[52] insisted that no profiling because of race or ethnicity was under any circumstances acceptable.

Mr. Mineta and his family, during World War II, were among those Japanese Americans rounded up by the United States government and placed in internment camps. The lesson taught by this experience has clearly remained with him and explains his unflinching opposition to racial profiling, even post-September 11th. In contrast, consider again the remarks of Floyd Abrams, one of the country's leading champions of the Bill of Rights, on the same segment as Mineta, responding to the notion of "no profiling" based on ethnicity.

> They've started with a perfectly correct legal and constitutional principal, and one that certainly I believe in deeply, which is that we better treat people the same, as a general proposition and better not throw people out or put people in jail just because they're this or that. Right now, we're in an emergency situation that we've been attacked, and one thing that the attackers have in common so far is their national origin and their sex and their language. And for us to say, "We'll—we'll just put that aside, because, call it political correctness, call it anything, we just won't think about it because . . . it makes us feel uncomfortable,". . . is an a—appalling malfeasance.[53]

Indeed, the federal government's skittishness about racial profiling would come back to haunt it. In May 2002, press reports about information in the possession of the FBI and CIA prior to September 11th regarding terrorism threats generally and specifically some of the tactics used in the September 11th attacks led many to question whether the Bush administration should have been able to foresee and therefore prevent the attacks. One particular area of inquiry involved the arrest of Zacarias Moussaoui, originally suspected of having been the "20th hijacker."[54] After the arrest of Moussaoui, FBI field agents in Minnesota, where the arrest took place, sought a search warrant to seize and inspect Moussaoui's personal effects, including his laptop computer. That request was denied by senior FBI officials in Washington. When it turned out that a review of Moussaou's computer would have revealed a tie to one of the key hijackers, questions—as well as particularly scathing criti-

cism by an FBI attorney from the field office that arrested
Moussaoui—were raised about the decision to refuse the request for the search warrant. Press reports had it that the initial refusal to authorize the search warrant was due to concerns of senior Justice Department lawyers that, if they
agreed to issue the warrant, the FBI would be criticized for
engaging in racial profiling.[55]

That, in turn, led to criticism of the FBI for *not* engaging
in racial profiling. Columnist Nicholas Kristof of the *New
York Times,* for example, criticized both the Justice Department officials and members of the media (including himself) who had "regularly excoriated law enforcement au-
thorities for taking shortcuts and engaging in racial
profiling." Kristof noted with approval that racial profiling
led to the arrest of Moussaoui in the first place:

> The bottom line is that Mr. Moussaoui was thrown in jail—thank
> God—not because there was evidence he had committed a
> crime but because he was a young Arab man who behaved sus-
> piciously and fit our stereotypes about terrorists. . . . [F]ortu-
> nately, the flight attendant [who alerted law enforcement about
> Moussaoui's flight training] had a—possibly racist and certainly
> accurate—hunch that Mr. Moussaoui was up to no good.

Kristof used the Moussaoui matter to criticize "the timidity
of bureau headquarters" who had refused the field office request for a search warrant and to argue that in light of the
special risks posed by terrorism exemplified by the September 11th attacks, "[w]e must . . . relax a taboo, racial profiling, for one of the lessons of the Moussaoui case is that it
sometimes works."[56]

Finally on this point, even among those who supported
the idea of increased scrutiny for certain groups in light of the
attacks, some took the opportunity raised by September
11th's re-opening the debate on racial profiling to suggest or
argue for more limited approaches to police tactics rather
than giving blanket approval to unbridled law enforcement
discretion. Floyd Abrams, for example, in endorsing brief
stops based on the attributes of passengers in airports, noted,

> There's a big difference . . . between being interned and being
> searched a little more at an airport. I mean we should be
> searching everybody. We should be looking at every bag.
> Maybe we can't do it 'cause it takes too long or it's too difficult.
> So if we use one factor—not the only one—the fact that the—
> that the person seems to look like the people we're looking for,
> it seems to me entirely appropriate.[57]

Peter Schuck, a professor at Yale Law School, writing shortly
after the attacks, presented an even more nuanced approach to the problem, in arguing that there are degrees of
intrusiveness in questioning and detaining individuals and
that a more general profile may be more defensible when
used for a less intrusive process:

> A sensible profiling policy will also recognize that safeguards
> become more essential as the enforcement process progresses.
> Stereotypes that are at the stage of deciding whom to screen for
> questioning may be unacceptable at the later stages of arrest
> and prosecution, when official decisions should be based on
> more individualized information and when lawyers and other
> officials can be taught about the many exceptions to even ser-
> viceable stereotypes, to recognize them when they appear, and
> to behave in ways that encourage those being screened not to
> take it personally.[58]

Racial Profiling in the Aftermath of the Attacks

Of course, there is nothing wrong with re-opening the debate over racial profiling or taking it in a different direction,
particularly in connection with so important a topic as terrorism. Reconsideration of racial profiling in the battle
against terrorism to a large extent raises again some of the
issues we have explored earlier, although in a radically new
setting. Whether the new debate clarifies any of the old issues remains to be seen.

Most important in this regard, there is the question, still
frequently skirted as this issue has been revisited, of what
exactly one means by racial profiling. Is it consideration of
race or ethnicity alone or consideration of race or ethnicity
as one of a number of factors?[59] Is it enough, for example,
to pull an Arab or a Muslim person off a commercial air-

plane based on that fact alone,[60] or does law enforcement need to know more, such as how long before the flight the person had been in the United States, what he did while he was in the United States, with whom he had associated, and/or whether he had taken flying lessons? For better or worse, based on some of the incidents in the wake of the attacks, it appears that a person's Middle Eastern ancestry alone has been enough to prompt action (at least by private citizens).[61]

Nonetheless, it is possible to envision use of racial profiling in the battle against terrorism consistent with some of the strictures laid down so far. We might begin with the assumption that stopping a person for questioning based solely on the fact that he or she appears to be Arab or Muslim is not permissible. However, as long as the Supreme Court and other federal courts remain wedded to the principle set forth in the *United States v. Martinez-Fuerte*,[62] that race or ethnicity may be one factor among many to be considered in the decision to stop someone, one might argue that a stop based on the fact that a person is Arab or Muslim combined with other factors, *could* be justified. But what are the "other factors" that could legitimately be added to the profile? Would it be enough that there was not just one person of Middle Eastern descent but a group of Arabs or Muslims? Does it strengthen or weaken the decision to stop if the group has congregated near an Arab American community in cities such as Brooklyn, New York, Dearborn, Michigan, or Paterson, New Jersey? Near an airport or reservoir? In any of the cities—for example, Boston, Massachusetts, or Daytona Beach, Florida—associated with those who carried out the September 11th hijackings?

Assuming that one can identify the appropriate "other factors" to be included in the profile, there is also the issue of what the investigative stop would entail. Questioning alone might not cross the line (although in the current climate it might be unrealistic to assume that such encounters will be or have been viewed as consensual police encounters by those approached[63]); treatment analogous to what

Japanese Americans suffered during World War II[64] clearly would (and no one has argued for that, yet). But what about a broad range of investigative tools in between? As Samuel Gross and Debra Livingston describe it,

> The range of things the government can do on the basis of racial or ethnic information is enormous. If mass imprisonment defines the high end (short of torture or execution), paying close attention may define the low end. After September 11, nobody could seriously complain about the FBI paying more attention to reports of suspicious behavior by Saudi men than to similar reports about Hungarian women—even though as a consequence many more Saudi men will set off false alarms. In between there are infinite gradations, as the government's conduct becomes increasingly intrusive, disruptive, frightening and humiliating.[65]

Assuming that law enforcement has stopped someone based on the fact that the person is Arab or Muslim *plus* the hypothetical "other factors" needed to justify the stop, how far, if at all, can police go to determine whether the person is up to anything? Evidence of the threat posed by the person in this setting might be more elusive than the type of evidence police routinely look for in a stop at an airport based on the drug courier profile or in connection with a traffic stop. How far beyond mere questioning, if at all, can police go to require a person to demonstrate proof of long-time residency in a location, significant ties to a mainstream community, allegiance to the United States (or no allegiance to Al- Qaeda), or any other fact that would allay concerns that prompted the stop in the first place? Could the police, for example, remove such a person from an airplane or train or insist that some members of the group take a later flight or train? At this point at least, we believe that even if attitudes towards racial profiling change, prompting more leeway for law enforcement to employ the practice, the intrusions that change occasions will stop short of the most extreme measures that are universally considered to be indefensible (such as what happened to Japanese Americans during World War II). But there is considerable play in how we balance the variables in this regard.

Samuel Gross and Debra Livingston, for example, suggest that in evaluating police conduct in this regard, we ask two questions: first, was the suspect directly confronted or was his privacy invaded covertly? Second, "Is the subject treated as one of us or as one of them, as a law abiding person to be checked out or as a criminal to be caught and punished?"[66] For some those may be the right questions; for others such considerations may reach too far or not far enough. To raise just two considerations consider the following. Gross and Livingston state that to gather information from a distance from public sources where the suspect is unaware that the police are doing so may be okay because "the worst consequences may be minimal. More often than not the suspect will never know."[67] However, some civil libertarians may prefer police conduct that is open and visible rather than conducted covertly. (To be fair, Gross and Livingston do not give a blanket endorsement to all such practices.) As for their second question, use of security checkpoints at airports or other venues that *everyone* must go through must confront the frequently voiced criticism that it makes no sense to stop and search little old grandmothers from Iowa, as opposed to Arab or Muslim men in their 20s, if one is looking for terrorists. In short, exactly where the line will be drawn and whether that will be consistent with cherished attitudes toward civil liberties or a significant compromising of those attitudes has become a central issue in the new debate.

Other issues in the current debate also loom in this new setting. Of course, there is the issue of whether a racial profile, however it is composed, actually increases the effectiveness of law enforcement in rooting out the problem. At this point, it is difficult to tell whether racial profiling will serve as anything more than a placebo, reflecting *some* action being taken by a nation hungry for such signs yet without any measure that the action is effective. Moreover, even if it is effective, are the psychological and other costs of racial profiling stressed by commentators such as Randall Kennedy[68] sufficiently high with regard to Arabs or Muslims so as to counsel against the practice? Or does the argument only apply to racial profiling as it came to be understood in the 1990s, largely against African Americans as a discrete and insular minority that has had a history of discrimination and mistreatment at the hands of law enforcement in this country?

But there is more. Consideration of the use of racial profiling in any efforts to prevent terrorism, in addition to restating familiar issues, raises new ones. The central one involves context. It is worth remembering that the new category of investigative stops created by Terry v. Ohio[69] that gave rise to what has evolved into racial profiling was borne out of a pragmatic balancing of the relative interests involved.[70] Without minimizing the problems associated with illegal drug use, few would question that the immediate physical threat posed by what occurred on September 11th exceeds—by a considerable amount—the threat posed by illegal drugs. Terrorism, in a word, convincingly trumps drugs. However one strikes the balance when a racial profile is used to stop drug couriers, the stakes appear much higher now. Where is the balance to be drawn when the conduct law enforcement hopes to detect and prevent could result in the deaths of thousands, if not more, and the disruption of major cities, financial centers, and government institutions?

This is, without doubt, the largest change in any assessment of the costs and benefits of racial profiling. Prior to September 11th, there were arguments to be made on both sides, but in an impressionistic way it appeared that the direction of policy, though not necessarily the law, was toward a more restrictive use of race in a profile. Indeed, as noted, the term "profiling" is quickly becoming almost synonymous with racism in the popular lexicon.[71]

September 11th changed all of this. The new world we found after the World Trade Center and Pentagon bombings legitimated for many the use of ethnicity in the same way race was used as part of a profile prior to September 11th. The problem of false positives remains though the context, costs, and benefits have changed dramatically. Whereas prior to September 11th the benefits to be obtained (if any) were reduction and deterrence of drug crimes, post-September 11th the stakes were obviously higher. Few would argue that though drugs pose a significant problem—particularly when cumulated over many offenses—the risks in most respects pale compared to the terror that September 11th brought to this country. The context for profiling is different, and this difference is reflected in the ways profiling was and is viewed.

Some comments underline this change. First, the observations again of Stuart Taylor:

> The police's stopping of people for "driving while black," for example, has rightly been discredited because the costs—both to the searched and to the long-term interests of law enforcement—far exceed any benefits. Stopping people for "driving while Arab" would be similarly unwarranted. *Flying while Middle Eastern poses a dramatically different cost-benefit calculus.*[72]

And Michael Kinsley expressed the same sentiment in stronger terms:

> [T]he considerations are practical. How much is at stake in forbidding a particular act of discrimination? . . . [W]e're at war with a terrorist network that just killed 6,000 innocents and has anonymous agents in our country planning more slaughter. Are we really supposed to ignore the one identifiable fact that we know about them?[73]

Finally Peter Schuck, after suggesting that the context of a situation determines the extent to which stereotypes are properly used, observes:

> A wise policy will insist that the justice of profiling depends on a number of variables. How serious is the crime risk? How do we feel about the relative costs of false positives and false negatives? How accurate is the stereotype? How practicable is it to pursue the facts through an individualized inquiry rather than through stereotypes?[74]

The story of post-September 11th policy and legislative enactments is too complex, too significant to be examined in detail in this little book. It is the subject for another volume, one in which security is weighed against civil liberties, one in which values are compared, and resulting practices examined. For our purposes, it is enough to observe how September 11th altered the profiling landscape. Given the change in circumstances, what was previously an unacceptable practice for many can now be legitimated on public safety grounds among other reasons.

This is the critical new issue that, in fact, overwhelms all others. Indeed, if we are engaged in a War Against Terrorism, much of the debate of the past couple of years becomes less relevant, or at least requires a decidedly different approach. *Inter arma, silen leges*—"in times of war, law is silent," goes the old expression. This may not be absolutely true, but just as the initial formulation of the "clear and present danger" test, in many regards hostile to free speech, was arguably influenced by the backdrop of World War I and the Red Scare,[75] so too the context in which racial profiling is now being considered is certain to raise a host of new questions and provoke answers to those questions different than the previous debate would suggest. Not only is there the question of *how* the balance is to be struck—including who is properly the target of racial profiling in this setting and what investigative practices we will allow—but perhaps more important is the question of *who* determines how the balance is struck.

Also, who in law enforcement should do the racial profiling: law enforcement officers trained in counter-terrorism measures or any law enforcement personnel assigned to guard airports, patrol the highways, or walk the streets? If the former, are there sufficient resources and manpower to accomplish anything meaningful and, just as important, satisfy the cry for action that has prompted the reconsideration of racial profiling? If the latter, can we be certain that racial profiling in this circumstance will involve the drawing of reasonable inferences based on years of relevant law enforcement experience or instead become the type of "hunch policing" that has appropriately attracted the harshest criticism?

There is yet another question raised by the prospect of

using racial profiling following September 11th related to the issue of context. September 11th may have changed the debate over racial profiling to some extent, but we should also learn from what has gone before. Specifically, it is not too pessimistic to fear that police conduct and the new investigatory rules developed after September 11th may have the same "us vs them" quality that was so much at issue in the pre-September 11th debate over racial profiling. Just as minority drivers seemed to bear the brunt of efforts to detect drug couriers on the nation's highways, so it is easy for America to adopt measures that will fall most heavily on Arabs and Muslims generally, even those who have long resided in this country and have no other allegiances. The stakes are higher now, and we have argued that is likely to and should affect how the balance is struck. But the increased stakes also raise the likelihood that racial and ethnic prejudice will be brought into play, even if unintentionally or below the surface. As one study recently expressed it:

> There are two parts to this calculation: How great is the harm we are fighting? And how likely is our conduct to be useful? When the danger is extreme, we may accept unpleasant methods that have only a slight chance of success. But it is one thing to sketch out these calculations on paper, and quite another to do so in a real emergency. We never actually know either the magnitude of the danger or the effectiveness of possible countermeasures. Urgency and fear do not improve our judgment. They may lead us to overestimate the danger or the value of preventive steps, or both. Racism and ethnic prejudice may color every step of the process. Most Americans probably feel particularly threatened because the September 11 suicide hijackers were foreign, and some may be especially fearful because they were Arabs. This fear may cause us to exaggerate the danger of future attacks in general, and of attacks by Middle Eastern terrorists in particular. As a result, we may overestimate the effect of racially specific security measures. And unfortunately, we are more willing to accept aggressive measures when they target small and politically disempowered groups, specifically racial and ethnic minorities, and foreign nationals.[76]

In this light, it is worth keeping in mind another lesson from what has gone before. Although we have just expressed some confidence that actions against Arab Americans in response to the terrorist attacks will not take a form as extreme as the internment of the Japanese Americans in World War II, it is worth remembering that the initial concern of those drafting the policy for the Roosevelt administration was more for the safety of the Japanese Americans, a concern for possible retaliation against them by other Americans, than that they would manifest overt disloyalty and assist the Japanese military in an invasion of the West Coast. Nonetheless, as public pressure grew, the policy eventually took a much more draconian form, not one to which German Americans or Italian Americans were subjected.[77] That same phenomenon—an initially unobjectionable or even benign practice growing into something much worse—should be guarded against today as well.

There is, however, one final issue. Assume that the imperatives of the fight to eradicate terrorism produce a consensus that racial profiling in some form is a legitimate law enforcement tool. Would that consensus be necessarily limited to the fight against terrorism, or would it expand, either as a theoretical matter or practical matter, to other areas of law enforcement? Can we realistically restrict the use of racial profiling only to the fight against terrorism, or is the reconsideration of the practice in this context going to prompt a sea of change in attitudes about racial profiling in general? Will those who approve of the practice become the dominant voices? This remains to be seen.[78]

Continuing the Assessment of Profiling: Data and Legislation

Setting aside outright racist or race-exclusive profiling activities, we have seen that reasonable people might disagree about whether race can be part of a set of variables the police use to focus on particular individuals. Whether experience as a law enforcement officer legitimates this kind of behavior and whether the data support (or do not support) it are matters we discuss above. But from these discussions something else emerged—namely, that wherever one came down on the profiling question, it was plain that the proverbial "more data are needed" refrain applied with a vengeance. The literature is long on criticisms of "profiling," but these criticisms mostly rest on the kinds of anecdotal information about individual stops or on the very limited amount of quantitative data produced in a few states (mostly the Lamberth data). So David Harris, one of the most knowledgeable, most visible (and most critical) scholars examining racial profiling, called in 1999 for each of the states to collect systematic data on traffic stops as well as for passage of the Traffic Stops Statistics Act in Congress. This bill, passed by the House in 1998 but not the Senate, also mandated collection of data on traffic stops, including data on the race of the driver. Moreover, it then required the Attorney General's office to conduct a study using these data and to assess the kinds of profiling matters addressed above.[79]

Simultaneously, eleven states have recently passed legislation regarding profiling, and even stronger bills have been introduced in an additional thirteen states. These bills and laws require additional data collection, sometimes for a specified time, sometimes indefinitely. The legislation also varies on what data are required to be collected.[80] Perhaps not surprisingly, although police unions have supported some efforts to pass legislation to deal with racial profiling, they appear more often to have opposed legislation and other efforts to deal with the issue, arguing that such legislation is unnecessary and will invite baseless complaints.[81]

Though it is possible to argue that these data were to be collected to deter police and/or to document an indefensible use of race, we think a fair reading of the analysis of the limited data suggests that more data were needed to understand (racism aside) how and why race might have been included in a suspect profile. This view now appears to have been swept aside. In its stead is the simple view that profiling is necessarily unacceptable and must be abolished. For example, in the past year Senators Hillary Clinton and Jon Corzine introduced S.989/H.R. 2074. This current version of the 1998 "collect data bill," though still calling for more data collection, is now titled, the "End Racial Profiling Act of 2001." Profiling has, in the popular lexicon, traveled from being a fuzzy practice, maybe an arguably defensible one under certain circumstances, to something very much the equivalent of racism. Data no longer are desired for analysis; their purpose is simply to document the extent to which race is used, and to the extent that it is, its use must self-evidently be proscribed.[82]

Suggestions for Further Research

The legislative response to racial profiling argues strongly for more research so that we may better understand what racial profiling is and what to do about it. Racial profiling is hardly the first problem for which the heat of the public debate and the perceived urgency of the problem led to some solutions that, in hindsight at least, could have benefited from more information and data to understand better the problem. Peter Irons, in his insightful study of the role of lawyers in the New Deal agencies, recounts similar experiences, especially with regard to the National Industrial Recovery Act,[83] and more recently, similar criticisms have been leveled at some of the legislative responses to the savings and loan crisis of the late 1980s and the War on Terrorism's USA Patriot Act. Even with additional information and data, the preferred solutions might not change; the end result might be policy initiatives that outlaw the use of racial profiling. But even so, that desired end might be approached by different means with a better understanding of what exactly has occurred.

So what are some research projects that might be useful to undertake? First, and most fundamentally, it is important to make certain that we understand who is doing what and why, and, to the extent that racial profiling is perceived to be and treated as a national problem, that we are sensitive to differences across regions, states, and communities. So far, much of what we know about racial profiling comes from the studies of John Lamberth in New Jersey and Maryland.[84] Those studies have been subjected to some criticism although they have also been accepted as compelling evidence by courts in both states. Still, even if one accepts Lamberth's studies, more work needs to be done. For one thing, his studies are limited to two nearly contiguous states in the Mid-Atlantic Region. It is important that similar studies (or at least studies seeking the same information) be conducted in different regions throughout the country. What would similar studies show in the Northwest, for example, or the Plains states? What would they show in New England or the Deep South? The insights from comparative studies are likely to be valuable.

But let us take this further. Even if accurate, Lamberth's data are not without problems. We do not know, for example, details about what police recovered during the successful searches. Nor do we know about the percentage of stops that lead to searches (in contrast to the percentage of successful searches or stops). Even David Harris, the nation's leading scholar (and critic) of racial profiling acknowledges problems with the data though he also maintains that the data taken as a whole provide rather compelling evidence of racial profiling. Among the criticisms that he anticipates will be made about the existing data are that we need data on all stops, not just on stops on selected sections of a highway; that we need more data on variation in offenses committed by those who are stopped; and that we need to weigh percentage differences in stops by race by police assignment patterns. Harris concedes that more data are needed but feels that in the interim we ought to grant a presumption of validity to the data we do have while we collect more data on matters that remain inconclusive.[85]

Harris' observations suggest another approach for future studies: those that more precisely define exactly what police are doing and why they are doing it. The State of New Jersey—both in its study of the problem of "racial

profiling" and its settlement and adoption of a consent decree with the Department of Justice—attempted to address every stop in which the race of the driver was involved. That may have been the right approach in New
Jersey, but that approach does cover police actions that
may go far beyond profiling *per se*. What would be useful
are studies that looked at exactly what police were and are
doing and why. Do different police departments handle
situations differently? Is racial profiling considered appropriate for some crimes, but not others (e.g., serial murder
vs. drug dealing). If so, what accounts for the differences?
Is geographic location important? Is it training? Is it department philosophy? Is it, more broadly, the political
leanings of the persons running the law enforcement
agencies?

In this regard, explanations of the data by police should
be noted. As we have seen, police frequently deny outright
that blacks are stopped simply because of their race, "Driving While Black." Instead the police offer multiple explanations that could account for some of the differences in the
stop-and-search rates. First, they maintain that they use
race, in conjunction with other variables, as predictors of involvement in a particular crime type (typically, drug trafficking on the highways). If as other data suggest, a higher percentage of minorities are involved in this type of crime, it
makes sense, say the police, to consider race, along with
other variables in their decision-making. A related argument is that race may be correlated with other factors that
suggest culpability to the police, and though it may look like
the defendant is being searched because of his race, it is
really these other factors that lead to the search.[86]

These areas of inquiry also point out the need for research that goes beyond simple gathering of data. Interviews with individual officers and focus groups should be
conducted. The challenge here is to get honest answers to
basic questions. Early on in the debate over profiling, police
seemed more willing to acknowledge certain practices with
an eye toward defending those practices. The backlash, at

least pre–September 11th may have silenced those who see some merit in profiling.[87] Any future studies must be sensitive to those dynamics and adjust accordingly.

What will new research initiatives accomplish? Perhaps they will reveal that there is a place for racial profiling, properly administered, as an effective law enforcement tool. On the other hand, as noted above, perhaps not much will change. In the end, the nation may still decide that racial profiling does more harm than good and is not a practice whose bad qualities can be cleansed, leaving only the good. But out of the new research might come more effective and efficient reforms, born out of a better understanding of the problem and an honest dialogue among all involved. It is worth a try.

Profiling: You've Come a Long Way, Baby!

In this book, we address, in varying degrees of detail, some rather complex matters. We were not be able to resolve to them all in this modest volume. What is important to leave with is a sense of the road that profiling has traveled. What once was, and still is, a laudable much-appreciated police practice to identify the attributes of particular offenders, became a term associated with selective highway and street police stops. What is of particular interest—and is still condoned by the case law—are profiles in which race is one, but not the only, factor. We have examined both the costs and the benefits of allowing race into a profile, and we have noted the effects of September 11th on the cost/benefit calculus. Finally, we noted the simultaneous increase in state profiling legislation with the tendency to equate profiling with racism and unequivocally call for its ban. This may be the correct "bottom line" conclusion but it was reached, we believe, without giving sufficient attention to definitions of profiling, without careful examination of extant case law, and without sufficient attention to what experienced police feel are appropriate predictors of potential criminal behavior.

Appendix

OCCUPANT IDENTIFIERS FOR A POSSIBLE DRUG COURIER

I. OCCUPANTS OF THE VEHICLE
   1. Columbian males
   2. Hispanic males
   3. Hispanic male and a black male together
   4. Hispanic male and female posing as a couple

*Any combination of sexes or races could be possible drug couriers, only a few of the common ones were listed above.

II. APPEARANCE OF THE OCCUPANTS
   1. The occupants will be fatigued from long driving.

   2. Occupants may not have showered for a few days

     A. Not shaven

     B. Greasy hair

     C. Dirty clothing

   3. Notice the clothing of the occupants

     A. Shorts in the winter

     B. Pastel clothing

III. ACTIONS OF THE OCCUPANTS

1. Be aware of the occupant that stares straight ahead while driving
2. Be aware of the occupant that exits his vehicle when he is stopped and walks back to your patrol unit (he may have something to hide)
3. Be aware of any odors coming from the occupant (heavy perfume, smell of marijuana, etc.)

VEHICLE IDENTIFIERS FOR A POSSIBLE DRUG COURIER

I. MOTOR VEHICLE INTERIORS

1. Fireworks
2. Untaxed cigarettes
3. Narcotics/paraphernalia
4. Odors

     A. Chemicals

     B. Mask odors (perfume, air fresheners)

5. Ledgers
6. Cellular phones
7. Tools
8. Items indicating route of travel

     A. Maps

     B. Newspapers

     C. Toll tickets

9. Rear seat out of alignment

10. Fresh weld marks on and under vehicle

11. Heavy undercoating

12. Missing screws from the plastic molding and dash board

13. Passenger in the back seat and sleeping

14. Newly registered vehicle

15. Rental vehicle

16. Police decal in the window

17. Logos or bumper stickers on the vehicle against using drugs

18. Air shocks on the vehicle

19. Anti static sheets (bounce)

20. Roll of duck tape

21. Fast food wrappers

22. Pillows

23. Screw driver (tools)

24. Ignition key only

25. friendly dialog

INDICATIONS AND LOCATIONS OF CONCEALMENT ZONES

1. Scratches around screws

2. Check if the windows roll down

3. Natural bodily cavities on the vehicle

4. Behind the back seat

5. Carpet in the trunk

6. Taillight cavities

7. Bumpers

8. Rocker panels

9. Natural cavity behind and under the dash board

10. Velcro dash board

TITLE 39: STATUTES COMMONLY USED ON DRUG INTERDICTION STOPS

VIOLATION	STATUES
SPEEDING	39:4–98
FOLLOWING TOO CLOSELY	39:4–89
FAILURE TO DRIVE WITHIN A SINGLE LANE, OR UNSAFE LANE CHANGE	39:4–88b
FAILURE TO OBSERVE TRAFFIC SIGNAL	39:4–81
FAILURE TO KEEP TO THE RIGHT SIDE OF THE ROADWAY	39:4–82
THROWING OF OBJECTS OR DEBRIS FROM VEHICLE	39:4–64
IMPROPER , DEFECTIVE, OR NO MUFFLER (LOAD NOISE,ANNOYING SMOKE)	39:3–70
FAILURE TO DISPLAY INSPECTION APPROVAL	39:9–6
FAILURE TO HAVE VEHICLE INSPECTED	39:8–1
LIGHTS REQUIRED	39:3–47
IMPROPER OR NO MIRRORS	39:3–71
OBSTRUCTED VISION TO FRONT AND SIDE WINDOWS	39:3–74
IMPROPER MAINTENANCE OF ALL LAMPS AND REFLECTORS	39:3–66
IMPROPER DISPLAY OF LICENSE PLATES	39:3–33
SELLING OR USING UNAPPROVED EQUIPMENT (TINTED WINDOWS)	39:3–77
IMPROPER SAFETY GLASS (CRACKED OR TINTED)	39:3–75
D.W.I.	39:4–50

*DO NOT FORM A PATTERN ON YOUR STOPS

*DO NOT WRITE THE SAME SUMMONSES ON ALL THE VEHICLE STOPS YOU MAKE.

THIS WILL FORM A PATTERN AND CAN LATER BE USED AS A DEFENSE IN COURT.

NOTES

Introduction

1. Brent Turvey, *Criminal Profiling* (San Diego: Academic Press 1999), 2–3.
2. *Jim Crow Policing 1999*, ACLU-NJ Civil Liberties Report, 2nd Quarter, 1999, 1.
3. Mindy Cameron, "Profiling Is an Inherent Part of Police Work," *Seattle Times*, September 30, 2001, B10.
4. Senator Corzine's speech is reprinted as "End Racial Profiling," *Seton Hall Legislative Journal* 26 (2001), 55, 56.
5. *Washington v. Lambert*, 98 F.3d 1181, 1183 n.1 (9th Cir. 1996) (describing incidents involving actors Wesley Snipes and Blair Underwood and athletes Joe Morgan, Jamaal Wilkes and Al Joyner).
6. For the specifics on this evolution of the concept, see Chapter 4.

7. See Adam Nagoursky, "Bradley and Gore Trade Jabs in Fiercest
    Campaign Debate," *New York Times,* Feb. 22, 2000, A16; John
    Derbyshire, "In Defense of Racial Profiling," *National Review,*
    February 19, 2001, 19; < *www.usembassy.it/file2000_10/alia/a010
    1209.htm* > (April 25, 2002). For a more detailed review of the
    public debate on racial profiling, see Milton Heumann and Lance
    Cassak, "Profiles in Justice?—Police, Discretion, Symbolic Assai-
    lants and Stereotyping," *Rutgers Law Review* 53 (Summer 2001):
    911, 971.

Chapter 1

1. William Stuntz, "Local Policing After the Terror," *Yale Law Journal*
    111 (June 2002), 2138, 2142.
2. W. B. Yeats, "The Second Coming," in Richard J. Finneran (ed.),
    The Poems of W. B. Yeats (New York: Collier Books, 1983), 187.
3. Perhaps the most famous formulation of this is in Edward Levi's
    classic work, *An Introduction to Legal Reasoning* (Chicago: Univer-
    sity of Chicago Press, 1949). In that work, Dean Levi illustrates
    the process in discussions of a number of examples drawn from
    the common law, statutory law, and constitutional law. Examples
    of this phenomenon can be seen in our basic freedoms. Take the
    right to counsel set forth in the Sixth Amendment to the United
    States Constitution. What exactly does that guarantee? At a time
    when the right to counsel encompassed nothing more than a
    defendant's right to hire an attorney he or she could afford, a de-
    cision by the United States Supreme Court in the notorious
    Scottsboro case in the early 1930s introduced a defendant's right,
    under certain limited circumstances, to have counsel appointed
    by the court and paid for by the government if the defendant
    could not afford to pay for counsel. In a series of cases beginning
    a decade later, defendants, in different factual settings, raised the
    issue of whether that right extended any further and, if so, how
    far: in a capital case (yes); in a felony prosecution (yes), for a mis-
    demeanor (no, unless the punishment involves imprisonment).
    See *Powell v. Alabama,* 287 U.S. 45 (1932); *Betts v. Brady,* 316 U.S.
    455 (1942); *Gideon v. Wainwright,* 372 U.S. 335 (1963); *Arger-
    singer v. Hamlin,* 407 U.S. 25 (1972). Another example is freedom
    of speech, which is guaranteed by the First Amendment. But
    what exactly constitutes "speech" entitled to protection? What
    about criticism of local public officials in a newspaper advertise-
    ment? Burning the American flag? Burning a draft card? Offen-
    sive speech? What about a donation to your favorite politician?

The answers (yes, yes, no, maybe, don't ask) have developed more or less piecemeal over the past half-century. See, *New York Times v. Sullivan*, 376 U.S. 254 (1964); *Texas v. Johnson*, 491 U.S. 397 (1989); *United States v. O'Brien*, 391 U.S. 367 (1968); *Cohen v. California*, 403 U.S. 15 (1971); *F.C.C. v. Pacifica Foundation*, 438 U.S. 726 (1978); *Buckley v. Valeo*, 424 U.S. 1 (1976).

4. Brent Turvey, *Criminal Profiling* (San Diego: Academic Press, 1999), 1.

5. John E. Douglas and Mark Olshaker, *Mindhunter: Inside the FBI's Elite Serial Crime Unit* (New York: Scribner, 1995), 32–33. Popular novels have also embraced profiling, especially as it was practiced during these early years. See Caleb Carr, *The Alienist* (New York: Random House, 1994).

6. Ibid., 33–34; Turvey, *Criminal Profiling*, 7.

7. John Douglas, who later played a leading role in the development of criminal profiling at the FBI has labeled Brussel a "trailblazer" in the field and Brussel's work in the Mad Bomber case "a real landmark in what came to be called behavioral science in criminal investigation." See Douglas & Olshaker, *Manhunter*, 34; Turvey, *Criminal Profiling*, 8.

8. On Teten, his colleague and the early development of the FBI's BSU see Turvey, *Criminal Profiling*, 9–10. See also, Douglas & Olshaker, *Manhunter*, 10–24, 159–60, which, not surprisingly, discusses Douglas' own contributions to the BSU.

9. Ibid., 2.

10. Scott Ingram, "If the Profile Fits: Admitting Criminal Psychological Profiles Into Evidence In Criminal Trials," *Washington University Journal of Urban & Contemporary Law* 54 (1998): 239.

11. Ibid., 244–47 (footnotes omitted).

12. See Eli Lehrer, "Profiles in Confusion," *The Weekly Standard*, November 4, 2002, which includes the quote from Murphy. Indeed, much criticism of profiling was elicited by the events surrounding two snipers who terrorized the suburbs of Washington, D.C., shooting thirteen people and killing ten in the space of a few weeks in 2002. "Profilers" of all sorts and qualifications made their way to the cable television news programs with widely varying predictions, including that the sniper was white, between the ages of 20 and 30, working alone and otherwise held a steady job. In fact, the persons arrested and charged with the sniping (as this book goes to press) were two African Americans, one of whom was 41 and the other a teenager, and without long term ties to the community. The errors by the media profilers provoked criticism of the practice. See Ibid.; Brendan L. Koerner, "Did Criminal Profilers Blow It in the Sniper

Case?" *Slate,* available at *www.slate.msn.com,* posted October 25, 2002. Some even objected that the incorrect identification of the snipers' race was the product of pernicious racial profiling. Andrew Sullivan, "The Fruits of Racial Profiling," available at *www.andrewsullivan.com,* posted October 25, 2002. Some of the criticism based on the sniper case may overstate the limitations of profiling properly executed. It is doubtful, for one thing, that the television pundit profilers had all of the information the police had about the case and that a profiler actually working on the case would use.

13. Charles E. Becton, "The Drug Courier Profile: '"All Seems Infected that the Infected Spy, as all Seems Yellow to the Jaundic'd Eye,'" *North Carolina Law Review* 65 (1987): 424–26.

14. 392 U.S. 1 (1968).

15. See general discussions in Fred P. Graham, *The Self-Inflicted Wound* (New York: Macmillan, 1970); Lucas A. Powe, Jr., *The Warren Court and American Politics* (Cambridge: Harvard University Press, 2000), 379–411; Yale Kamisar, "The Warren Court and Criminal Justice," in *The Warren Court; A Retrospective,* Bernard Schwartz, ed. (New York: Oxford University Press, 1996), 116–158.

16. Graham, *Self-Inflicted Wound,* 65.

17. U.S. Const., Amend. IV.

18. *Brinegar v. United States,* 338 U.S. 160, 180–81 (1949) (Jackson, J. concurring).

19. This was due to the Supreme Court's holding in *Barron v. Baltimore,* 32 U.S. (7 Pet.) 243 (1833) that the restrictions on government action in the Bill of Rights applied only to the federal government, not the states.

20. *Mapp v. Ohio,* 367 U.S. 643 (1961).

21. Indeed, the harsher critics of Fourth Amendment jurisprudence have dismissed it as "an embarrassment" and "a mess." See Akhil Reed Amar, *The Constitution and Criminal Procedure; First Principles* (New Haven: Yale University Press, 1997), 1; Ronald Dworkin, "Fact Style Adjudication and the Fourth Amendment: The Limits of Lawyering," *Indiana Law Review* 48 (1973): 329; see generally, Anthony G. Amsterdam, "Perspectives on the Fourth Amendment," *Minnesota Law Review* 58 (1974): 349.

22. See generally, Amsterdam, "Perspectives," 356–60; Charles Whitebread and Christopher Slobogin, *Criminal Procedure: An Analysis of Cases and Concepts,* 4th ed. (New York: Foundation Press, 2000), 70–147.

23. Chilton died after the case went through the state courts but before the Supreme Court decided it; otherwise this very important

case would have been known as *Chilton v. Ohio.* See 392 U.S. 1,
4, n.2 (1968).

24. Ibid., 4–7.

25. Ibid., 8. For a more complete discussion of the lower state court
rulings, see Stephen A. Saltzburg, "*Terry v. Ohio:* A Practically Perfect Doctrine," *St. John's Law Review* 72 (1998): 914–17.

26. 392 U.S. 1 (1968), 15.

27. Ibid., 16.

28. Ibid., 20–21.

29. Ibid., 22.

30. Ibid., 22–23.

31. This is the usual formulation of the ruling in *Terry.* See, *Florida v.
Royer,* 460 U.S. 491, 498 (1983). See also, Whitebread and Slobogin, *Criminal Procedure,* 244; David Harris, "Particularized Suspicion, Categorical Judgments: Supreme Court Rhetoric Versus
Lower Court Reality Under *Terry v. Ohio,*" *St. John's Law Review*
72 (1998): 975.

32. Warren ultimately stated the holding of the case as follows:

> We merely hold that where a police officer observes un-
> usual conduct which leads him reasonably to conclude in
> light of his experience that criminal activity may be afoot
> and that the persons with whom he is dealing may be
> armed and presently dangerous, where in the course of in-
> vestigating this behavior he identifies himself as a police-
> man and makes reasonable inquiries, and where nothing
> in the initial stages of the encounter serves to dispel his
> reasonable fear for his own or others' safety, he is entitled
> for the protection of himself and others in the area to con-
> duct a carefully limited search of the outer clothing of such
> persons in an attempt to discover weapons which might be
> used to assault him.

392. U.S. at 30.

33. See John Q. Barrett, "Deciding the Stop and Frisk Cases: A Look
Inside the Supreme Court's Conference," *St. John's Law Review* 72
(1998): 816.

34. On this point, see Earl C. Dudley, Jr., "*Terry v. Ohio,* the Warren
Court and the Fourth Amendment: A Law Clerk's Perspective," *St.
John's Law Review* 72 (1998): 896–7; Philip S. Greene and Brian
W. Wice, "The D.E.A. Drug Courier Profile: History and Analysis,"
South Texas Law Journal 22 (1981): 267.

35. The exclusionary rule prevents evidence obtained as the result of
a violation of a defendant's constitutional rights—for example,
an admission elicited from a coerced confession or drugs or

other physical evidence gotten in the course of an illegal search—
from being introduced at the defendant's criminal trial.

36. Compare Dudley, "Terry, the Warren Court and the Fourth
Amendment," 903, and Bernard Schwartz, *SuperChief* (New
York: New York University Press, 1983), 684–92 (arguing that
Terry is consistent with the earlier Warren Court decisions, in-
cluding *Miranda*), with Graham, *The Self-Inflicted Wound;* Powe,
Jr., *The Warren Court and American Politics;* Yale Kamisar, "The
Warren Court and Criminal Justice," Tracy Maclin, *"Terry v. Ohio's*
Fourth Amendment Legacy: Black Men and Police Discretion,"
St. John's Law Review 72 (1998): 1276–77 (describing *Terry* as a
break with earlier Warren Court decisions that had favored the
rights of defendants over the interests of law enforcement).

37. William Stuntz, "Local Policing After the Terror," *Yale Law Journal*
111 (June 2002), pp. 2138, 2153; Greene and Wice, "The D.E.A.
Courier Drug Profile," 267.

38. David F. Musto, *The American Disease: Origins of Narcotics Control*
(New Haven: Yale University Press, 1973), Chapter 1; Steven B.
Duke and Albert C. Gross, *America's Longest War: Rethinking Our
Tragic Crusade Against Drugs* (New York: Putnam, 1993), 78–84;
Lawrence M. Friedman, *Crime and Punishment in American His-
tory* (New York: Basic Books, 1993), 354–57.

39. Musto, *American Disease,* 54–68; Friedman, *Crime and Punishment,* 354–57.

40. Friedman, *Crime and Punishment,* 354–57; Ted Gest, *Crime and
Politics: Big Government's Erratic Campaign for Law and Order*
(New York: Oxford University Press, 2001), 109–110. On the
Treasury Department's responsibility for enforcing federal prohi-
bition laws, including the Volstead Act, one study pointed out that
Treasury was allocated $2 million toward enforcement efforts
and the Justice Department only $100,000. See Richard Hamm,
*Shaping the Eighteenth Amendment: Temperance Reform, Legal
Culture, and the Polity, 1880–1920* (Chapel Hill: University of
North Carolina Press, 1995), 253–54. Hamm also notes that in
some circles, it was assumed that the states, not the federal
government, would take the lead on enforcement of Prohibition.
On the problems with and ineffectiveness of Treasury's efforts to
enforce Prohibition, see Michael E. Parrish, *Anxious Decades:
America in Prosperity and Depression, 1920–1941* (New York:
W.W. Norton, 1992), 98–105; James H. Timberlake, *Prohibition
and the Progressive Movement, 1900–1920* (Cambridge: Harvard
University Press, 1963), 181–183.

41. On Johnson's unsuccessful efforts to get the federal government
more involved in combating illegal drugs, see Dan Baum, *Smoke*

and Mirrors; The War on Drugs and the Politics of Failure (Boston: Little, Brown, 1996), 8–9; on the paucity of drug prosecutions in the 1960s, see William Stuntz, "Local Policing After the Terror," 2151. That would change once the War on Drugs got into full swing, and arrests for drug offenses quintupled between 1968 and 1988.

42. On the difficulties Nixon had with using the Vietnam War as a campaign issue and his use of a law and order theme as a campaign issue, see Baum, *Smoke and Mirrors,* 9–11; Stephen Ambrose, *Nixon* (New York: Simon & Schuster, 1991); Graham, *The Self-Inflicted Wound.*

43. Baum, *Smoke and Mirrors,* 11–12.

44. Ibid., 21.

45. One recent study summarizes the major themes in the current literature as follows:

> There seem to be three links between drugs and crime. First, there are the crime-facilitating effects of drug use itself: the intoxication and addiction that, in certain circumstances, appear to encourage careless and combative behavior. The second and third drugs-crime connections stem from policies of drug prohibition and enforcement: the crimes that attend the workings of the black market—violence among dealers and corruption of law enforcement—and the crimes committed by users to obtain money with which to buy drugs.

David Boylum and Mark A.R. Kleiman, "Alcohol and Other Drugs," in *Crime,* James Q. Wilson and Joan Petersilia, eds. (San Francisco: ICS Press, 1995), 295–326 (quote on 296–97) Nearly all of the studies cited by Boylum and Kleiman are from the 1990s and 1980s. See also Duke and Gross, *America's Longest War,* 103–21, again citing studies from the 1980s and 1990s in support of the causal link between drug use and other crimes.

46. Baum, *Smoke and Mirrors,* 17–19.

47. See Ramsey Clark, *Crime in America* (New York: Simon & Schuster, 1970), 56–67, 85–100; James Q. Wilson, *Thinking About Crime* (New York: Vintage Books, 1975), 140–180; Richard H. Blum, "Drugs, Behavior and Crime," *Annals of the American Academy of Political and Social Science* (November 1967): 135–146 (quoted 145); Michael Tonry, *Malign Neglect: Race, Crime and Punishment in America* (New York: Oxford University Press, 1995), 18–19.

48. Baum, *Smoke and Mirrors,* 71–72.

49. On drug use as an aspect of the 1960s, particularly associated

with the rise of the counterculture, see, William L. O'Neill, *Coming Apart: An Informal History of America in the 1960's* (Chicago: Quadrangle Books, 1971), 233–243; Todd Gitlin, *The Sixties: Years of Hope, Days of Rage* (New York: Bantam Books, 1987), 195–221; Allen J. Matusow, *The Unraveling of America: A History of Liberalism in the 1960's* (New York: Harper & Row, 1984), 275–307.

50. Baum, *Smoke and Mirrors,* 13–66.
51. Ibid., 83.
52. Ibid., 82–84; Gest, *Crime and Politics,* 110–111.
53. Ibid., 111; Baum, *Smoke and Mirrors,* 80–85.
54. Ibid., 16.
55. Ibid.
56. William Manchester, *The Glory and the Dream* (Boston: Little, Brown, 1973), 1182.
57. *United States v. Lopez,* 328 F. Supp. 1077, 1082 (E.D.N.Y. 1971). The following description of the creation of the profile and its features is drawn primarily from the court's decision and findings in the *Lopez* case.
58. Ibid., 1083. For airport officials today, profiling is still an essential tool for winnowing down and focusing in on particular potential threats, and, if anything, it has taken on special importance because of the events of September 11, 2001. As Todd Hauptli, spokesman for the American Association of Airport Executives puts it, "'Everyone gets all freaked out' when they hear about profiling [. . .] [b]ut finding someone who intends to hijack or blow up a plane is like looking for a needle in a haystack [. . .] and 'you've got to figure out how to make the haystack smaller.'" See Matthew Wald, "At Airports, a Search for Better Security," *New York Times,* May 26, 2002, TR5, 13. This is not to say that the profiles currently employed in the wake of September 11th are precisely the same as the one devised by the Task Force in the late 1960s. We deal at greater length with the effects of September 11th on profiling and racial profiling in Chapter 6.
59. 328 F. Supp. at 1083–86.
60. Ibid., 1084.
61. Ibid.
62. Ibid., 1084, 1093–99.
63. Ibid., 1100.
64. Ibid. Despite the fact that the people introducing the improper elements into the profile were employees of a private corporation, and hence not technically government agents, the court still found the defendant's constitutional rights violated because under the FAA procedures, the airline employees were "acting as

government agents insofar as they designated" persons who fit the profile and called the marshals.

65. *United States v. Skipwith,* 482 F.2d 1272, 1275 (5th Cir. 1973).

66. *United States v. Moreno,* 475 F.2d 44, 48–49 (5th Cir. 1973).

67. Morgan Cloud, "Search and Seizure by the Numbers: The Drug Courier Profile and Judicial Review of Investigative Formulas," *Boston University Law Review* 65 (November 1985): 843, 873–74.

68. See, e.g., Jerome H. Skolnick, *Justice Without Trial: Law Enforcement in Democratic Society* (New York: Macmillan, 1967) and James Q. Wilson, *Varieties of Police Behavior* (Cambridge: Harvard University Press, 1968).

69. We do not claim that the typology implicit in the continuum is a typology in the formal sense of the term. Our categories are neither exhaustive nor mutually exclusive and thus do not meet the standard conditions for a typology; the typology design is adopted simply to highlight the range of police behavior.

70. There might be something worthwhile in allowing the police on patrol, and the judge in sentencing, to occasionally (and, of course, defining "occasionally" is part of the problem) act on his/her instincts or hunches—assuming that there is no improper variable such as race being used.

71. This stated equilibrium between permissible and impermissible policing assumes that one can "negotiate" between experience and law. This may not be true. The federal government's position regarding the interaction of race and profiling, for example, can be difficult to pin down at best and often inconsistent. On the one hand, the federal government, through agencies such as the Drug Enforcement Agency, has evidenced an equivocal approval of racial profiles. See, e.g., David Kocieniewski, "New Jersey Argues That the US Wrote the Book on Racial Profiling," *New York Times,* November 29, 2000, A1; Ron Marisco and Kathy Barrett Carter, "State Ties Profiling to Advice on Crime Fighting," *Star-Ledger* (Newark), November 28, 2000, 26. On the other hand, the courts have sent a much more mixed, and at times muddled, message—to the extent they have sent one at all. These issues will be discussed in more detail in Chapters 4 and 5.

72. Skolnick, *Justice,* 45–47, 83.

73. Roy R. Roberg and Jack Kuykendall, *Police and Society* (Roxbury: Roxbury Press, 1993), 163.

74. William K. Muir, Jr., *Police: Streetcorner Politicians* (Chicago: University of Chicago Press, 1977), 153–156.

75. Wilson, *Varieties,* 38, 40; see also Milton Heumann and Lance Cassak, "Profiles in Justice?—Police, Discretion, Symbolic Assailants and Stereotyping," *Rutgers Law Review* 53 (Summer 2001): 925–26.

76. Jonathan Rubinstein, *City Police* (New York: Farrar, Straus and Giroux, 1973), 262–263; and see Heumann and Cassak, "Profiles in Justice?," 925–29.

77. Consider, for example, the comments of Bernard Parks, then police chief of Los Angeles: "It's not the fault of the police when they stop minority males or put them in jail. It's the fault of the minority males for committing the crime. In my mind it is not a great revelation that if officers are looking for criminal activity, they're going to look at the kind of people who are listed on crime reports." Race, he argues is legitimately included in this kind of profile. See Jeffrey Goldberg, "The Color of Suspicion," *New York Times Magazine,* June 20, 1999, 53–54.

    See, as well, Egon Bittner, *Aspects of Police Work* (Boston: Northeastern University Press, 1990) 98–99. Bittner, while objecting in principle to police decisions linked to age, class, and race, feels that under public pressure the police inevitably weigh differences in crime rates for individuals in these different categories, and as a result "even the most completely impartial policeman who merely takes account of probabilities, as these probabilities are known to him, will feel reasonably justified in being more suspicious of the young-poor-black than of the old-rich-white . . ." (99).

78. *Brown v. Texas,* 443 U.S. 47, 52 (1979).

79. *United States v. Condelee,* 915 F.2d 1209 (1990).

80. *State v. Citarella,* 154 N.J. 272 (1998), quoting *State v. Thomas* 110 N.J. at 10–11, 69 A.2d 808.

81. *Illinois v. Wardlow,* 528 U.S. 119 (2000). Indeed, such confidence in the practical street experience of police was important in the Supreme Court's decision in *Terry v. Ohio,* 392 U.S. 1, 21–23 (1968). Anthony Thompson emphasized how *Terry* used the "police officer as expert" contention to demonstrate that the decision applied to more than mere police hunches. See "Stopping the Usual Suspects: Race and the Fourth Amendment," *New York University Law Review* 74 (1999): 956.

CHAPTER 2

1. On the influence of the skyjacker profile in the development of the drug courier profile, see Philip S. Greene and Brian W. Wice, "The D.E.A. Drug Courier Profile: History and Analysis," *South Texas Law Journal* 22 (1981): 269; Charles E. Becton, "The Drug Courier Profile: "'All Seems Infected that the Infected Spy, as all Seems Yellow to the Jaundic'd Eye,'" *North Carolina Law Review*

65 (1987): 426. Numerous courts and commentators identify Markonni as the creator of the drug courier profile. See, e.g., *United
States v. Ehlebracht*, 693 F.2d 333, 335 n.3 (5th Cir. 1982); *United
States v. Berry*, 639 F.2d 1075, 1079 n.6 (5th Cir. 1981); Becton,
"Drug Courier Profile," 426–28; Greene and Wice, "D.E.A. Drug
Courier Profile," 269–274; Morgan Cloud, "Search and Seizure by
the Numbers: The Drug Courier Profile and Judicial Review of Investigative Formulas," *Boston University Law Review* 65 (November 1985): 847–49. One prominent scholar who has written ex-
tensively on racial profiling also credits another DEA agent, John
Marcello, with co-creating the drug courier profile, based on an
interview with Mr. Marcello. See David Harris, *Profiles in Injustice:
Why Racial Profiling Cannot Work* (New York: New Press, 2002),
20. Even those who identify Markonni as the father of the drug
courier profile readily concede he had help in devising it.

2. Becton, "The Drug Courier Profile," 426–427. Other cases in
which the skyjacker profile resulted in an arrest for drugs include
United States v. Skipwith, 482 F.2d 1272, 1275 (5th Cir. 1973);
United States v. Moreno, 475 F.2d 44, 48–49 (5th Cir. 1973) and
United States v. Legato, 480 F.2d 408 (5th Cir. 1973).

3. For a description of the procedures used in connection with the
airport drug courier profile see, Cloud, "Search and Seizure By
the Numbers"; Becton, "The Drug Courier Profile"; Greene and
Wice, "The DEA Drug Courier Profile."

4. Compare *United States v. Van Lewis*, 409 F. Supp. 535, 538
(E.D.Mich. 1975):

> Testimony taken in open court indicated that the following
> constitute some of the characteristics of a drug courier: (1)
> the use of small denomination currency for ticket pur-
> chases, (2) travel to and from major drug import centers, es-
> pecially for short periods of time; (3) the absence of luggage
> or use of empty suitcases on trips which normally require
> extra clothing; and (4) travel under an alias. For purposes of
> this opinion, the court refers to these and other characteris-
> tics testified to in camera as the "'courier profile.'"

with *United States v. Elmore*, 595 F.2d 1036 (5th Cir. 1979) (identifying eleven characteristics of the drug courier profile); see also,
Becton, "The Drug Courier Profile," 430–32.

5. *United States v. Elmore*, 595 F.2d 1036 (5th Cir. 1979); Greene and
Wice, "D.E.A. Drug Courier Profile," 272; Cloud, "Search and Seizure by the Numbers," 871–72 (relying upon eight "shared" characteristics and a few other similar although not perfectly identical characteristics drawn from the *Elmore* case and the court's

opinion in *United States v. Ballard,* 575 F.2d 913 (5th Cir. 1978) to identify the characteristics of the DEA drug courier profile); Becton, "Drug Courier Profile," 432. The primary characteristics have been described as those that "derive from logical deductions about the practicalities of the drug business." The secondary characteristics cannot claim that pedigree and "have less of an empirically based common sense component." Ibid.

6. *United States v. McCaleb,* 552 F.2d 717, 719 (6th Cir. 1977); *United States v. Price,* 599 F.2d 494, 502 n.10 (2d Cir. 1979); Becton, "The Drug Courier Profile," 418.

7. See Milton Heumann and Lance Cassak, "Profiles in Justice?—Police, Discretion, Symbolic Assailants and Stereotyping," *Rutgers Law Review* 53 (Summer 2001): 920–21 (citing cases and sources); Becton, "Drug Courier Profile," 433.

8. William V. Conley, "Mendenhall and Reid: The Drug Courier Profile and Investigative Stops," *University of Pittsburgh Law Review* 42 (1981): 839.

9. Becton, "Drug Courier Profile," 433.

10. *Derricott v. Maryland,* 578 A.2d 791, 797 (Md. Ct. Spec. App. 1990), *rev'd* 611 A.2d 592 (Md. 1992).

11. Becton, "Drug Courier Profile," 433.

12. *United States v. Hooper,* 935 F.2d 484, 499–500 (2d Cir. 1991). Judge Pratt's description of the airport drug courier profile as "chameleon-like" is taken, ironically, from the opinion of the United States Court of Appeals for the Ninth Circuit in *United States v. Sokolow,* 831 F.2d 1413, 1418 (9th Cir. 1987), which the Supreme Court later reversed in its most extensive consideration of profiling, *United States v. Sokolow,* 490 U.S. 1 (1989). We will have more to say about the Supreme Court's decision in the *Sokolow* case later.

13. See David Cole, *No Equal Justice: Race and Class in the American Criminal Justice System* (New York: New Press, 1999), 47–49; Heumann and Cassak, "Profiles in Justice?", 920, n.55.

14. *United States v. Chambliss,* 425 F. Supp. 1330, 1333 (E.D. Mich. 1977); *United States v. Westerbaum-Martinez,* 435 F. Supp. 690 (E.D.N.Y. 1977); *United States v. Taylor,* 917 F.2d 1402, 1409 (6th Cir. 1990), *rev'd en banc* 956 F.2d 572 (6th Cir. 1992).

15. *Pennsylvania v. Daniels,* 599 A.2d 988, 990 n.1 (Pa. Super. Ct. 1991).

16. *United States v. McCranie,* 703 F.2d 1213, 1218–19 (10th Cir. 1983) (McKay, dissenting).

17. Becton, "Drug Courier Profile," 446.

18. See, e.g., *State v. Washington,* 364 So.2d 958 (La. 1979).

19. Compare *United States v. Van Lewis,* 409 F. Supp. 535, 538

(E.D.Mich. 1975) and *United States v. Price*, 599 F.2d 494 (2d Cir. 1979) with *United States v. Cordell*, 723 F.2d 1283, 1287–88 (7th Cir. 1983), *cert. den.* 465 U.S. 1029 (1984). It is difficult to assess the reliability of the assessment offered by the *Van Lewis* court. For one thing, the court does not indicate the source of its statistics, but more importantly, it represents a very early assessment of the drug courier profile. Later cases and studies do not provide any evidence as to the reliability or effectiveness of the drug courier profile. See, *United States v. Place*, 660 F.2d 44 (2d Cir. 1981); Joseph P. D'Ambrosio, "The Drug Courier Profile and Airport Stops: Reasonable Intrusions or Suspicionless Stops?" *Nova Law Review* 12 (1987): 276–77; Conley, "Mendenhall and Reid," 839–40; Cloud, "Search and Seizure by the Numbers."

20. Cole, *No Equal Justice*, 49–50.
21. Sheri Lynn Johnson, "Race and the Decision to Detain a Suspect," *Yale Law Journal* 93 (1983): 234.
22. See James Alan Fox and Jack Levin, "Multiple Homicide: Patterns of Serial and Mass Murder," *Crime and Justice* 23 (1998): 413.
23. See Ralph Lerner, "The Supreme Court as Republican Schoolmaster," *Supreme Court Review* (1967): 127 (characterizing the Court as a "republican schoolmaster"); Eugene Rostow, "The Democratic Character of Judicial Review," *Harvard Law Review* 66 (1952) (conducting a "vital national seminar"): 208; Alexander Bickel, *The Least Dangerous Branch: The Supreme Court and the Bar of Politics* (Indianapolis: Bobbs-Merrill, 1962), 24–26. The observation that the Supreme Court does not always take advantage of this function is from Ralph Rossum, "The Supreme Court as Republican Schoolmaster: Freedom of Speech, Political Equality and the Teaching of Political Philosophy," in *Taking the Constitution Seriously: Essays on the Constitution and Constitutional Law,* Gary McDowell ed. (Dubuque, Iowa : Kendall/Hunt Publishing Company, 1981), 125.
24. The studies by the Hon. Charles Becton and Morgan Cloud identify a large number of the cases. See Becton, "Drug Courier Profile" and Cloud, "Search and Seizure by the Numbers."
25. Compare *United States v. Buenaventura-Ariza*, 615 F.2d 29, 32–33 (2d Cir. 1980) (discussing development of relaxed factors governing law of airport searches in the Second Circuit) with *United States v. McCaleb*, 552 F.2d 717, 720 (6th Cir. 1977) (discussing the use of drug courier profiles for airport searches). A recent assessment of the constitutionality of the use of the drug courier profile identified more than a dozen cases throughout the federal Circuit Courts of Appeal in which the use of drug courier profiles had played an "important" role. Significantly, all of the decisions

but one predated the Supreme Court's decision in *Reid*. See Dey,
"Drug Courier Profiles: An Infringement of Fourth Amendment
Rights," *University of Baltimore Law Review* 28 (1998): 3 n.9.

26. 594 F.2d 320, 326 (2d Cir. 1979). The *Rico* court also shows, however, that such praise did not necessarily mean that the court
would find that the stop and search in question passed constitutional muster, as the stop and search in that case was struck
down as a violation of the defendant's Fourth Amendment rights.

27. *State v. Grant*, 461 A.2d 524, 525 (Md. App. 1983), *cert. dismissed*
473 A.2d 455 (1984).

28. See *United States v. Ehlebrecht*, 693 F.2d 333, 335 n.2 (5th Cir.
1982); *United States v. Williams*, 647 F.2d 588, 589 (5th Cir. 1981);
United States v. Berd, 634 F.2d 979, 981 (5th Cir. 1981).

29. See *United States v. Price*, 599 F.2d 494, 501 (2d Cir. 1979); *United
States v. Oates*, 560 F.2d 45, 49 (2d Cir. 1978).

30. *United States v. Pulvano*, 629 F.2d 1151, 1155 n.1 (5th Cir. 1980).

31. *United States v. Vasquez*, 612 F.2d 1338, 1349–52 (2d Cir. 1979)
(Oakes, J., dissenting). Judge Oakes' reference to the *Terry-Adams*
exception was to the scope of investigatory stops allowed by the
United States Supreme Court in *Terry v. Ohio*, 392 U.S. 1 (1968)
and *Adams v. Williams*, 407 U.S. 143 (1972). The reference to a
"very active DEA agent" was apparently to DEA agent Gerald
Whitmore (not Paul Markonni), whose name appeared in and
whose conduct was at issue in a number of cases in the Second
Circuit besides the *Vasquez* case.

32. Mendenhall was traveling from Los Angeles, a "source city"; she
deplaned last and appeared nervous when she got off the plane;
she had checked no luggage, and she changed airlines for her return flight to Los Angeles. 446 U.S. 544, 547 (1980).

33. Ibid., 547–549.

34. Among the questions the Court agreed to decide was whether
"federal narcotics agents violate the Fourth Amendment by ap-
proaching someone and requesting identification on the basis of
facts that in their experience indicate that a person may be a narcotics courier but that are also consistent with innocent behavior." 444 U.S. 822 (1979).

35. 446 U.S. 544 (1980): 550–557.

36. Ibid., 560–566.

37. Ibid., 566–577.

38. See Becton, "Drug Courier Profile," 464; Greene and Wice,
"D.E.A. Drug Courier Profile," 280.

39. 448 U.S. 438, 439–41 (1980).

40. Ibid., 440.

41. Ibid., 441.

42. Ibid., 440.
43. Ibid., 441.
44. Ibid.
45. See Becton, "Drug Courier Profile," 463–64.
46. See, e.g., *United States v. Corbin,* 662 F.2d 1066 (4th Cir. 1981) (discussing cases); *United States v. Rico,* 594 F.2d 320 (2d Cir. 1979); *United States v. Post,* 607 F.2d 847 (9th Cir. 1979).
47. To sketch the broad outlines roughly, a Lexis-Nexis search for lower court cases in which the drug courier profile played a role in evaluating a defendant's claims under the Fourth Amendment showed an increase in such cases from a little more than 40 in the 1970s, to almost 160 in the 1980s and more than 230 in the 1990s.
48. See, e.g., *United States v. Berry,* 670 F.2d 583, 600–601 (5th Cir. 1982).
49. See, e.g., *United States v. Harrison,* 667 F.2d 1158 (4th Cir. 1982); *United States v. Hanson,* 801 F.2d 757 (5th Cir. 1986). At least in the immediate wake of *Reid,* some courts continued to hold that use of a profile by itself was enough to justify a stop, although such decisions are of doubtful validity after the Supreme Court decision. See, e.g., *Brooker v. Georgia,* 298 S.E.2d 48, 50 (Ga. Ct. App. 1982); *Berry v. Georgia,* 294 S.E.2d 562, 566 (Ga. Ct. App. 1982). See Cloud, "Search and Seizure by the Numbers," 850–51.
50. *United States v. Saperstein,* 723 F.2d 1221, 1229 n.11 (6th Cir. 1983).
51. *United States v. Berry,* 670 F.2d 583, 588 (5th Cir. 1982).
52. Becton, "Drug Courier Profile," 463 (footnotes omitted). One reason for the lower courts' cursory treatment of the issues was the number of times suspects "inexplicably consented to searches they knew would uncover drugs." Ibid. For another useful discussion of the lower court treatment of the use of drug courier profiles after *Mendenhall* and *Reid,* see also Cloud, "Search and Seizure by the Numbers."
53. 460 U.S. 491, 525 (1983).
54. 490 U.S. 1 (1989).
55. The following discussion of the *Sokolow* decision is heavily indebted to Norman Anker's unpublished manuscript "Profiling," a paper that deals in great depth with a variety of legal issues surrounding profiling.
56. 490 U.S. at 4–5.
57. *United States v. Sokolow,* 831 F.2d 1413, 1419 (9th Cir. 1987).
58. Ibid., 1419–21.
59. 490 U.S. at 5–7.
60. Ibid., 9, 7 (quoting its earlier decisions in *Reid v. Georgia* and *Terry v. Ohio,* respectively).

61. Ibid., 8–9.
62. Ibid., 10.
63. Ibid., 16 (Marshall, J. dissenting).
64. Ibid.
65. Ibid.
66. Ibid.
67. Ibid., 13 (Marshall, J., dissenting).
68. Ibid (quoting *Terry v. Ohio*).
69. Ibid., 13.
70. 528 U.S. 119 (2000).
71. 528 U.S. at 132–33 (Stevens, J., dissenting) (footnotes omitted).
72. Ibid., 133, n.10. We discuss the New Jersey experience in some detail in the chapters that follow.
73. 532 U.S. 318 (2001).
74. 532 U.S. at 589 (O'Connor, J., dissenting). It should be noted that, notwithstanding Justice O'Connor's concern about racial profiling, the petitioner in the *Atwater* case was white. See Linda Greenhouse, "Divided Justices Back Full Arrests on Minor Charges," *New York Times* April 25, 2001, A1.
75. William Stuntz, notes that the case was decided by a 5–4 majority and that the majority was careful, in reaction to Justice O'Connor's invocation of racial profiling, "to premise its holding on the absence of large-scale strategic behavior" that had come to be labeled "racial profiling," such as the use of pretextual traffic stops to find those engaged in illegal drug sales. William Stuntz, "Local Policing After the Terror," *Yale Law Journal* 111 (June 2002), p. 2158. On pretextual traffic stops and racial profiling, see Chapter 4.
76. The Court's decision in *Bush v. Gore,* 531 U.S. 98 (2000), which effectively resolved the razor-close 2000 presidential election, is only the most recent example of the Court's getting involved in an issue of paramount contemporary importance. Some have argued that the Court's foray in *Bush v. Gore* saved the country from a constitutional crisis; others contend that by taking the case and deciding it as it did, the Court intruded into the political arena in a manner that was unwarranted and for which it was ill suited. The literature on *Bush v. Gore,* only a year after the decision, is already huge, but a good starting place reflecting, *inter alia,* the differing attitudes just described are the essays collected in Cass R. Sunstein and Richard A. Epstein, *The Vote: Bush, Gore & the Supreme Court* (Chicago: University of Chicago Press, 2001).
77. For example, some state courts, following the decision in *Sokolow,* mistakenly read the Supreme Court's decision as allowing use of a profile, by itself, to be sufficient to create reasonable

suspicion to justify a stop and search; other courts recognized that use of a profile was not enough and that a law enforcement officer had to articulate the basis for the stop but failed to insist that the officers in the case before it do so. For a fuller discussion of such cases, see Heumann and Cassak, "Profiles in Justice?," n.198.
78. We have addressed this issue and the many questions raised thereby at greater length in "Profiles in Justice?," 138–43.
79. Cloud, "Search and Seizure by the Numbers," 855–869.

Chapter 3

1. *Brinegar v. United States,* 338 U.S. 160, 182 (Jackson, J. concurring).
2. *United States v. Johnston,* 497 F.2d 397, 398 (9th Cir. 1974). See also, *United States v. Whitehead,* 849 F.2d 849 (4th Cir.), *cert. den.* 109 S. Ct. (1988); William V. Conley, "Mendenhall and Reid: The Drug Courier Profile and Investigative Stops," *University of Pittsburgh Law Review* 42 (1981): 836, n.5.
3. For the different approaches to drug enforcement by the Carter and Reagan administrations, see Dan Baum, *Smoke and Mirrors; The War on Drugs and the Politics of Failure* (Boston: Little, Brown, 1996), chapters 6 and 11; Ted Gest, *Crime and Politics: Big Government's Erratic Campaign for Law and Order* (New York: Oxford University Press, 2001), 111–122.
4. Baum, *Smoke and Mirrors,* 169; David A. Harris, "Driving While Black, Racial Profiling on Our Nation's Highways, " ACLU Special Report (1999).
5. Gary Webb, "DWB" *Esquire,* April 1999, 122–23.
6. Baum, *Smoke and Mirrors,* 194; Harris, "ACLU Special Report"; Morgan Cloud, "Search and Seizure by the Numbers: The Drug Courier Profile and Judicial Review of Investigative Formulas," *Boston University Law Review* 65 (November 1985): 854–55; Webb, "DWB," 122–23; David Rudovsky, "Law Enforcement by Stereotypes and Serendipity: Racial Profiling and Stops and Searches Without Cause," *University of Pennsylvania Journal of Constitutional Law* 3 (2001): 296, n.78. There is some conflict in the sources as to the timing of events. Harris, for example, asserts that use of profiles in highway stops by the Florida Highway Patrol began in 1984 and claims that the DEA launched Operation Pipeline in 1986. Dan Baum, however, places the beginning of the efforts of the Florida Highway Patrol in 1983, and Morgan Cloud alludes briefly to Operation Pipeline in his extensive study of the airport drug courier profile, published in 1985, while also

suggesting that Florida began using aggressive highway stops in 1984.

7. The following description of police practices is primarily drawn from Webb, "DWB," 122, and Harris "ACLU Special Report." See also, Janet Koven Levit, "Pretextual Traffic Stops: *United States v. Whren* and the Death of *Terry v. Ohio*," *Loyola University Chicago Law Journal* 28 (1996): 146, and Peter Verniero and Paul H. Zoubek, *Interim Report of the State Police Review Team Regarding Allegations of Racial Profiling* (1999), although neither of the last two sources purport to describe Operation Pipeline specifically and the *Interim Report* describes the procedures for stops on the New Jersey roadways in general, not exclusively those conducted under Operation Pipeline.

8. This argument was presented by someone writing shortly after Operation Pipeline commenced. See Mark Ledwin, "The Use of the Drug Courier Profile in Traffic Stops: Valid Police Practice or Fourth Amendment Violation?", *Ohio Northern University Law Review* 15 (1988): 596 ("Although no court has held that a traffic stop based solely on a drug courier profile match fails to meet the Terry standard and is thus per se unconstitutional, it is probably a reasonable conclusion, since it is difficult, if not impossible, to come up with a list of objective characteristics which will distinguish a drug courier from an innocent motorist as they are driving on the highways.") The argument carries some merit, although if made too forcefully, it would cast doubt on the drug courier profile not for constitutional reasons but for practical ones, namely that the factors that comprise the profile have no effect or utility. That probably argues for too much. It is more accurate to say that characteristics giving rise to a reasonable suspicion are more difficult to observe in a moving vehicle, though not impossible to observe.

9. Webb, "DWB," 122–23. For cases in which courts were critical of Vogel's methods, see *United States v. Smith*, 799 F.2d 704 (11th Cir. 1986) and *United States v. Miller*, 812 F.2d 546 (11th Cir. 1987).

10. The "plain view" doctrine is one of the many well-established exceptions to the general Fourth Amendment requirement that law enforcement officials have a warrant before seizing a person's property. It is generally allowed when the initial stop of the person is independently justified, and, in the course of conducting that initial stop, the officials see something that is readily visible and that is immediately apparent as evidence of a crime. See *Horton v. California*, 496 U.S. 128 (1990). The plain view doctrine has frequently been invoked to justify the discovery and seizure of illegal drugs in drug cases, drawing skeptical reactions from

defense attorneys and some judges. In a widely circulated (and perhaps apocryphal) story, one judge in New York City is said to have observed that if there was as much cocaine lying in plain view as police officers testify to in court, the residents of New York would be ankle deep in the stuff.

11. See, e.g., *Michigan v. Long*, 463 U.S. 1032 (1983); *United States v. Trigg*, 925 F.2d 1064 (7th Cir. 1991) (upholding seizure of cocaine found in search incident to traffic arrest); *United States v. Scopo*, 19 F.3d 777 (2d Cir. 1994) (upholding seizure of illegal firearm found in search of defendant's "grab space" and in plain view following stop for violating various motor vehicle laws).

12. For a good description of the search options available to law enforcement officials following a traffic stop, see Janet Koven Levit, "Pretextual Traffic Stops: *United States v. Whren* and the Death of *Terry v. Ohio*," *Loyola University Chicago Law Journal* 28 (1996): 150–155.

13. Brief of Defendants in appeal in *State of New Jersey v. Soto*, available at *www.whbuckman.com* (April 2002).

14. "Occupant Identifiers for a Possible Drug Courier." A copy of this document is reproduced in the appendix of this book. It was part of the case in the litigation that produced the New Jersey court case, *State v. Soto*, 734 A.2d 350 (1996). We will discuss *Soto* in greater detail later.

15. Webb, "DWB," 122. This is not to suggest that Operation Pipeline, either on its own terms or as practiced, operated in a monolithic fashion. Nor was Operation Pipeline the only, or even the first, effort by law enforcement to develop procedures for catching drug traffickers on the highway (development of Operation Pipeline by DEA agents was itself influenced by efforts by law enforcement in New Mexico and New Jersey to catch drug dealers on the highways in the early 1980s). Operation Pipeline was, as noted, primarily concerned with funding and training local law enforcement efforts. It did not attempt to dictate how the program should be carried out, nor did it create procedures that had to be followed. As with any program disseminated to and administered by hundreds of state and local law enforcement agencies, law enforcement officials made adjustments to meet local priorities or needs. Thus, for example, in Pinellas County, Florida, local law enforcement officials operated the practice not by selecting only suspicious-looking vehicles to stop and search but instead by stopping *every* driver who violated the motor vehicle code, except for minor speeders, regardless of whether the troopers were suspicious of the driver, and subjected every driver to the same post-stop procedures to try to insulate the practice from challenge

as discriminatory treatment. And in New Jersey, troopers had begun stopping motorists on the New Jersey Turnpike as part of an effort to search for drugs before Operation Pipeline was created. New Jersey nonetheless got involved in Operation Pipeline in 1986 to stop passenger cars and continued with the program until 1991. After a two-year hiatus, it picked up the program again in 1993; this second time focusing on commercial vehicles and trucks. See Memorandum, George Rover to Alexander Waugh Jr. of New Jersey Department of Law and Public Safety, Re: State Police, April 22, 1997; *United States v. Holloman,* 113 F.3d 192, 193 (11th Cir. 1997); Kenneth Gavsie, "Making the Best of "Whren": The Problems with Pretextual Traffic Stops and the Need for Restraint," *Florida Law Review* 50 (1998): 395–96.

16. Webb, "DWB," 122.

17. See "Occupant Identifiers for a Possible Drug Courier."

18. David A. Harris, "'Driving While Black' and All Other Traffic Offenses: The Supreme Court and Pretextual Traffic Stops," *Journal of Criminal Law & Criminology* 87 (1997): 545.

19. *United States v. Hassan El,* 5 F.3d 726, 730 (4th Cir. 1993).

20. See *United States v. Smith,* 799 F.2d 704 (11th Cir. 1986). In fact, unlike D.E.A. agent Markonni, who was frequently the recipient of admiring remarks by lower court judges for his work with the airport drug courier profile, Trooper Vogel was more often the object of criticism by judges. In addition to *Smith* see *United States v. Miller,* 812 F.2d 546, 550 (11th Cir. 1987) ("The record does not reveal how many unsuccessful searches Trooper Vogel has conducted or how many innocent travelers the officer has detained. Common sense suggests that those numbers may be significant. As well as protecting alleged criminals who are wrongfully stopped or searched, the Fourth Amendment to the Constitution protects these innocent people as well."). That is not to say that every court disapproved of Vogel's methods. At least one court painted him as a lone figure in the battle against drug dealers. One judge, lamenting the failure of the Florida legislature to do more in the fight, wrote, "In effect, Trooper Vogel has been left alone to fight a war without tactical support from Tallahassee in the way of legislative armament." *Cresswell v. State,* 524 So.2d 685, 686 (Fla. Dist. Ct. App. 1988) (Cobb, J., concurring). And, as would be expected, other courts expressed no opinion of Vogel one way or the other. See, e.g., *Esteen v. State,* 503 So.2d 356 (Fla. Dist. Ct. App. 1987). Nor is it to say that when criticism came Vogel was the only recipient; the actions of other law enforcement officials were also questioned. See *United States v. Valdez,* 931 F.2d 1448 (11th Cir. 1991).

21. 799 F.2d at 707–08.
22. See Levit, "Pretextual Traffic Stops," 159–63.
23. *Whren v. United States*, 517 U.S. 806 (1996). *Whren* is a case of tremendous importance to the development of racial profiling and we discuss it at greater length in Chapter 5.
24. See Levit, "Pretextual Traffic Stops," 150–155. Some courts, mostly state courts, have ruled that a stop for a motor vehicle violation does not by itself justify an extensive search of the car or its occupants for evidence of additional crimes, which must still be judged by the more limiting standards of *Terry*, but this approach is not the one generally followed. Compare *Whren* with *Cresswell v. State*, 564 So.2d 480 (Fla. Sup. Ct. 1990); *Whitehead v. State*, 698 A.2d 1115 (Md. App. 1997). On Vogel's reasons for changing tactics, see Webb, "DWB."
25. Levit, "Pretextual Traffic Stops," 155, and Harris, "Driving While Black," 545.
26. See discussion in Chapter 2.
27. See *State v. Johnson*, 561 So.2d 1139, 1140, n.2 (Fla. 1990). In describing his profile, Vogel did not describe specific characteristics that prompted him to suspect drivers of carrying drugs but only ten general factors, such as the age of the driver, the type and year of the vehicle, the presence of CB or radar detectors and the time of day he saw the car. The court noted that Vogel's profile differed in some regards from the Florida Highway Patrol's own profile, upon which Vogel claimed he did not rely. Ibid., 1141.
28. Gary Webb, *Report on "Operation Pipeline,"* prepared for California Legislature Task Force on Government Oversight (1999), 13. Available at *www.aclunc.org/discrimination/webb-report.html* (April 2002).
29. The characteristics listed in the next few paragraphs are drawn from the following sources: "Vehicle Identifiers for a Possible Drug Courier," distributed by the New Jersey State Police to its troopers—produced as a document in the case of *State of New Jersey v. Soto*, and available at the website of attorney William H. Buckman *www.whbuckman.com* (April 2002); a profile distributed by the DEA office in Miami and reprinted in) Joseph P. D'Ambrosio, "The Drug Courier Profile and Airport Stops: Reasonable Intrusions or Suspicionless Stops?" *Nova Law Review* 12 (1987), 289 n.120; a list of profile characteristics available online at *www.ncseedexpress.com* (April 2002); Webb, "California Operation Pipeline Report"; Webb, "DWB," 122–23; Baum, *Smoke and Mirrors*, 193.
30. In *United States v. Smith*, 80 F.3d 215 (7th Cir. 1996), a hanging air freshener not only led the police to suspect the driver was carrying

drugs but was also the basis for the stop as an unlawful obstruc-
tion of the windshield. Characterizing it as a close call, the court
upheld the stop as a valid traffic stop.

31. Harris, "Driving While Black," 546.

32. DEA Briefing Book, DEA Programs "Foreign Cooperative Investi-
    gations," available at *www.usdoj.gov/dea/briefingbook* (April
    2002), 15.

33. See David Kocieniewski, "New Jersey Argues That the U.S. Wrote
    the Book on Race Profiling," *New York Times,* November 29,
    2000, A1; and Ron Marisco and Kathy Barrett Carter, "State Ties
    Profiling to Advice on Crime Fighting," *Star-Ledger* (Newark), No-
    vember 28, 2000, 26; David A. Harris, *Profiles in Injustice* (New
    York: The New Press, 2002), 48–50.

34. Drug Enforcement Administration, *New Jersey Field Division
    Threat Assessment* (1995), 9–12.

35. U.S. Department of Justice Drug Enforcement Administration,
    "The National Narcotics Intelligence Consumers Committee Re-
    port 1996," 2; Jeffrey Goldberg, "The Color of Suspicion," *New
    York Times Magazine,* June 20, 1999, 50–57.

36. Compare Harris, *Profiles In Injustice,* p. 49, with Memorandum,
    George Rover to Alexander Waugh and Jack Fahy, April 22, 1997,
    p. 4. Harris' assessment that the message from the DEA was
    "mixed" is further compromised for, as even he notes, the DEA
    also taught local police that race could be one of many factors
    they considered.

37. See "Vehicle Identifiers for a Possible Drug Courier"; Ambrosio,
    "The Drug Courier Profile and Airport Stops," n.120; Baum,
    Smoke and Mirrors, 192; Harris, *Profiles in Injustice,* 61.

38. The case is reported at 734 A.2d 350 (N.J.Super.Ct.Law Div.
    1996). We discuss *Soto* more fully in Chapter 5.

39. See Brief of Appellee, *State v. Soto.* Available at *www.whbuck
    man.com* (April 2002). Testimony to this effect by the New Jersey
    State Troopers was also noted in the local media at the time it
    was offered. See, e.g., Tom Hester, "Using Race To Stop Cars Is Al-
    leged," *Star-Ledger* (Newark), March 12, 1996.

40. "Memorandum," Debra Stone to Paul Zoubek, Re: Problems and
    Issues in Division of State Police, February 22, 1999.

41. "Memorandum," Debra Stone to Paul Zoubek, Re: Interview with
    State Police, March 5, 1999.

42. Harris, *Profiles in Injustice,* 48–49; *United States v. Harvey,* 16 F.3d
    109, 113 (6th Cir. 1993) (Keith, J., dissenting); "Presumed Guilty:
    Part Two: The Way You Look Tonight" *Pittsburgh Post-Gazette,*
    February 27, 1991; David Cole, *No Equal Justice: Race and Class in
    the American Criminal Justice System* (New York: New Press,

1999), 49; Angela Anita Allen-Bell, "The Birth of the Crime: Driving While Black," *Southern University Law Review* 25 (Fall 1997) 195; Gene Callahan and William Anderson, "The Roots of Racial Profiling," *Reason* 4 (Aug/Sept. 2001), 36; Angela J. Davis, "Race, Cops and Traffic Stops," *University of Miami Law Review* 51 (1997): 432 (discussing Ohio lawsuit); Tracey Maclin, "Race and the Fourth Amendment," *Vanderbilt Law Review* 51 (1998): 344–46 (1998) (discussing Avon, Connecticut, incident quoting Kathleen Gorman, "Avon Police Target Black, Hispanic Drivers, Report Says," *Hartford Courant,* April 13, 1994, A1). The Avon, Connecticut, effort is a variation on the theme, in that the supposed purpose of the targeting in that instance was not to catch and arrest drug dealers but rather to keep minority drug dealers (and perhaps minorities engaged in other conduct) out of the community. Ibid.

43. "California Operation Pipeline Report," 3.
44. See Jeff Brazil and Steve Berry, "Color of Driver is Key to Stops in I-95 Videos," *Orlando Sentinel,* August 23, 1992; Sean Hecker, "Race and Pretextual Traffic Stops: An Expanded Role for Civilian Review Board," *Columbia Human Rights Law Review* 28 (Spring 1997): 559–651.
45. See American Civil Liberties Union Freedom Network, Report of John Lamberth, Ph.D. (1996), available at *www.aclu.org/court/Lamberth.htm* [hereinafter "Lamberth Report"], prepared in connection with *Wilkins v. Maryland State Police,* No. CCB-93–468 (D.Md.) (settlement approved January 5, 1995) For a summary of these suits, see Milton Heumann and Lance Cassak, "Profiles in Justice?—Police, Discretion, Symbolic Assailants and Stereotyping," *Rutgers Law Review* 53 (Summer 2001). Note also that these are data collected on highways and not from police stops on the streets. For a discussion of what the authors see as discriminatory order maintenance policing in New York City, see Jeffrey Fagan and Garth Davies, "Street Stops and Broken Windows: *Terry,* Race, and Disorder in New York City," *Fordham Law Review* 28 (2000): 464.
46. Ibid.
47. Ibid.
48. Ibid.
49. Ibid.
50. Ibid. ("5,354 of 5,741, or 93.3% . . . were violating traffic laws . . . ").
51. Ibid. ("Of the violators, 17.5% were black, and 74.7% were white").
52. Ibid. ("Between January 1995 and September 1996, the Maryland State Police reported searching 823 motorists on I-95 . . .").

53. Ibid.
54. See Kathy Barrett Carter and Michael Raphael, "Minority Arrests Spur Probe of Troopers," *Star-Ledger* (Newark), February 11, 1999, 1; Milton Heumann and Lance Cassak, "Profiles in Justice?—Police, Discretion, Symbolic Assailants and Stereotyping," *Rutgers Law Review* 53 (Summer 2001) (discussing the Lamberth Report).
55. See *State of New Jersey v. Soto,* 734 A.2d at 352 (referring to a 1993 survey whereby 98.1% of vehicles that violated traffic laws, 15% contained black occupants); Heumann and Cassak, "Profiles in Justice?" (discussing the Lamberth Report).
56. Kathy Barrett Carter and Michael Raphael, "Minority Arrests"; see also *State of New Jersey v. Soto,* 734 A.2d. 350 (N.J. Super. Ct. Law Div. 1996).
57. See Lamberth Report ("Data reported by MSP for motorist searches conducted outside the I-95 corridor is markedly different from that reported by troopers patrolling I-95").
58. Ibid.
59. Ibid. (finding that 12 out of 13 state troopers "searched blacks and other minority motorists at much higher rates than these motorists travel on the highway").
60. Ibid. (reporting results in table form—Table 2).
61. Ibid.
62. Indeed, a recent report argues specifically that racial profiling is quite inefficacious: "Racial profiling not only constitutes discrimination against people of color, it is also simply an unsound, inefficient method of policing." See "Components of Racial Profiling Legislation" (Mar. 5, 2001) available online at: *www.1.umn.edu/irp/publications/racialprofiling.html*. The percentage of cars stopped for pretextual reasons that are found to be actually carrying contraband is extremely low. In 1991, the California Patrol Canine Unit stopped and searched 34,000 vehicles as part of Operation Pipeline. Of the 34,000 vehicles stopped, only 2% contained any illegal drugs. Programs such as Operation Pipeline have been frequently cited as relying heavily on racial profiling.
    A comparable argument has been made by David Harris:

    > Other statistics on both drug use and drug crime show something surprising in light of the usual beliefs many hold: blacks may not, in fact, be more likely than whites to be involved with drugs. The U.S. Customs Service, which is engaged in drug interdiction efforts at nation's airports, has used various types of invasive searches from pat downs to body cavity searches against travelers suspected

of drug use. The Custom Service's own nationwide figures show that while over 43% of those subjected to these searches were either black or Hispanic, "hit rates" for these searches were actually lower for both blacks and Hispanics than for whites.

See David A. Harris, "The Stories, The Statistics, and the Law: Why 'Driving While Black' Matters," *Minnesota Law Review* 84 (1999): 269–75.

A competing argument suggests the deterrent effect that results from a profiling policy. Jonathan Alter notes that the former New York City Policy Commissioner William Bratton opposes profiling, while also calling attention to its deterrent effect. Restating Bratton's position and the views of a number of other prosecutors with whom Alter spoke, Alter notes their view that "in recent years young blacks in Harlem have known the police were stopping them and searching for guns, so they stopped carrying weapons, a major contributor to the reduction in crime." Jonathan Alter, "Hillary Raises Her Profile," *Newsweek*, June 25, 2001, 34.

63. See Lamberth Report.
64. Ibid. It should be noted that a recent paper raises questions about the assertion that cops on I-95 in Maryland are participating in racial profiling. See generally John Knowles et al., "National Bureau of Economic Research, Working Paper 7449: Racial Bias in Motor Vehicle Searches: Theory and Evidence" (Dec. 1999). Available at: *www.nber.org/papers/w7449*. The authors contend that the higher search rate of blacks may not be due to race, at least not directly, but rather to other unobservable traits that may be indirectly correlated with race, and they label this practice "statistical discrimination." In effect, under statistical discrimination, the cost for the police officer of searching white or black motorists is equal [TA = TW], but the probability of the two races being searched by a police officer is not equal [Y(C,W) does not = Y(C,A)] because of the C term. The variable C is probative about the possible guilt of defendants, which determines stops and searches; C may correlate with race, but under the theory of statistical discrimination, it is the examination of a variable, not race, which explains stops and searches. Therefore, police officers looking to maximize their efficiency and arrest numbers will be particularly keen on motorists with a certain C, as opposed to those not characterized by C. Consequently, blacks who are stopped and searched, are stopped and searched because they disproportionately display C, not because of race. It

should be noted that there is no contention by the authors that this practice is not discriminatory. Rather, the point the authors are trying to make is that economic or statistical discrimination motivates police behavior, not racial discrimination

This issue of fairness in this type of policing remains. The data from I-95 in Maryland that Lamberth collected indicated that while the guilt rates of African Americans and whites are comparable, a much greater number of African Americans are pulled over than whites. See Lamberth Report. This incongruity in data leads one to question whether efficiency or the guilt rate would be sacrificed if police officers conducted stops and searches of African Americans at a number proportional to their population as motorists.

The supplementary data provided by Knowles et al. seemed to suggest the answer is "no." Furthermore, additional data collected from Maryland showed that the rate of recovery of contraband during searches of African Americans was 28.4% while it was 28.8% for whites; however, blacks were searched at a disproportionately higher rate. See Lamberth Report. Comparable results can be obtained from the New Jersey Turnpike arrest data, which shows that 10.5% of searches involving white motorists resulted in arrest, and 18.5% of searches involving blacks resulted in arrests. Deborah Ramirez et al., "A Resource Guide on Racial Profiling Data Collection Systems: Promising Practices and Lessons Learned," (Nov. 2000). This minimal difference in fruitful searches suggests that the disproportionate rate of stopping blacks may be difficult to defend. Before any conclusive theory can be maintained, however, more research needs to be conducted on the change in proportion of stops and searches of blacks and the consequent decline, increase, or steadiness of the guilt rate.

Finally, we note a controversial study of driving patterns on the New Jersey Turnpike suggests that minorities are stopped more frequently simply because they drive at higher speeds. See David Kocieniewski, "Study Suggests Racial Gap in Speeding in New Jersey," *New York Times*, March 21, 2002, B1. However, as one commentator has pointed out, even if one assumes minority drivers were more often guilty of the traffic offenses than white drivers, that still does not mean that race was not a factor in the decisions of police to stop them, given the broad discretion the law affords police in this area and the large percentage of drivers violating the law who are not stopped. See Sean Hecker, "Race and Pretextual Traffic Stops: An Expanded Role for Civilian Review Board," *Columbia Human Rights Law Review* 28 (Spring 1997): 566–70.

65. For more detailed discussions of these data, see Heumann and Cassak, "Profiles in Justice?", 929–34; Tracey Maclin, "Race and the Fourth Amendment," *Vanderbilt Law Review* 51 (1998): 341–352; Lamberth Report. For a more general discussion of stop and arrest data demonstrating unjustifiable profiling, see Peter Verniero and Paul Zoubek, "Interim Report of the State Police Review Team Regarding Allegations of Racial Profiling," April 20, 1999.

66. The differential stop rate by race is not limited to the United States. A recent study in Great Britain found that blacks were over seven times more likely to be stopped than were whites despite the fact that the arrest rates for blacks and whites were close to equal. See Deborah Ramirez et al., "A Resource Guide on Racial Profiling Data Collection Systems," 8.

67. See for example the comments made by the head of the New Jersey State Police, Colonel Carl Williams, who, by identifying certain countries and ethnic groups with the drug trade, raised the issue of experience-based assessments of ethnic associations of particular crimes. Robert D. McFadden, "Whitman Dismisses Police Chief for Race Remarks," *New York Times*, March 1, 1999, A1. Were the comments of the 35-year veteran chief of the New Jersey State Police about ethnic associations with particular crimes legitimate experienced-based assessments or inappropriate ethnic and racial stereotyping? For more on Williams' comments and their fallout, see chapter 4.

68. John Lambert, "Driving While Black: A Statistician Proves That Prejudice Still Rules the Road," *Washington Post*, August 16, 1998; "Fattah, Foglietta Attack 'Profiling'" *Philadelphia Tribune*, August 9, 1996; David A. Harris, "Driving While Black, Racial Profiling on Our Nation's Highways, " ACLU Special Report (1999), 18–24, Heumann and Cassak, "Profiles in Justice?"; James Forman, Jr., "Arrested Development," *The New Republic*, September 10, 2001; David A. Harris, "When Success Breeds Attack: The Coming Backlash Against Racial Profiling Studies," *Michigan Journal of Race & Law* 6 (2001): 244–47.

69. Sunni Khalid, "Morning Edition," *National Public Radio*, September 30, 1997.

70. See Brazil and Berry, "Color of Driver"; "Without Just Cause," WWOR Television Report (1989); "Presumed Guilty: Part Two: The Way You Look Tonight," *Pittsburgh Post-Gazette*, February 27, 1991; Christo Lassiter, "Eliminating Consent from the Lexicon of Traffic Stop Interrogations," *Capital University Law Review* 27 (1998): 115–122. The *Pittsburgh Post-Gazette* series actually discussed a variety of police tactics in addition to stops on the highway, including stops at airports and seizure of money.

71. Peter Noel, "Driving While Black," *The Village Voice*, June 9, 1998; Heumann and Cassak, "Profiles in Justice?", 901–02; J. Zamgba Browne, "ACLU To Challenge Maryland State Police over Racial Profiling," *New York Amsterdam News*, June 17, 1998.

72. See David A. Harris, "The Stories, The Statistics, and the Law: Why 'Driving While Black' Matters," *Minnesota Law Review* 84 (1999), 269–75.

73. For these and other stories, see Davis, "Race, Cops and Traffic Stops," 438, 440; Jennifer A. Larabee, "'DWB (Driving While Black)' and Equal Protection: The Realities of an Unconstitutional Police Practice," *Journal of Law & Policy* 6 (1997): 291; Harris, *Profiles in Injustice*, pp. 48–72. Ibid., "ACLU Special Report"; Noel, "Driving While Black"; Heumann and Cassak, "Profiles in Justice?" We discuss the response of New Jersey officials to allegations of racial profiling in the next chapter.

CHAPTER 4

1. David Rudovsky, "The Impact of the War on Drugs on Procedural Fairness and Racial Equality," *University of Chicago Legal Forum* (1994): 237; Michael Tonry, *Malign Neglect: Race, Crime and Punishment in America* (New York: Oxford University Press, 1995), 81–123; Milton Heumann and Lance Cassak, "Profiles in Justice?—Police, Discretion, Symbolic Assailants and Stereotyping," *Rutgers Law Review* 53 (Summer 2001): 917–18.

2. For a brief summary, see Angela Anita Allen-Bell, "The Birth of the Crime: Driving While Black (DWB)," *Southern University Law Review* 25 (Fall 1997): 195; see also Chapters 2 and 3.

3. See Wayne R. LeFave, "Controlling Discretion by Administrative Regulations: The Use, Misuse, and Non-use of Police Rules and Policies in Fourth Amendment Adjudication," *Michigan Law Review* 89 (1990): 442, 502–506; Sean Hecker, "Race and Pretextual Traffic Stops: An Expanded Role for Civilian Review Board," *Columbia Human Rights Law Review* 28 (Spring 1997): 551, 555–58.

4. David Cole, "See No Evil, Hear No Evil," quoted in Craig J. Glantz, "Could This Be the End of the Fourth Amendment for Motorists: *Whren v. United States* 116 S.Ct. 1769 (1996)" *Journal of Criminal Law and Criminology* 87 (Spring 1997): 884.

5. Wesley MacNeil Oliver, "With an Evil Eye and an Unequal Hand: Pretextual Stops and Doctrinal Remedies to Racial Profiling," *Tulane Law Review* 74 (2000): 1412.

6. Janet Koven Levit, "Pretextual Traffic Stops: *United States v. Whren* and the Death of *Terry v. Ohio*," *Loyola University Chicago*

Law Journal 28 (1996): 155; Glantz, "Could This Be the End of the Fourth Amendment for Motorists," 885. See also David A. Harris, "'Driving While Black' and All Other Traffic Offenses: The Supreme Court and Pretextual Traffic Stops," *Journal of Criminal Law & Criminology* 87 (1997): 544–47; Hecker, Race and Pretextual Traffic Stops," 555–558.

7. Remarks of Reverend Donald Jackson, "Colonel Williams Speaks," *60 Minutes II,* October 19, 1999.

8. "Jim Crow Policing," *ACLU-NJ Civil Liberties Report,* 2nd Quarter (1999), 1.

9. Ira Glasser, "American Drug Laws: The New Jim Crow," *Albany Law Review* 63 (2000): 706. For an analysis that attempts to place profiling, including airport drug courier profiles and highway drug courier profiles, within the context of other types of racial discrimination by law enforcement, see Erika L. Johnson, "'A Menace to Society': The Use of Criminal Profiles and Its Effect on Black Males," *Howard Law Journal* 38 (1995): 629.

10. David A. Harris, "The Stories, The Statistics, and the Law: Why 'Driving While Black' Matters," *Minnesota Law Review* 84 (1999): 292.

11. Lisa Walter, "Eradicating Racial Stereotyping from *Terry* Stops: The Case for an Equal Protection Exclusionary Rule," *University of Colorado Law Review* 71 (2000): 276.

12. Hecker, "Race and Pretextual Traffic Stops," 566–71.

13. David Cole, "Race, Policing, and the Future of the Criminal Law," *Human Rights* (Summer 1999), 3.

14. Forman, "Arrested Development," *The New Republic* September 10, 2001.

15. Harris, "Stories and Statistics," 273.

16. Jackson is quoted and his encounter with the police is recounted in Randall Kennedy, *Race, Crime and the Law* (New York: Pantheon Books, 1997), 152.

17. Harris, "Stories and Statistics," 271–72, 274; Maurice Possley, "Minority Drivers Feel Like Moving Targets," *Chicago Tribune,* April 4, 1999.

18. See Kennedy, *Race, Crime and the Law,* 144–163.

19. Verniero quoted in Kathy Barrett Carter, "Verniero Documented His Own Indifference," *Star-Ledger (Newark),* November 28, 2000, p. A1. On the repeated denials of New Jersey officials, even after court rulings and other evidence of racial profiling, see Tom Hester, "Using Race to Stop Cars Is Alleged," *Star-Ledger (Newark),* March 12, 1996; "State to Challenge Ruling Troopers Targeted Drivers," *The Record,* May 2, 1996; David Kocieniewski, "U.S. to Open Civil Rights Inquiry in New Jersey Turnpike Shooting," *New*

York Times, November 4, 2000; David Kocieniewski and Robert Hanley, "Racial Profiling Was Routine, New Jersey Finds," *New York Times,* November 28, 2000. The state court case finding a practice of targeting minority drivers in *State of New Jersey v. Soto.*

20. Robert D. McFadden, "Whitman Dismisses State Police Chief for Race Remarks," *New York Times,* March 1, 1999, A1; Heumann and Cassak, "Profiles in Justice?", 912; David Harris, *Profiles in Injustice: Why Racial Profiling Cannot Work* (New York: New Press, 2002), 53–60. On racial profiling specifically, Williams said, "As far as racial profiling is concerned, that is absolutely not right. It never has been condoned in the State Police and it never will be condoned in the State Police." It has been suggested that the comments by Williams may have been a politically correct defense of racial profiling, condemning it specifically but indirectly claiming that the practice works. See Samuel R. Gross and Debra Livingston, "Racial Profiling Under Attack," *Columbia Law Review* 102 (June 2002): 1413, 1421–22.

21. Peter Verniero and Paul H. Zoubek, *Interim Report of the State Police Review Team Regarding Allegations of Racial Profiling* (1999), 3–7.

22. On criticism of Verniero and Whitman see, e.g., David Kocieniewski, "Whitman and Verniero Face Charges of Hiding Information," *New York Times,* October 10, 1999; David Kocieniewski, "Bias Permeates State Police, Whitman Admits," *New York Times,* July 3, 1999; Paula Zahn, "New Jersey Governor Christie Todd Whitman Gets Caught Up in Racial Profiling," *Fox News, The Edge With Paula Zahn,* July 11, 2000; Wendy Ruderman, "Verniero Facing Probe on Profiling Documents," *The Record,* October 17, 2000; David Kocieniewski, "Race Profiling by Troopers Under Review by Legislature," *New York Times,* October 17, 2000; Mark Mueller and Kathy Barrett Carter, "The Road Ahead; After Revelations of Bias Can the State Police Steer From a Stormy Past Toward Reform?" *Star-Ledger (Newark),* December 3, 2000; "Posturing on the Racial Issue; Gore and Bradley Fence on Profiling By Police," *The Record,* February 25, 2000; "The Frisking Photo; Smart Woman, Foolish Choice," *The Record,* July 13, 2000. On Whitman's problems going through the confirmation process, see, "Minority Leaders Assail EPA Nominee Whitman," *San Diego Union Tribune,* January 12, 2001. On state officials' efforts to blame the DEA, see David Kocieniewski, "New Jersey Argues That the U.S. Wrote the Book on Race Profiling," *New York Times,* November 29, 2000. Verneiro also attempted (largely unsuccessfully) to shift blame to the state troopers accused of racial profiling. Kathy Barrett Carter, "Verniero Answers Racial Profiling Critics on Work as AG," *Star-Ledger (Newark),* December 2, 2000.

23. We discuss the Department of Justice's efforts in New Jersey and other states in greater detail, including a description of the terms of the consent decree, in Chapter 5.

24. Mark Mueller and Kathy Barrett Carter, "The Road Ahead; After Revelations of Bias Can the State Police Steer From a Stormy Past Toward Reform?" *Star-Ledger (Newark)*, December 3, 2000; Kathy Barrett Carter, "Profiling Evidence Uncovered in 1989; Kean Aide Says He Regrets His Silence," *Star-Ledger (Newark)*, June 14, 2001.

25. Harris, *Profiles in Injustice*, 48–62; Hecker, "Race and Pretextual Traffic Stops," 559–64.

26. Jeffrey Goldberg, "The Color of Suspicion," *New York Times Magazine*, June 20, 1999, 56.

27. Heather MacDonald, "The Myth of Racial Profiling," *City Journal* 11 (Spring 2001). MacDonald's defense was given much broader circulation, though in summary form, by nationally syndicated columnist George F. Will. See *Seattle Post-Intelligencer*, April 19, 2001.

28. Clayton Searle, "Profiling in Law Enforcement," posted at *www.inia.org/whats-new-presidents.htm*.

29. Jackson Toby, "'Racial Profiling' Doesn't Prove Cops Are Racist," *Wall Street Journal*, March 11, 1999, B5.

30. Jill Labbe, "Still, Profiling Fills a Societal Purpose in Fighting Crime," *Akron Beacon Journal*, April 24, 2001; see also MacDonald, "The Myth of Racial Profiling."

31. Fred McGuiggan, Jr., "Racial Profiling: Who Is Stereotyping Whom?" Available online at: *www.domelights.com/racprof1.htm* (April 2002).

32. Jeffrey Goldberg, "The Color of Suspicion," 54.

33. Ibid.

34. Ibid.

35. Ibid.

36. William Stuntz, "Local Policing After the Terror," *Yale Law Journal* 111 (June 2002) 2137, 2178–79. Stuntz made the point as part of an argument that preventing police from considering race is probably impossible and not the right focus in any event; what should be regulated, he claims, is not *whom* the police decide to stop but *how* they conduct those stops. See Chapter 6.

37. For the first such articles, see "Utah Troopers Seize Couriers in Cocaine Lane," *San Diego Union-Tribune*, October 8, 1987; "Utah Route Rough For Drug Couriers; State Patrol Denies Targeting Hispanics," *Washington Post*, December 25, 1987.

38. The first use of the term racial profiling as a type of police conduct in the media that we found, employing Westlaw as a search

engine, was a very brief reference in the "Public Pulse" section of the *Omaha World-Herald*, October 24, 1994, and again two months later in Jon Nordheimer, "New Jersey Troopers Accused of Bias in Traffic Stops," *Patriot Ledger*, December 23, 1994.

39. See Henry Louis Gates, "Thirteen Ways of Looking at a Black Man," *The New Yorker*, October 23, 1995, 59. The characterizations also expanded as different ethnic groups added other formulations. Some in the southwestern United States, for example, insisted that there was also the offense of 'Driving While Mexican." See Victor C. Romero, "Racial Profiling: 'Driving While Mexican' and Affirmative Action," *Michigan Journal of Race and Law* 6 (Fall 2000): 195.

40. In a law review article published in 1997, David Harris commented on the phrase "Driving While Black," indicating that he had heard the phrase used by clients he represented from the minority community before it had become used regularly in the media. See Harris, "'Driving While Black' and All Other Traffic Offenses: The Supreme Court and Pretextual Traffic Stops," 546, n.10. The same is almost certainly true of the phrase "racial profiling" as well; it probably was used informally in casual conversation before being picked up by the media.

41. *Washington v. Lambert*, 98 F.3d 1181, 1182, n.2 (9th Cir. 1996); Rudovsky, "Law Enforcement by Stereotypes and Serendipity," 298, n.25.

42. According to *web.lexis-nexis.com/universe*, when the search term "racial profiling" was entered in 1998, it returned 177 matches; in 1999, the same search returned 927 matches; and in 2000 and 2001 matches surpassed 1,000.

43. The shootings on the New Jersey Turnpike received considerable coverage, or at least mention, in newspapers beyond the New Jersey and metropolitan New York papers that cover New Jersey as a regular part of their territory. Coverage of the Turnpike shootings was frequently grouped with other instances of alleged racial profiling. See, e.g., Richard Weizel, "Police Memo Sparks Review on Alleged Targeting of Blacks," *Boston Globe*, July 19, 1998 (discussing New Jersey shootings and incidents in Maryland); Michael Paul Williams, "Report Cites Human Rights Ills in U.S.," *Richmond Times Dispatch*, October 26, 1998; Michael Janofsky, "Suit Accuses Maryland Police of Prejudice," *Portland Oregonian*, June 5, 1998. Interest in the Turnpike shootings "had legs" as the saying goes, beyond the initial incident. Thus, when the troopers involved were indicted for their actions, that, too, received mention nationwide. See, e.g., Katherine Shaver, "On Patrol, Race Shadows Police; Montgomery Officers Say Experience Colors,"

Washington Post, September 26, 1999; "NJ Troopers Indicted in Racial Profiling Case; Three Wounded in '98 Incident," *Cincinnati Post,* September 9, 1999; "Two Troopers Charged in Shootings of Minority Motorists," *Chicago Tribune,* September 8, 1999.

44. The incident in Trumbell found its way into the *Chicago Tribune* and the Associated Press Wire Services. See Maurice Possley, "Minority Drivers Feel Like Moving Targets," *Chicago Tribune,* April 4, 1999; Adam Gorlick, "FBI Finds Insufficient Evidence of Racial Profiling in Trumbull," Associated Press Newswires, July 24, 1999. See also Erin Texeira, "Racially-motivated Traffic Stops May Be Easier to Prove with Bill," *Houston Chronicle,* August 16, 1998 (discussing events in Maryland).

45. *New Jersey Interim Report,* 53.

46. Rudovsky, "Law Enforcement by Stereotypes and Serendipity," 299, n.27; Fred McGuiggan, Jr., "Racial Profiling: Who Is Stereotyping Whom?"

47. Jeffrey Goldberg, "The Color of Suspicion," 85; Gaiutra Bahadur, "Civil Rights Leaders Ask Texas for Death Penalty Moratorium," *Austin American Statesman,* August 30, 2000, 23; "March Will Protest Racial Profiling, Execution," *St. Louis Post-Dispatch,* June 24, 2000, 23; Gail Collins, "The Case of Wen Ho Lee Unravels," *Pittsburgh Post-Gazette,* August 30, 2000, sec. A23; Vernon Loeb and Walter Pincus, "Lee Could Be Freed on Bail Friday," *Washington Post,* August 30, 2000, sec. A3. "Dolpho, the Police Dog Cleared of Racial Profiling Charges," *Associated Press Newswires,* August 17, 2002.

48. Neely Tucker, "Domino's Wins DC Bias Suit Ruling; Customer Fought Delivery Policy," *Washington Post,* October 11, 2000; Stuart Taylor, Jr., "Cabbies, Cops, Pizza Deliveries, and Racial Profiling," *National Journal,* June 17, 2000.

CHAPTER 5

1. David A. Sklansky, "Traffic Stops, Minority Motorists, and the Future of the Fourth Amendment," *Supreme Court Review* (1997): 316; Michael Klarman, "The Racial Origins of Modern Criminal Procedure," *Michigan Law Review* 99 (2000): 48.

2. Adina Schwartz, "'Just Take Away Their Guns': The Hidden Racism of *Terry v. Ohio,*" *Fordham Urban Law Journal* 23 (1996): 317; James T. Patterson, *Grand Expectations* (New York: Oxford University Press, 1996), 664; Irwin Unger and Debi Unger, *Turning Point: 1968* (New York: Scribner, 1988), 184–85.

3. See Anthony Thompson, "Stopping the Usual Suspects: Race and

the Fourth Amendment," *New York University Law Review* 74 (1999): 956. Others have also noted the importance of the petitioners' race to the decision. See also Tracey Maclin, "Race and the Fourth Amendment," *Vanderbilt Law Review* 51 (1998): 1271; Ibid., "Race and the Fourth Amendment," 333; Schwartz, "Just Take Away Their Guns," 317.

4. Schwartz, "Just Take Away Their Guns," 336–38.
5. 392 U.S. at 14 and n.11.
6. Ibid., 23.
7. Schwartz, "Just Take Away Their Guns," 339, 341; Thompson, "Stopping the Usual Suspects," 971.
8. 422 U.S. 873, 886–87 (1975).
9. 428 U.S. 543, 563 (1976). In its opinion, the Court also cited statistical data suggesting that border patrol officers considered more than merely race in deciding whom to stop. Ibid., 563–64, n.16, 17.
10. 517 U.S. 806 (1996).
11. See discussion in Chapter 3.
12. Among the many commentators to focus on the treatment of race in the decision in *Whren* are Sklansky, "Traffic Stops, Minority Motorists, and the Future of the Fourth Amendment," 271; David A. Harris, "'Driving While Black' and All Other Traffic Offenses: The Supreme Court and Pretextual Traffic Stops," *Journal of Criminal Law & Criminology* 87 (1997): 544; Angela J. Davis, "Race, Cops and Traffic Stops," *University of Miami Law Review* 51 (1997): 432; Maclin, "Race and the Fourth Amendment," 344–46; Anthony Thompson, "Stopping the Usual Suspects: Race and the Fourth Amendment," 956.
13. 517 U.S. at 813, 817.
14. Among those making this point are Sklansky, "Traffic Stops, Minority Motorists, and the Future of the Fourth Amendment," 278–79; Maclin, "Race and the Fourth Amendment," 362; Thompson, "Stopping the Usual Suspects: Race and the Fourth Amendment," 981–82; Abraham Abramovsky and Jonathan I. Edelstein, "Pretext Stops and Racial Profiling After *Whren v. United States:* The New York and New Jersey Responses Compared," *Albany Law Review* 63 (2000): 732–33.
15. See, for example, *Delaware v. Prouse,* 440 U.S. 658 (1979), in which the Court ruled that random road stops—those based on neither a reasonable suspicion that a crime had been committed nor upon witnessing a violation of the motor vehicle code—were impermissible under the Fourth Amendment, and *Tennessee v. Garner,* 471 U.S. 1 (1985), dealing with the use of deadly force in stopping a fleeing felon. For fuller discussions of this feature of

the Court's criminal justice jurisprudence, see Maclin, "Race and the Fourth Amendment," 338–40; Thompson, "Stopping the Usual Suspects: Race and the Fourth Amendment," 974–83

16. Sklansky, "Traffic Stops, Minority Motorists, and the Future of the Fourth Amendment," 291.

17. David A. Harris, "'Driving While Black,'"550–552; Sklansky, "Traffic Stops, Minority Motorists, and the Future of the Fourth Amendment," 326; David Rudovsky, "The Impact of the War on Drugs on Procedural Fairness and Racial Equality," *University of Chicago Legal Forum* (1994): 353–58; Sean P. Trende, "Why Modest Proposals Offer the Best Solution for Combating Racial Profiling," *Duke Law Journal* 50 (2000): 350–53; Hecker "Race and Pretextual Traffic Stops," 586–92.

18. 221 F.3d 329 (2d.Cir. 2000).

19. 221 F.3d at 334–35.

20. Samuel R. Gross and Debra Livingston, "Racial Profiling Under Attack," *Columbia Law Review* 102 (June 2002) pp. 1413, 1435–36. Gross and Livingston do not describe *Brown* as an instance of racial profiling, but they do include it with a number of cases or situations involving police conduct that raise issues similar to the ones raised in racial profiling.

21. See R. Richard Banks, "Race Based Suspect Selection and Colorblind Equal Protection Doctrine and Discourse," *UCLA Law Review,* 48 (June 2001) pp. 1075, 1078, n.8. Banks argues that race-based suspect identifications can be just as harmful a type of discrimination as racial profiling, and as such warrant heightened scrutiny under the Equal Protection Clause.

22. 221 F.3d at 336–41.

23. Milton Heumann and Lance Cassak, "Profiles in Justice?—Police, Discretion, Symbolic Assailants and Stereotyping," *Rutgers Law Review* 53 (Summer 2001): 956–58, 965–68.

24. See Chapter 3.

25. Thompson, "Stopping the Usual Suspects: Race and the Fourth Amendment," 1008; Sean Hecker makes the same point in a slightly different way. It is at least possible under the "reasonable suspicion" test that police might have to defend the use of race in a decision to stop a motorist, argues Hecker, but not so for a traffic stop after *Whren:* "By using pretext stops, police avoid having to defend their use of race altogether." Sean Hecker, "Race and Pretextual Traffic Stops: An Expanded Role for Civilian Review Board," *Columbia Human Rights Law Review* 28 (Spring 1997): 569–70.

26. 734 A.2d 350 (N.J.Super.Ct.Law.Div. 1996).

27. 734 A.2d at 352–57. We discuss some of that testimony and statistical evidence in Chapter 3.

28. Ibid., 361 (citing *New Jersey v. Kuhn*, 517 A.2d 162 [N.J. Super. Ct. App. Div. 1986]).
29. Ibid., 360.
30. Ibid.
31. Ibid., 357.
32. Ibid., 360–61. For those unfamiliar with New Jersey, the Turnpike is the name given to that stretch of I-95 that traverses the state.
33. According to one recent study, only one state high court—the Washington Supreme Court—has rejected *Whren*, relying on its own state constitution to do so. This study also cites one lower appellate state court—from New York—that has also refused to follow *Whren*. See Abramovsky and Edelstein, "Pretext Stops and Racial Profiling After *Whren v. United States:* The New York and New Jersey Responses Compared," 738–39; see also Harris, "Addressing Racial Profiling in the States," 376–77. This is so despite the fact that in other areas regarding police practices, many state courts had been willing to draw upon state constitutional provisions to extend protections further than the rights spelled out by the Supreme Court under the Constitution. See Hecker, "Race and Pretextual Traffic Stops," 583–85.
34. At the time, a number of lower federal courts had held that use of race alone to justify an investigative stop was unconstitutional, a result essentially compelled by the Supreme Court's decision in the *Brignoni-Pierce* case. See, e.g., *United States v. Travis*, 62 F.3d 170 (6th Cir. 1995); *United States v. Manuel*, 992 F.2d 272 (10th Cir. 1993).
35. On the reaction to *Brown v. Board of Education*, including resistance by local communities, including some, although not all, lower federal courts, see James T. Patterson, *Brown v. Board of Education, A Civil Rights Milestone and Its Troubled Legacy* (New York: Oxford University Press, 2001), 86–146; J. Harvie Wilkinson III, *From Brown to Bakke* (New York: Oxford University Press, 1979), Ch.5; J.W. Peltason, *Fifty-Eight Lonely Men* (Urbana, Illinois: University of Illinois Press, 1961); Jack Bass, *Unlikely Heroes* (New York: Simon and Schuster, 1981).
36. See Hecker, "Race and Pretextual Traffic Stops": 581–83.
37. Randall S. Susskind, "Race, Reasonable Articulable Suspicion, and Seizure," *American Criminal Law Review* 31 (994): 335.
38. *United States v. Laymon*, 730 F.Supp. 732, 338–39 (D.Colo. 1990)
39. *United States v. Bridges*, No. 00-CR-210, 2000 WL 1170137 at 5 (S.D.N.Y. 2000); *United States v. Montero-Camargo*, 208 F.3d 1122, 1139 (9th Cir. 2000).
40. See, e.g., *United States v. Taylor*, 917 F.2d 1402 (6th Cir. 1990), rev'd 956 F.2d 572 (6th Cir. 1992); *United States v. Avery*, 137 F.3d

343 (6th Cir. 1997); *Martinez v. Village of Mount Prospect,* 92 F.Supp.2d 780 (N.D.Ill. 2000)

41. *United States v. Coleman,* 450 F. Supp. 433 (E.D.Mich. 1978).
42. *United States v. Weaver,* 966 F.2d 931, 934 n.2 (8th Cir. 1992).
43. *United States v. Armijo,* 781 F.Supp. 1551 (D.N.M. 1991).
44. *Jones v. United States Drug Enforcement Administration,* 819 F.Supp. 698 (M.D.Tenn. 1993).
45. 949 F. 2d 220 (6th Cir. 1993).
46. Ibid., 223.
47. Ibid., 222.
48. See *New Jersey v. Patterson,* 637 A.2d 593 (N.J. .Super.Ct.Law.Div. 1993) *aff'd* 637 A.2d 599 (N.J.Super.Ct.App.Div. 1994); *New Jersey v. Letts,* 603 A.2d 562 (N.J. .Super.Ct.Law.Div. 1992). See also, Abramovsky and Edelstein, "Pretext Stops and Racial Profiling After *Whren v. United States,*" 745–56.
49. See *New Jersey v. Ballard,* 752 A.2d 735, 742 (N.J. Super. Ct. App. Div. 2000). In that case, the court, based on its findings of a policy, allowed discovery of information from the state to explore further the key issues.
50. 788 A.2d 746 (2002).
51. See, e.g., Rocco Cammarere, "Profiling or Valid Search at Airport?" *New Jersey Lawyer,* September 10, 2001, 1.
52. 2002 WL 334169 (N.J. 2002). The New Jersey Supreme Court also cited a decision from Hawaii, handed down prior to both *Soto* and *Whren* that also required that law enforcement have reasonable suspicion of wrongdoing before allowing a search following a traffic stop. *State v. Quino,* 840 P.2d 358 (Haw. 1992), *cert den.* 507 U.S. 1031 (1993).
53. See, e.g., Laura Mansnerus, "High Court in New Jersey Strictly Limits Auto Searches," *New York Times,* March 5, 2002, B1.
54. *Martinez v. Village of Mount Prospect,* 92 F.Supp.2d 780, 782 (N.D. Ill. 2000).
55. 92 F. Supp.2d at 784.
56. David Cole, *No Equal Justice,* 34–36; Davis, "Race, Cops and Traffic Stops," 425; David A. Harris, *Profiles in Injustice* (New York: The New Press, 2002), 60–72. It should be noted that talking about success in these kinds of cases often comes with a caveat or qualifier. The *Wilkins* litigation produced, among other things, a consent order pursuant to which Maryland agreed to stop using race in decisions by police regarding whom to stop on the highways and to compile data on traffic stops in Maryland on the I-95 corridor: that is, who the police were stopping and why. Compilation of that data (including the study in Maryland done by John Lamberth, discussed in Chapter 3) nonetheless, led to accusations

that the police had not stopped targeting minority drivers, denial of those accusations by state officials, and follow-up litigation to sort out the problems. See Sean Hecker, "Race and Pretextual Traffic Stops," 561–64.

57. Harris, *Profiles in Injustice,* 60–72; Trende, "Modest Proposals"; Gary Webb, "DWB," *Esquire,* April 1999, 127.

58. For example, if a pizza delivery man crashes his car into your neighbor's porch, your neighbor has standing to bring suit for the damages suffered, not you, unless, of course, you were standing on the porch at the time.

59. Compare *Maryland State Conference of NAACP Branches v. Maryland Department of State Police,* 72 F.Supp.2d 560 (D.Md. 1999) with *Washington v. Vogel,* 156 F.R.D. 676 (M.D.Fla. 1994). See also Trende, "Modest Proposals," 342–49; Rudofsky, "Law Enforcement by Stereotypes and Serendipity," 355–58.

60. For competing views of the likelihood of success of civil lawsuits challenging racial profiling, compare *Martinez v. Village of Mount Prospect,* 92 F.Supp.2d 780, 782 (N.D. Ill. 2000) with Trende, "Modest Proposals," 342–57; Rudofsky, "Law Enforcement by Stereotypes and Serendipity," 352–58. See also, Harris, *Profiles in Injustice,* 60–72.

61. Angela Anita Allen-Bell, "The Birth of the Crime: Driving While Black (DWB)," *Southern University Law Review* 25 (Fall 1997): 195.

62. See website for the Department of Justice, Civil Rights Division Special Litigation section. Available at: *www.usdoj.gov/crt/split* (April 2002).

63. Ibid. See also Harris, *Profiles in Injustice,* 201–07; Rudofsky, "Law Enforcement by Stereotypes and Serendipity," 358–63.

64. The consent decree entered into between the DOJ and New Jersey can be found at the DOJ's website.

65. See e.g., Harris, *Profiles in Injustice,* 201–07; Rudofsky, "Law Enforcement by Stereotypes and Serendipity," 358–63.

66. Angela Couloumbis, "Improvements Seen in Stops by State Police," *Philadelphia Inquirer,* January 24, 2002. Police representative quoted in Lori Hinnant, "Report: Consent Searches Down Sharply on Turnpike," *Associated Press Newswires,* March 8, 2002. Buckman quoted in "Blacks Still Pulled Over at High Rate on Turnpike," *Star-Ledger (Newark),* June 27, 2002.

67. Alexander Bickel, *The Least Dangerous Branch: The Supreme Court at the Bar of Politics* (Indianapolis: Bobbs Merrill, 1962), pp. 23–28.

68. See, e.g., *City of Boerne v. Flores,* 117 U.S. 2157 (1997). On the current Court's insistence on having the last and perhaps only say on the scope of constitutional rights, see generally, Larry Kramer,

"We the Court," *Harvard Law Review* 115 (November 2001); David Cole, "The Value of Seeing Things Differently: *Boerne v. Flores* and Congressional Enforcement of the Bill of Rights," *Supreme Court Review* (1997): 31; Robert Post and Reva Seigel, "Equal Protection by Law: Federal Antidiscrimination Legislation After *Morrison* and *Kimel*," *Yale Law Journal* 110 (2000): 441.

69. For example, some have claimed that a series of cases in the mid- to late 1960s involving issues related to, but not directly addressing, the constitutionality of the death penalty sent a signal that the Court was prepared to address a direct challenge to that practice, which it did shortly thereafter in *Furman v. Georgia*, 408 U.S. 238 (1972). See Michael Meltsner, *Cruel and Unusual: The Supreme Court and Capital Punishment* (New York: Random House, 1973).

70. See Chapter 3.

71. "Justices OK Wider Police Power to Jail," *Houston Chronicle*, April 25, 2001, sec. 1A.

72. See Gerald Rosenberg, *The Hollow Hope* (Chicago: University of Chicago Press, 1991).

73. See Michael Klarman, "The Backlash Theory," *Journal of American History* 81 (1994): 118. Even some who support the decision in *Brown* for the message it sent on racial equality have criticized it for its impact on educational opportunities for African Americans and have questioned whether its integrationist ideals did not also send a demeaning message of racial inferiority. See, e.g., Derrick Bell, *And We Are Not Saved* (New York: Basic Books, 1987). See James Patterson, *Brown v. Board of Education*.

74. See, e.g., *Adarand Constructors, Inc. v. Pena*, 515 U.S. 200 (1995).

75. See, e.g., *Bray v. Alexandria Women's Health Clinic*, 506 U.S. 263 (1993); *Wards Cove Packing Co., v. Antonio*, 490 U.S. 642 (1989); *Grove City College v. Bell*, 465 U.S. 555 (1984).

Chapter 6

1. Thurgood Marshall, dissenting in *Skinner v. Railway Labor Executives Assoc.*, 489 U.S. 602, 635 (1989).

2. Samuel R. Gross and Debra Livingston, "Racial Profiling Under Attack," *Columbia Law Review* 102 (June 2002): 1413, 1414. The same point was made in an article written before the events of September 11th, 2001, that the political and legal elites had expressed "almost universal condemnation" of racial profiling. David Rudovsky, "Law Enforcement by Stereotypes and Serendipity: Racial Profiling and Stops and Searches Without Cause,"

University of Pennsylvania Journal of Constitutional Law 3 (2001): 364.

3. On racial profiling as an issue in the 2000 election, we high-lighted some of the more colorful exchanges earlier. See the Introduction.

4. The word "silly," for example, originally meant "blessed" and, later, "simple" or "innocent"; in Elizabethan times, "wit" meant "knowledge" rather than cleverness or humor. See John McWhorter, "The Uses of Ugliness," *The New Republic,* January 14, 2002. Nor is this a distinctly pre-Enlightenment phenomenon: When is the last time you used the word "gay" to describe someone who was happy and light-hearted?

5. To put it another way, assume a suspect matches all five factors of a carefully devised profile based on objective data drawn from the historical record. If, in the absence of consideration of race, there is not sufficient grounds to stop the suspect, does knowledge of the suspect's race add enough to justify the stop? If so, does that mean that it has become the critical factor in justifying the stop?

6. William Stuntz, "Local Policing After the Terror," *Yale Law Journal* 111 (June 2002), pp. 2137, 2169–80. Stuntz's argument is based in part on the work of Tom Tyler, who argues that attitudes toward law enforcement are shaped more by whether one is treated fairly by police than by the outcome of any police conduct. Id. *p.* 2173. Justice Stewart's definition of pornography is from *Jacobellis v. Ohio,* 378 U.S. 184, 197 (1964) (Stewart, J. concurring).

7. Peter Schuck raises the possibility that the racial piece of a profile can be the determinative one, at least in a close case. See Schuck, "A Case for Profiling," *The American Lawyer,* January 2002, 2. See also Randall Kennedy, *Race, Crime and the Law* (New York: Pantheon Books, 1997), 136–163, who argues that race will always be the key piece of a profile and that therefore it is a smokescreen to argue for profiles in which race is only one component.

8. Evan P. Schultz, "Racial Profiling Is Back but It Is Not the Answer to Terrorism," *American Lawyer, Media LP, Fulton County Daily Report,* October 2, 2001.

9. Sean Hecker, "Race and Pretextual Traffic Stops: An Expanded Role for Civilian Review Board," *Columbia Human Rights Law Review* 28 (Spring 1997): 551–52. See also: Randall Kennedy, *Race, Crime and the Law,* 136–145; David A. Sklansky, "Traffic Stops, Minority Motorists, and the Future of the Fourth Amendment," *Supreme Court Review* (1997), 80–81; and Deborah Ramirez et al., "A Resource Guide on Racial Profiling Data Collection Systems: Promising Practices and Lessons Learned" (Nov. 2000), 4–5.

10. Hecker, "Race and Pretextual Traffic Stops," 52–553. Hecker is citing other research. To be exact this is the text from Hecker: "The real and perceived inequality in police stops poses perhaps the single greatest threat to the legitimacy of the criminal justice system." Hecker also asserts that the belief among a substantial segment of the population that law enforcement officers act with bias or prejudice undermines the authority and effectiveness of law enforcement and threatens the rule of law. For additional discussion of how profiling can damage attitudes toward the police, see Peter Verniero and Paul Zoubek, "Interim Report of the State Police Review Team Regarding Allegations of Racial Profiling," April 20, 1999, 45–48 and Chapter 4.

11. See e.g., Heather MacDonald, "The Myth of Racial Profiling," *City Journal* 11 (Spring 2001): 5–7.

12. See, e.g., Jackson Toby, "Are Police the Enemy?" *Society* 37 (May/June 2000), 38–42; James Q. Wilson and Heather Higgins, "Profiles in Courage," *The Wall Street Journal*, January 10, 2002. For an extended discussion of the statistical evidence and an effort to address the counterarguments, see David A. Harris, "When Success Breeds Attack: The Coming Backlash Against Racial Profiling Studies," *Michigan Journal of Race & Law* 6 (2001): 237.

13. See Kennedy, *Race, Crime, and the Law,* 136–163, and Kennedy, "Race, the Police and 'Reasonable Suspicion,'" in *Perspective on Crime and Justice: 1997–1998 Lecture Series,* National Institute of Justice, November 1998.

14. See Kennedy, *Race, Crime, and the Law,* 136; ibid., "You Can't Judge a Crook by His Color," *The New Republic,* September 13, 1999, 5–6.

15. Jerome Skolnick, "The Color Line of Punishment," *Michigan Law Review* 96 (May 1998): 1479. Recall as well the argument of William Stuntz discussed earlier in this chapter that it is unrealistic to attempt to prevent police from using race and, in any event, the psychological harm from profiling comes not in being singled out, even on racial grounds, but in being treated coercively or rudely when stopped. William Stuntz, "Local Policing After the Terror."

16. Anthony Thompson, "Stopping the Usual Suspects: Race and the Fourth Amendment," *New York University Law Review* 74 (1999): 24.

17. Precisely that type of economic argument was presented to and rejected by the Supreme Court in *Heart of Atlanta Motel v. United States,* 379 U.S. 241 (1964).

18. See, e.g., Tracey Maclin, "Race and the Fourth Amendment," *Vanderbilt Law Review* 51 (1998); David A. Harris, "The Stories, The

Statistics, and the Law: Why 'Driving While Black' Matters," *Minnesota Law Review* 84 (1999); and David A. Harris, "'Driving While Black' and All Other Traffic Offenses: The Supreme Court and Pretextual Traffic Stops," *Journal of Criminal Law & Criminology* 87 (1997); Kennedy, *Race, Crime & the Law;* Erika Johnson, "'A Menace to Society': The Use of Criminal Profiles and Its Effects on Black Males," *Howard Law Journal* 38 (1998), 629.

19. Professor Victor Romero sees an interesting irony (or hypocrisy) in the differing attitudes and responses both liberals and conservatives have brought to Affirmative Action and racial profiling:

> The liberal asserts the irrelevance of race in the automobile stop context for the same reason that the conservative pans affirmative action: race is not an accurate predictor in evaluating a particular individual; put another way, "racial profiling" does not work. Yet both groups adopt a different perspective when arguing for race relevance: race is relevant in "Driving While Mexican" cases, the conservative claims, because while respectable individuals . . . might unfortunately (but rarely) be targeted, they are part of a larger group that contains non-respectable individuals (drug smugglers and undocumented immigrants) who should properly be targets of law enforcement. Analogously, the liberal contends that rich Black individuals who might not be the most worthy recipients of affirmative action preferences nonetheless belong to a class whose members are disproportionately disadvantaged by university admissions processes and standards.
>
> Who is right? Is race relevant in only one context but not the other? Both our hypothetical conservative and liberal should take a cue from former Justice Lewis Powell's writings in the automobile stop and affirmative action contexts, and admit and make clear that race is irrelevant in both situations.

Victor C. Romero, "Racial Profiling: 'Driving While Mexican' and Affirmative Action," *Michigan Journal of Race and Law* 6 (Fall 2000) 200. Affirmative Action is not the only current topic in which such a dichotomy or paradox appears to surface. The same is true comparing competing attitudes on the death penalty and racial profiling. As with Affirmative Action, those who believe you cannot extrapolate from statistical data on the highways to justify stops have urged courts to do exactly that in determining whether considerations of race played an improper role in imposing the death sentence, while their ideological opponents have rejected the statistical argument in death penalty challenges despite valuing the statistical models at the heart of racial profiling efforts. See Milton Heumann and Lance Cassak, "Profiles in Justice?—Police, Discretion, Symbolic Assailants and Stereotyping," *Rutgers Law Review* 53 (Summer 2001): 968, n.289.

20. We say "at least nineteen" because that is the number of terrorists who actually boarded the airplanes and rode them into the World Trade Center, the Pentagon, and a field in Pennsylvania. As this book goes to press, one other person, often described as "the twentieth hijacker" in the media, has been arrested and charged with helping to plan the September 11th attacks. It is almost certain that there were other persons involved in the attacks, at least in planning or other phases.

21. In the context in which it is raised in connection with the September 11th attacks, it probably makes more sense to describe this as ethnic rather than racial profiling. However, partly because of how it played out in the popular media after September 11th, we will use the more common term of racial profiling.

22. William Stuntz, "Local Policing After the Terror," p. 1262.

23. Remarks of Dennis M. Lormel, Chief, Financial Crimes Section, Federal Bureau of Investigation before the House Committee on Financial Services Subcommittee on Oversight and Investigations, delivered February 12, 2002. Available online at: *www.fbi. gov/congress02/lormel021202* (April 2002). The description of the Hijacker Financial Profile set forth hereinafter comes from Mr. Lormel's remarks.

24. Within three weeks of September 11th, no fewer than eleven articles appeared in major newspapers asking whether attitudes towards racial profiling would change in light of the terrorist attacks.

25. In fact, across the country there are complaints of several minorities who are not of Middle Eastern descent but fall victim to profiling because they are perceived to be, including Latinos and South Asians. Annie Nakao, "Arab Americans Caught in Profile Snare; Detained, Denied Boarding or Kicked off Planes for Looking Middle Eastern," *San Francisco Chronicle,* September 28, 2001, A1.

26. Linda Greenhouse, "A Nation Challenged: The Supreme Court; in New York Visit, O'Connor Foresees Limits on Freedom," *New York Times,* September 29, 2001, B5.

27. Ibid.

28. Ibid.

29. Kathy Barrett Carter, "Some See New Need for Racial Profiling," *Star-Ledger (Newark),* September 20, 2001, 24. Likewise, New Jersey's Attorney General indicated that some level of profiling

may be necessary or desirable in the interest of securing our safety as we face the new threat of mass terrorism. See John Farmer, Jr., "Now Is the Time to Reconsider Profiling," *The Record,* September 26, 2001, L11.

30. Barrett Carter, "Some See New Need for Racial Profiling," 24 (quoting Floyd Abrams). For a discussion of airline profiling approaches developed since September 11th, see David Armstrong and Joseph Pereira, "Flight Risks: Airlines Adopt Aggressive Passenger Profiling Systems," *Ann Arbor News,* Oct. 28, 2001, A-3.

31. Kathy Barrett Carter, "State Ties Profiling to Advice on Crime Fighting," *Star-Ledger* (Newark), November 28, 2000, 24.

32. Michael Kinsley, "When Is Racial Profiling Okay?," *Washington Post,* September 30, 2001, B7.

33. Chris Mooney, "Smart—and Stupid—Profiling," *American Prospect,* October 23, 2001. Available online at: *www.americanprospect.com/webfeatures/2001/10/mooney-c-10–23.html* (April 2002).

34. Sam Howe Verhovek, "A Nation Challenged: Civil Liberties; Americans Give in to Race Profiling," *New York Times,* September 23, 2001, A1.

35. This echoes comments made by many in law enforcement at the time racial profiling was coming under intense scrutiny, that every one engages in racial profiling and that they are being unfairly criticized for the practice. See Jeffrey Goldberg, "The Color of Suspicion," *New York Times Magazine,* June 20, 1999, 51.

36. Stuart Taylor, Jr., "Politically Incorrect Profiling: A Matter of Life or Death," *National Journal* 33 (2001), posted at *www.nationaljournal.com/members/buzz/2001/openingargument/110501.htm.*

37. Verhovek, "Civil Liberties," A1.

38. Ibid.

39. Ibid.

40. Clarence Page, "My, Oh My, Look Who's Profiling Now," *Chicago Tribune* October 3, 2001, N23.

41. Fedwa Malti-Douglas, "Let Them Profile Me," *New York Times,* February 6, 2002.

42. See Page, "My, Oh My, Look Who's Profiling Now," N23.

43. Samuel R. Gross and Debra Livingston, "Racial Profiling Under Attack," 1423–24 (reporting the results of a poll taken by the *Washington Post* and ABC News reflecting 79% approval for that initiative.)

44. Page, "My, Oh My, Look Who's Profiling Now." Attorney Ronald Kuby, who has made a career in progressive causes including representing minority defendants in high-visibility cases, was asked why African Americans seemed to support racial profiling after the September 11th attacks. He surmised that since the tar-

gets of the new racial profiling were members of another group, African Americans no longer felt victimized by the practice but instead had become part of the "us" in the "us vs. them" scenario. See the "Curtis & Kuby" radio broadcast (77WABC, Oct. 5, 2001). Available at: *www.curtisandkuby.net.*

45. See Taylor, "Politically Incorrect Profiling."

46. Kirk D. Richards, "Middle Eastern People Being Booted off Planes," *Columbus Dispatch,* September 28, 2001, 1A (quoting Nihan Awad, Director of the Council on American-Islamic Relations in Washington, D.C.).

47. Raymond Hernandez, "New Racial Profiling Debates Puts Legislators to the Test," *New York Times,* September 30, 2001, NJ14.

48. David Cole and James X. Dempsey, *Terrorism and the Constitution* (New York: The New Press, 2002), 168–71; Alan M. Dershowitz, "Why Fear National ID Cards?" *New York Times,* October 13, 2001, A23.

49. For a brief summary, and criticism of the various tactics, see Ronald Dworkin, "The Bush Threat," *New York Review of Books,* February 28, 2002, 44; Linda Greenhouse, "A Penchant for Secrecy," The Week in Review, *New York Times,* May 5, 2002, 1.

50. Chertoff's testimony is reprinted at *www.politechbot.com* (October 4, 2002). For other accounts of Chertoff's rejection of racial profiling while defending other Department of Justice initiatives in the War On Terrorism, see Frank Davies, "Top Terrorist Investigation Official Defends Tribunals, Emergency Powers," *Knight-Ridder Tribune Business News,* November 29, 2001; Rebecca Carr, "Sweeping Anti-Terrorism Powers Questioned," *Atlanta Journal and Constitution,* November 29, 2001; Sharon Behn, "Congress Critical of Bush Administration Anti-Terrorism Measures," *Agence France-Presse,* November 28, 2001. See also Dan Eggen, "Ashcroft Undaunted As Criticism Grows, Higher Profile Brings Controversy," *Washington Post,* November 29, 2001, for similar comments by Attorney General John Ashcroft.

51. Samuel R. Gross and Debra Livingston, "Racial Profiling Under Attack," p. 1419–20.

52. See Joshua Green, "The Mineta Myth," *Slate Magazine,* On line, posted at *www.slate.msn.com,* April 1, 2002, describing not only Mineta's vehement and expletive-laden order that planes be brought down immediately (and that the decision not be left to the discretion of the pilots in the individual airplanes) but also the fact that Mineta's order had been already been issued by one of his top aides, making his order somewhat superfluous.

53. "That Dirty Little Word 'Profiling,'" *60 Minutes* transcript (December 2, 2001), 4.

54. As this book is going to press before Moussaoui's trial, his precise identity and role have been subject to different descriptions. As noted, he was originally described as the "20th hijacker." Later, however, information simply suggested that he had ties to Al-Qaeda, may have known the September 11th hijackers, and had been engaged in flight school training similar to what the September 11th hijackers had taken. This led some, although not everyone, to identify him as other than the 20th hijacker. See Kate Taylor, "Was Zacarias Moussaoui Really the 20th Hijacker?" *Slate Magazine,* posted on the web on May 30, 2002.

55. See, e.g., Williams Safire, "The Rowley Memo," *New York Times,* May 27, 2002.

56. Nicholas D. Kristof, "Liberal Reality Check," *New York Times,* May 31, 2002, A 23.

57. "That Dirty Little Word 'Profiling,'" *60 Minutes* transcript (December 2, 2001), 4. Abrams' reference to internment is to the experience of Japanese Americans in World War II.

58. Peter Schuck, "A Case for Profiling," *The American Lawyer,* January 2002, 2. See also, William Stuntz, "Local Policing After the Terror" (arguing that we should regulate how police conduct the stops rather than whom they decide to stop).

59. See Mooney, "Smart—and Stupid—Profiling" (finding profiling based on race and religion acceptable).

60. See, e.g., Katherine Corcoran and John Hubner, "Haunted by Plane Attacks, Some Struggle with Suspicion," *San Jose Mercury News,* September 24, 2001, 1A (identifying a new offense, "Flying While Arab," obviously influenced by the "Driving While Black" of more traditional profiling).

61. See Kinsley, "When Is Racial Profiling Okay?" (describing efforts of passengers to remove three Arab passengers who had already cleared security).

62. 428 U.S. 543, 566 (1976).

63. Samuel R. Gross and Debra Livingston, "Racial Profiling Under Attack," 1424: "The interviews are described as purely voluntary, though that is something of an exaggeration. The constitutional regulation of stops and searches is based in part on the premise that the average citizen feels free to ignore an armed police officer who asks for identification, or to look in the trunk and that the nearly universal compliance with such demands is voluntary. This is a convenient fiction under even ordinary circumstances, let alone in this context. The typical recipient of one of these letters [asking the person to come to the local United States Attorney's Office for an interview]—a foreign student on a temporary visa from a country with an authoritarian and sometimes

abusive government—must be forgiven if he interprets the request for an interview as an order. Worse, he may be right to do so."

64. See, e.g., *Korematsu v. United States*, 323 U.S. 214 (1944); Peter H. Irons, *Justice at War: The Story of the Japanese American Internment Cases* (New York: Oxford University Press, 1983).

65. Samuel R. Gross and Debra Livingston, "Racial Profiling Under Attack," 1425.

66. Ibid.

67. Ibid.

68. See Chapter 4.

69. 392 U.S. 1 (1968).

70. See Chapter 1.

71. See Chapter 4; Heumann and Cassak, "Profiles in Justice?"

72. Stuart Taylor, "Politically Incorrect Profiling: A Matter of Life or Death," *The National Journal*, November 5, 2001, available *www.nationaljournal.com/members/buzz/2001/openingargument/ 110501*.

73. See Kinsley, "When Is Racial Profiling Okay?"

74. Peter Schuck, "A Case for Profiling."

75. See, e.g., *Abrams v. United States*, 250 U.S. 616 (1919); *Debs v. United States*, 249 U.S. 211 (1919); *Schenck v. United States*, 249 U.S. 47 (1919). On the wartime background on these cases and the development of this doctrine, see Paul L. Murphy, *World War I and the Origins of Civil Liberties in the United States* (New York: Norton, 1979); Richard Polenberg, *Fighting Faiths: The Abrams Case, The Supreme Court, and Free Speech* (Ithaca: Cornell University Press, 1987). But see David M. Rabban, *Free Speech in Its Forgotten Years* (New York: Cambridge University Press, 1997) (arguing that restrictive elements of the clear and present danger test had their roots in pre-war developments and thought).

76. Samuel R. Gross and Debra Livingston, "Racial Profiling Under Attack," 1430.

77. See Greg Robinson, *By Order of the President: FDR and the Internment of Japanese Americans* (Cambridge, Mass.: Harvard University Press, 2001), especially ch. 3.

78. See William Stuntz, "Local Policing After the Terror," arguing that the rules engaged for ferreting out terrorists will be applied by police and approved by judges to all sorts of crimes not related to terrorism.

79. David Harris, *Driving While Black: Racial Profiling on Our Nation's Highways: An American Civil Liberties Union Special Report*, 26–28.

80. See Institute on Race and Poverty, "Memo: Components of Racial Profiling Legislation"; to Senator Linda Berglin, Senator Jane Ranum,

and Representative Greg Gray (March 5, 2001). See "Racial Profiling Update," available online at: *www.calea.org/newweb/newsletter/ No.%2075/racial_profiling_update.htm* and/or *www.theiacp.org/leg policy/legupdate/states2001.htm* .

81. On the efforts of police and police unions to prevent legislation dealing with racial profiling, see, e.g., Kathy Barrett Carter, "Racial Profiling Laws in Sight But Out of Reach," *Star-Ledger* (Newark), July 29, 2001; John McAlpin, "Profiling Bills Die in Assembly," *Associated Press Newswires,* January 7, 2002; Gary Fields, "Police Union Has Friends in White House," *Wall Street Journal,* August 1, 2002; "Police Feel; Eyes of Big Brother," *Chicago Daily Herald,* April 6, 2001; Kit Wagar, "Panel Reacts To Profiling Law," *Kansas City Star,* December 12, 2000; Joe Mahoney, "Cops Fight Profiling Law," *New York Daily News,* May 31, 2001. Police unions also tried to block the efforts of the Department of Justice to investigate and reach settlements based on its findings. See, e.g., Tina Daunt, "Talks With U.S. Officials Over LAPD Bog Down," *Los Angeles Times,* October 26, 2000; Mark O'Keefe, "Blue Wall of Silence," *Sunday Patriot-News Harrisburg,* May 7, 2000. On police unions' cooperation with efforts to pass anti-profiling legislation, see Kevin Osborne, "Traffic Stop Data To Include Race," *Cincinnati Post,* March 8, 2001 (noting that police union helped draft legislation, although the police had initially opposed legislative efforts they ultimately supported), Kevin Osborne, "Profiling Data Flawed, Police Say," *Cincinnati Post,* March 6, 2001); Carol Kreck, "Racial Profiling Study on Fast Track," *Denver Post,* February 26, 2001.

82. Again, though, this was before September 11th. It is not clear how much support there is post–September 11th. Public opinion polls are equivocal, and we think depend very much on the wording of the questions. Somewhat surprisingly during the week of September 19th, 77% of the respondents in a nationwide Harris poll were either highly or moderately concerned that "[t]here would be broad profiling of people and searching them based on their nationality, race or religion." Yet, a week earlier, when asked if "[u]sing profiling by age, race and gender to identify suspicious [airport] passengers," 57% felt this was acceptable. A small note: with respect to the latter question, we were actually surprised that 38%, even just a few days after the World Trade Center, felt it was not acceptable. See Roper Center for Public Opinion, University of Connecticut. Available at: *www.ropercenter.uconn.edu/ ipoll.html.*

83. Peter Irons, *The New Deal Lawyers* (Princeton: Princeton University Press, 1983).

84. There are studies and data for other communities available (David Harris, *Profiles in Injustice: Why Racial Profiling Cannot Work* (New York: New Press, 2002); David A. Harris, "Driving While Black, Racial Profiling on Our Nation's Highways," ACLU Special Report (1999); *Report on "Operation Pipeline"*) but none has yet had the impact of Lamberth's studies.
85. Harris, "When Success Breeds Attack," 6–10.
86. See Hecker, "Race and Pretextual Stops," 566. On general police responses to accusations of racial profiling, see Chapter 4.
87. For an indication of early willingness by police to talk freely on this subject, see Goldberg, "The Color of Suspicion." More recently, we have found it difficult to find members of law enforcement who would speak on behalf of racial profiling as a legitimate law enforcement technique. Once, in attempting to line up a speaker for a seminar in which racial profiling was one of the topics, a contact at the FBI advised us that he knew of no FBI officer who cared about his job who would voluntarily speak to our class in defense of racial profiling.

Index